Twayne's United States Authors Series

Sylvia E. Bowman, *Editor*

INDIANA UNIVERSITY

Edmund Wilson

EDMUND WILSON

by

CHARLES P. FRANK

For nearly fifty years Edmund Wilson has been supreme in American letters as a perceptive reporter on literature, ideas, and life. An intellectual without academic sanctuary, objecting repeatedly to the abuses of his age, and an individualist insisting on personal freedom while exemplifying social responsibility, Wilson has been one of the most courageous writers of his time. His views have been attacked and praised, but seldom ignored. Yet, in the excitement generated by his formidable presence in American letters, his contribution to literature tends to be overlooked. Only one book has previously been devoted to Wilson, and its emphasis is biographical rather than critical.

Dr. Frank provides a systematic analysis and evaluation of Wilson's major and minor work — his criticism, fiction, drama, poetry, and journalism. The selections reveal that his criticism is less historical than is commonly recognized, with a strong biographical and psychological preoccupation, and that it suggests in its moral attitudes a closer affinity to the criticism of the Humanists than he would admit. Dr. Frank shows, furthermore, that Wilson's fiction is serious and undeservedly neglected.

EDMUND WILSON

By CHARLES P. FRANK
University of Puget Sound

 152

Twayne Publishers, Inc.   ::   New York

To the Memory of
W. Howard Dawe
1902-1963

ABOUT THE AUTHOR

Charles P. Frank is an associate professor of English at the University of Puget Sound. After receiving the Ph.D. from the University of Michigan in 1964, he taught English and American literature for four years at Indiana University in Fort Wayne, where he wrote this book. His current scholarly interests center on narrative fiction and on contemporary philosophy.

Preface

ARTICLES on the writings of Edmund Wilson reveal two peculiarities. The first is a (perhaps traditional) hostility expressed by the non-academic toward the academic faction in American letters. The non-academic, or "professional," side claims Wilson as its exclusive property and resents criticism directed at him from the universities. When Frederick C. Crews of the University of California at Berkeley reviewed Wilson's *The Bit Between My Tooth* for the *New York Review of Books* (November 25, 1965) and, while admiring Wilson's criticism, raised certain questions regarding its deficiencies, he was scolded in the December 23 issue of the *Review* by Elizabeth Hardwick, a distinguished if sometimes confused representative of the non-academic group. Then, in the January, 1966, issue of *Holiday*, Clifton Fadiman also felt obliged to rescue Wilson from the arrows of academia.

Although Wilson himself has encouraged ill will by making contemptuous remarks about academic provinciality, he has long been respected in the universities; and some of the most eulogistic recent commentaries—such as another review of *The Bit Between My Teeth*, by R. W. B. Lewis of Yale, in the *New York Times Book Review* (December 12, 1965)—come from teachers. The much-deserved attention paid to *Patriotic Gore*, which received nearly fifty reviews in American journals, came mainly from grateful university people. Indeed, members of the non-academic group turned their coats when they attacked *The Cold War and the Income Tax*, which seemed to embarrass them.

The second oddity is that writers on Wilson are usually more concerned with what he stands for, what he symbolizes even, than with the quality of his work. Relatively few articles deal thoroughly with his writings, and far too many are preoccupied with such sentiments as "What Wilson Means to Me"—as if, like Charles Dickens, he were already canonized and enshrined in the hearts of the people. The review by R. W. B. Lewis mentioned above and one of *Patriotic Gore* by Elizabeth Hardwick imply that one just has to love such a wonderful old man who has put us all in his debt forever. This attitude is, of course,

Contents

Contents

Sylvia Salmi

EDMUND WILSON

Acknowledgments

Edmund Wilson has generously permitted me to quote freely from his work.

Four critical and encouraging readers of the text were my wife Suzanne Frank; my colleague Mary Catherine Bodden; Dr. Sylvia Bowman, the editor; and Robert Milch, the copy editor.

The typists who made my manuscript legible were Linda Flatley (on a grant from Indiana University), Clare McAfee, Mary Waller, Etta Krumwiede, and Sandy Shroyer.

I particularly wish to thank Louise Sample, the expert reference librarian at Indiana University's Fort Wayne Campus, who graciously and promptly found so much material for me—more than I was able to include.

preferable to Stanley Hyman's vilification of 1947 in *The Armed Vision;* but it naturally tends to overlook the work itself.

To some extent Wilson himself is responsible for the personal interest taken in him, for his own approaches to his topics are highly personal. As Louis D. Rubin, Jr., says in his good review of *Patriotic Gore* (*Sewanee Review,* January-March, 1963), Wilson "has a way of seeming to be discovering everything for the first time, of assuming that until he, Edmund Wilson, has read a book, it hasn't really been properly evaluated." But Rubin also says that Wilson has "one of the most original minds of the twentieth century," and—although Wilson's intellect is probably more formidable than original—it *is* exciting to watch it at work on material that it has not considered before. As a critic, Wilson lacks René Wellek's erudition, Northrop Frye's imagination, John Crowe Ransom's discrimination, and Austin Warren's brilliance; yet the latest essay by him in *The New Yorker* or the *New York Review of Books* is always an event which perhaps no other living Western writer except Jean-Paul Sartre or André Malraux could bring about, and it always excites strong personal feelings ranging from pleasure to annoyance.

But the only aspect of Wilson that has in the long run any valid claim on the beleaguered attention of the literary student is the work—his criticism, poetry, drama, fiction, and journalism—which this monograph analyzes and evaluates. Because I have wanted to be as thorough in a limited number of pages as Wilson's writings demand, I have had to omit consideration of *To the Finland Station, The Scrolls from the Dead Sea, Red, Black, Blond and Olive, Apologies to the Iroquois,* and *O Canada;* and I have had to be selective about much of his other work.

This study is not constructed on any thesis, which would, I think, have made objectivity very difficult. It is hard enough to be objective when the Wilson apotheosized by other writers stands at one's shoulder, and when the personality of the real Wilson appears and reappears, attractively and not, in his pages.

CHARLES P. FRANK

University of Puget Sound

Chronology

1895   May 8, Edmund Wilson, Jr., born in Red Bank, New Jersey, to Edmund and Helen Mather (Kimball) Wilson; only child.

1908   Attended The Hill School in Pottstown, Pennsylvania, until 1912; contributed to and edited the *Hill School Record*. First trip to Europe in summer, 1908, during which young Wilson wrote impressions of the Azores, Spain, Italy, Germany, and France in a diary—the beginning of a lifelong interest in travel writing.

1912   Attended Princeton; received A.B. in 1916; contributed to and edited the *Nassau "Lit"*; met his esteemed mentor, Christian Gauss (1914); became friends with other promising young writers, such as John Peale Bishop and F. Scott Fitzgerald.

1916   Reporter on the *New York Evening Sun* at fifteen dollars a week until 1917.

1917   August, enlisted as a private in the army, served with Base Hospital Unit 36 and then, as sergeant, with the Intelligence Corps, in France; until July, 1919.

1920   Managing editor of *Vanity Fair* until 1921; met Edna St. Vincent Millay.

1921   Drama critic for the *New Republic*, with which he would be associated for nearly twenty years.

1922   *The Undertaker's Garland*, in collaboration with John Peale Bishop.

1923   Married actress Mary Blair; daughter, Rosalind; divorce, 1928. Death of Wilson's father.

1924   *The Crime in the Whistler Room* produced on October 9 by the Provincetown Players in Greenwich Village; starred Mary Blair as "Bill." In October reviewed Ernest Hemingway's *Three Stories and Ten Poems* and *In Our Time* in the *Dial*—the first article on Hemingway published in the United States.

1926   *Discordant Encounters*. Associate editor of the *New Republic* until 1931.

1929　*Poets, Farewell!* and *I Thought of Daisy.* Nervous breakdown in New York in February.

1930　Literary battles with the Humanists. Married Margaret Canby, who died from a fall in Santa Barbara, September 30, 1932; no children, although Margaret had a son by a previous marriage.

1931　*Axel's Castle,* published piecemeal since 1924, established Wilson's reputation as an important literary critic.

1932　*The American Jitters,* an account of Wilson's nationwide investigations into poverty, racism, industry, and reclamation.

1935　May to October, trip to Russia on a Guggenheim Fellowship for the thwarted purpose of studying Marxism and the Russian Revolution at the Marx-Engels Institute in Moscow; the trip culminated in scarlet fever and a six-week sojourn in a hospital in Odessa.

1936　*Travels in Two Democracies;* the Russian half of this book, comprising selections from the diaries he kept on the Soviet trip, barred him from Russia.

1937　*This Room and This Gin and These Sandwiches.* Open literary war with the Marxists.

1938　*The Triple Thinkers.* Married writer Mary McCarthy; son, Reuel; divorce, 1946.

1939　Taught at University of Chicago summer school.

1940　*To the Finland Station,* published piecemeal since 1932. Broke his long association with the *New Republic* over the pro-war policy of its owner.

1941　*The Boys in the Back Room* and *The Wound and the Bow.*

1942　*Note-Books of Night.*

1943　*The Shock of Recognition.* Succeeded Clifton Fadiman as literary editor for *The New Yorker,* until 1948.

1945　Trip to Europe in the summer as a reporter for *The New Yorker.*

1946　*Memoirs of Hecate County,* suppressed as obscene soon after publication in Boston, New York, Philadelphia and other places. Married Elena Thornton, his present wife; daughter, Helen.

1947   *Europe Without Baedeker,* resulting from *New Yorker* trip, brought charges of Anglophobia from reviewers. Trip to New Mexico for *The New Yorker* to visit the Zuñi (and Navaho) Indians for a month and to observe their Shálako festival.

1948   Revised and enlarged *Triple Thinkers.*

1949   Trip to Haiti for a month for the *Reporter.*

1950   August 15, *The Little Blue Light* produced by the Brattle Theater Company at the Cambridge (Mass.) Summer Playhouse. *Classics and Commercials.* Death of Christian Gauss.

1951   April 29, *The Little Blue Light* at the American National Theater and Academy Playhouse in New York (eight performances).

1952   *The Shores of Light.*

1954   *Five Plays.* Trip to Palestine for *The New Yorker* to investigate the Dead Sea Scrolls findings.

1955   *The Scrolls from the Dead Sea.* Awarded the gold medal for essays and criticism by the American Academy of Arts and Letters (Van Wyck Brooks made the presentation).

1956   *Red, Black, Blond and Olive* and *A Piece of My Mind.*

1958   *The American Earthquake.* In serious trouble with the Internal Revenue Service for failure to file income tax returns from 1946 to 1955.

1959   *Apologies to the Iroquois.* Unexpurgated *Memoirs* republished. Taught Harvard seminar on Civil War literature, until 1960.

1961   *Night Thoughts.*

1962   *Patriotic Gore.*

1963   *The Cold War and the Income Tax.* One of thirty-three recipients of the Presidential Medal of Freedom, the highest civilian honor in the United States; John F. Kennedy presided.

1964   Awarded the Edward MacDowell Medal "for his outstanding contribution to literature" at the MacDowell artists' colony, Peterborough, New Hampshire; Aaron Copland presided.

1965 *O Canada* and *The Bit Between My Teeth.*

1966 Awarded the National Medal for Literature "for the excellence of his total contribution to literature" (including five thousands dollars tax free, so that, in Wilson's words, "not a penny of it will be demanded for the infamous war in Vietnam"). Also awarded the Emerson-Thoreau Medal "for distinguished achievement in the field of literature."

1967 *Galahad* and *I Thought of Daisy,* in one volume; and *A Prelude.*

1969 *The Fruits of the MLA, The Duke of Palermo and Other Plays,* and *The Dead Sea Scrolls: 1969.*

CHAPTER 1

Edmund Wilson: An Introduction

EDMUND WILSON has distinguished himself for nearly fifty years as a reporter—principally of modern authors and their work, of American life during the Boom and the Depression, and of himself. His interests are far-ranging, and many of his writings have little in common with each other thematically. His social journalism, for example, has almost nothing to do with his very small body of poetry or his eight volumes of essays on literature. And other interests—in history and biography, in archaeology and religion, in anthropology and travel—are more or less distinct from one another.

Nevertheless, his writings reveal a general attitude of social dissent, which has moved from one political direction to another. The first tendency, toward the left, touched five different kinds of books, as well as separate pieces, between 1922 and 1936: *The Undertaker's Garland,* a book of stories and poems written in collaboration with John Peale Bishop; *Discordant Encounters,* a group of dialogues which included his first long play; his first novel, *I Thought of Daisy,* and much of his second novel, *Memoirs of Hecate County* (1946), whose longest part is set in the 1930's; his first collection of articles on Depression life, *The American Jitters;* and his disillusioned reports on America and Russia in *Travels in Two Democracies.*

Near the middle of his career stands *To the Finland Station* (1940), in which he evinces admiration for the great founding Marxists and their desire to rid humanity of class privilege and economic degradation but yet deplores the "dictatorship in the interests of the proletariat," which he had found in Russia in 1935. Since *Europe Without Baedeker* (1947), the social dissent has clearly moved in the other direction; and Wilson's attitude has become increasingly reactionary: in a play, *The Little Blue*

Light; a collection of personal essays, *A Piece of My Mind,* and a study of Civil War literature, *Patriotic Gore;* a polemic, *The Cold War and the Income Tax;* his "notes on Canadian culture," *O Canada;* and the 1967 edition of *Europe Without Baedeker.* The dissent in both directions is perhaps the dominant motif of Wilson's career. His relationship with the United States is one of concern with social problems and defiance of the government.

I *Estrangement*

Wilson's first enthusiasm was for literature. When he attended The Hill School at Pottstown, Pennsylvania, he was, in the opinion of "Mrs. Meigs," whose husband operated the school, too bookish. When she once held private talks with each of the boys, she warned him against becoming so absorbed in his studies as to neglect his relation to his fellows.[1] But Wilson does not seem to have been discouraged by her concern, and in 1910 and 1911 he published a short story and a poem, respectively, in the *Hill School Record.*

Shortly after he entered Princeton in 1912, he apparently knew what kind of literature he preferred. His favorite professor, Christian Gauss, who taught French and Italian, said years later in 1944, on the occasion of Wilson's being "bibliographed" at Princeton, that young Wilson had cared little for reform writers, such as G. B. Shaw and H. G. Wells, and had preferred Max Beerbohm and W. B. Yeats.[2] This statement is not wholly true, however, because Wilson himself remembers in *A Prelude* that Shaw was one of his heroes as early as prep school (*New Yorker* [April 29, 1967], 107), a point that he made in a letter to Gauss in 1944. Wilson's interest in writing was stimulated by the *Nassau Literary Magazine*—which he served as writer and editor— and by its other young contributors, such as T. K. Whipple, F. Scott Fitzgerald, and John Peale Bishop.

In the summer of 1915, between his junior and senior years, Wilson studied sociology and labor problems at Columbia University;[3] and after he had been graduated from Princeton, he became still more interested in social and political issues. An obvious reason for this change in him was one in the national life of America that began with World War I and extended through the Boom, the Depression, and World War II. It would have been impossible for even the narrowest of intellectuals to be unaware of these influences on American life, and, for a perceptive young man who already had an ideal of social justice, their effect was particularly disturbing. Even in college Wilson had sensed that his comfortable life was too restricted, that he was too far removed from human affairs. He enlisted in the army, he says in "The Case of the Author," "to get away from my old life. . . . My life had seemed to me both false and dull; and though I disliked the army extremely, I got a good deal of satisfaction out of it" (*Devil Take the Hindmost*, 306-7).[4] Wilson was alienated from a well-bred though confining life to which he would always be attracted but to which he could never return. He writes in *A Prelude*: "I also had leisure [in the army] to think, and it suddenly became very clear to me that I could never go back to my former life—that is, that I could never go back to the habits and standards of even the most cultivated elements of the world in which I had lived. I felt now that I had never quite believed in that world, that I had never, in fact, quite belonged to it" (*New Yorker* [May 13, 1967], 154, 157).

To understand both the alienation from the respectability of the past and the formation of Wilson's social conscience, which in turn estranged him from the present, is to comprehend something of Wilson's youth and family. In three fine essays—"The Old Stone House," "At Laurelwood," and "The Author at Sixty"— as well as in his most recent memoir, *A Prelude*, he has written about his early life and its influence on his response to the problems of living in the United States. "The Old Stone House" appears almost too tranquil in tone to be included among the thirteen American pieces in *Travels in Two Democracies*.[5] It lies between "Sunshine Charley"—a firsthand account of the 1933 trial of Charley Mitchell, securities salesman, for income-tax evasion (see Chapter 5)—and "The Second Battle of Oriskany," another firsthand account, of a milk strike by New York farmers and the machine gunning of them by state police. The tranquility, however, is superficial: the author strolls through his paternal home at Talcottville, not far from the strike; he examines the antique furnishings ("A footstool innocently covered in white, which, however, when you step on a tab at the side, opens up into a spittoon"—*Travels*, 70); he reflects upon his great-grandfather, a farmer and state legislator, and upon his grandfather, a doctor.

But beneath this charming inventory of memory and legend lies uneasiness. His boyhood summers were spent happily with cousins at this house, but the romance is gone: in his solitude, the large families of the past oppress him. The past, despite its nostalgic appeal, provides no strength for the present. The essay balances on the tension between the attraction and the repulsion of the past: "Along with the memory of exaltation at the immensity and freedom of that countryside, I have also memories of horror at its loneliness ... the dark nights and the prisoning winters. . . . And I would not go back to that old life if I could: that civilization—why idealize it?—was too lonely, too poor, too provincial" (76).

Nor does he belong to the present. His urbanized cousins are members of the big business world, but they are "too scrupulous and decent" to make any "conquests of real importance." And Wilson himself, in an "old, cramped, sour frame house" between First and Second Avenues in New York, has been unable to obtain from "the American big business era the luxuries and the prestige which I should unquestionably very much have enjoyed" (75, 78). He is caught between two worlds but would not feel at home in either.

Nevertheless, by Depression standards of living, Wilson was reasonably prosperous. In a less melancholy and more jocular vein he wrote in *Devil Take the Hindmost* (1932): "And since the war I have never been uncomfortable—though I have never by prosperity standards had very much money. I have worked mostly for highbrow magazines: my top salary was $7,500 a year, and I didn't get that very long. I have always managed, however, to live slightly beyond my income, and have been rescued by small family inheritances which have allowed me a margin for classical reading, liquor and general irresponsibility. And as I have got used to these bourgeois luxuries, I naturally shrink from the prospect of an era where everybody will have to earn all he gets" (308). Despite his taste for bourgeois luxuries, however, he was never able to reconcile his conscience with the unscrupulousness of big business or with the general irresponsibility of the 1920's. Impossible as it was for him as a grown man to live in the old Talcottville house for longer than part of the summer, it nevertheless represented stability, order, and decency—values as dated, apparently, in the twentieth century as the furnishings.

[20]

The second essay, "At Laurelwood," also concerns a house, that of his mother's parents in New Jersey.[6] With its flowers, books, and games of chess, the Laurelwood house represented the good life. But it also had its bizarre aspects: the worldly uncle (Uncle Reuel of *A Prelude*) who always turned up with a different woman, whom he would casually introduce as his fiancée: "He had brown eyes, round, bland and humorous, a handsome mustache in the style of Guy de Maupassant, and an attractive *blagueur* manner; his great retort was the baffling 'You don't say!'"(*Night Thoughts,* 165).

The charm of the Laurelwood house contrasts to the somewhat brutal power of a neighboring rich family. On a visit one day to their lavish estate, young Wilson was shocked when the rich boy his own age ordered the footman to get him some apples from under a tree and then told the governess, "These men must do their duty, Anna!" (172). This early lesson in the reality of class conflicts was the kind that would lead him to write in 1932: "...there is no hope for general decency and fair play except from a society where classes are abolished" (*Devil Take the Hindmost,* 307).

The rich family was a degenerating member of that "society after the Civil War, when all the forces of exploitation had cut loose and nothing as yet had been done to curb them." Wilson's mother's and father's families, with their "old professional education," had been out of place in that rich world, which "was a strain on the old-fashioned American" (*Night Thoughts,* 174).[7] Even the Laurelwood house itself was "a product of the impulse to keep up"; it was more than his grandfather, a doctor, needed and could afford; but his grandmother had wanted it. The *blagueur* uncle, also a doctor, overworked himself just to maintain the new standard of living and died of apoplexy. But Wilson's father "refused to keep up beyond a certain point and went on acting on a set of principles at a tangent from the accepted ones, to incur a certain isolation" (175).

Wilson himself incurred his father's isolation but turned it to advantage. It permitted him the perspective of a man standing somewhat apart from his society and therefore more able to see it wholly. What he called in *Devil Take the Hindmost* his "slightly outside point of view" was due to his family's "professional tradition" and to its never having "departed very far from the old American life of the countryside and the provincial" (305-6). Wilson could probably have withdrawn into the academic world; but he preferred to be free of teaching, although he has on occasion held temporary residence at a university, and it is possible that even then he possessed the contempt for academia that he has rather peevishly expressed in recent writings.[8] More important, perhaps, is that he may have needed the freedom to accept the challenges of his developing social consciousness. Its development was influenced by his father, a fighter for social justice and near-idol of the son.

It is to his father that Wilson devotes much of the third essay, "The Author at Sixty." An excellent and honorable lawyer, Edmund Wilson, Sr., was more than willing to take unpopular cases. As a Republican attorney general of Democratic New Jersey during Woodrow Wilson's governorship, he succeeded in prosecuting a number of Atlantic City criminals. But the brilliant and brave lawyer was also a hypochondriac and, surprisingly, lacked "objectives in life" (*A Piece of My Mind*, [1956], 217). As he grew older, his "eclipses" became longer, and his relationship with his wife became strained. Edmund, Jr., the only child, was monopolized by his mother; but, as he grew up, he came to understand his father and to appreciate his sense of honor, his professional integrity, his ideals of social justice, and his ability in a profession that he increasingly did not bother to practice.

Leon Edel has said that, although Wilson ostensibly writes about his father, his real subject is himself.[9] Certainly the son reflects the father in some ways: the younger Wilson's social ideals and his antagonism toward the "money power"; his passion for the world of ideas; his own depressions, which he likens to his father's illness; his common sense; and his separation from his own country and period. Edel even sees Wilson's writings as lawer's briefs: the evidence carefully arranged, the logic sound, the form short and compact.

The sense of not belonging, which Wilson "inherited" from his father, underlines "The Author at Sixty." Wilson is an alien in the world of *Life* magazine; he feels that he is instead a part of the eighteenth or the early nineteenth century (211, 239). And yet he says that he has had "a good many more uplifting thoughts, creative and expansive visions" in a modern American bathroom than in a European cathedral (61). Perhaps it is true, as Maxwell

Geismar has said, that Wilson's "old fogeyism" is a role.[10] Nevertheless, the alienation from the new America is genuine. The generation of his father was trained in the learned professions, "but they had then had to deal with a world in which this kind of education and the kind of ideals it served no longer really counted for much" (213). This pessimistic tone might justify the recent charge against Wilson that his "sentiments toward mankind have begun to resemble those of a village atheist."[11] But occasionally he reveals a gleam of optimism, as in an interview of 1959: "I was born in the 19th century, and, like most people born in the 19th Century, I still have—entirely instinctively—the belief in human progress, the conviction that the world won't fall apart, the faith in the value of reform."[12] But this confidence may not include America.

II *Protest*

Wilson's career was fairly launched by 1920, when he became the managing editor of *Vanity Fair* and began contributing articles to such periodicals as the *Dial*, the *Liberator*, and the *New Republic*. An earlier start—in 1916 as a reporter for the *New York Evening Sun* at fifteen dollars a week—had been interrupted when he joined the army in August, 1917, and served in France for two years, first in a hospital unit and later in the Intelligence Service, where he was promoted to sergeant. At this time he still viewed literature as he had at Princeton, as something disconnected from the social world. He had what he later called in *Devil Take the Hindmost* a "naive vision of science and poetry" as independent of and superior to social institutions (311). But not long after his return to the United States in 1919 he must have regarded literature as something other than a leisurely pursuit for disinterested intellectuals, for he and John Peale Bishop began writing and publishing the satirical poems and stories that appeared in *The Undertaker's Garland* (1922). This book, Wilson's first sustained protest, decried a moribund America whose obsession, it seemed, was to make money.

From this beginning it was only logical that, as a prolific reporter and literary critic, Wilson should have been alarmed during the 1920's and 1930's by his investigations of economic and social abuses. Nor is it surprising that for a time he found Marx-

ism attractive. In his polemic, "An Appeal to Progressives"
(1931), he asked whether "it may be henceforward impossible
for capitalism to guarantee not merely social justice but even
security and order?" (*The Shores of Light* [1952], 522). He
admired Marx, Engels, Lenin, and Trotsky for their courage,
intelligence, and serious interest in social problems. But he was
not entirely sympathetic with Marxism, and he thought that
Communism was too good for the Communists. He urged those
radicals and progressives "who repudiate the Marxist dogma and
the strategy of the Communist Party [to] take Communism away
from the Communists, and take it without ambiguities, asserting
that [your] ultimate goal is the ownership by the government of
the means of production" (532).

Wilson seems to have been unsympathetic with the Communists partly because of their factionalism, partly because he
could not believe that there were enough brains among the proletariat to govern anyone, and, finally, because he distrusted
Stalin as an anti-intellectual. *To the Finland Station* (1940)
shows that, after his visit to Russia in 1935, his distrust changed
to a loathing of Stalin as a tyrant:

> We who of recent years have seen the State that Trotsky helped
> to build in a phase combining the butcheries of the Robespierre
> Terror with the corruption and reaction of the Directory.... have
> seen the successor of Lenin undertake a fabulous rewriting of the
> whole history of the Revolution in order to cancel out Trotsky's
> part; pursue Trotsky from country to country, persecuting even
> his children and hounding them to their deaths; and at last, in
> faked trials and confessions more degrading to the human spirit
> than the frank fiendishness of Iván the Terrible, try to pin upon
> Trotsky the blame of all the mutinies, mistakes and disasters that
> have harassed his administration—till he has made the world con-
> scious of Trotsky as the accuser of Stalin's own bad conscience....
> (413)

The American Communists had gradually repudiated Wilson
with a bitterness all the more severe because they could have
used someone of his intellectual stature to add prestige to their
movement. At first, shortly after "An Appeal to Progressives,"
they were nervous; then they wrote laborious arguments for
New Masses to show that Wilson had misunderstood the Movement and to turn him from the error of his thinking. By the mid-

1930's, when Wilson's disillusionment with Russia was plain, they expressed resentment and dismay; and, by the end of the decade, they became plainly hostile and implied that Wilson was a Fascist.[13]

Granville Hicks, a disillusioned ex-Communist, wrote in 1946 that Wilson had become an "independent radical" soon after the 1932 elections and he attributed this to "his basic incapacity for cooperation with any group of human beings, organized or unorganized."[14] But Daniel Aaron has said more reasonably that Wilson did not affiliate with the Communists because he feared that they were using him. When he accompanied Waldo Frank's delegation of writers to Harlan County, Kentucky, in 1932 to investigate poverty, Wilson did not know until later that the expedition had been planned and directed by the Communist Party.[15]

In 1940, on the question of the United States's entry into World War II, Wilson was silenced. Because of its isolationist policy and its attacks on the Roosevelt administration, the *New Republic* was dissolved and reorganized by the order of a pro-war Englishman named Elmhirst, the second husband of a wealthy widow who had continued her first husband's financing of the magazine. Wilson was out of a job. (See "War" in *A Piece of My Mind.*) Although he replaced Clifton Fadiman as the literary editor of *The New Yorker* in 1943 and later traveled to Europe and the Southwest as its reporter, his career as an analyst and critic of the American scene was apparently as defunct as H. L. Mencken's. Furthermore, the lure of fiction seems to have been especially strong during the 1940's, and Wilson devoted much of his attention to his most ambitious work of the decade, *Memoirs of Hecate County* (1946).

But his involvement in national affairs was far from over. Indeed, in ten years it became more personal than it had ever been; for Wilson found himself in serious income tax trouble. He had not known that failure to file a tax return was a major federal offense, and during the 1940's and early 1950's he earned so little money (an average of two thousand dollars a year from 1947 to 1951) that he thought he should wait to pay his taxes until he made more. Therefore, he filed no return at all between 1946 and 1955; and he was eventually dunned by the government for sixty-nine thousand dollars, including penalties and interest. He discusses the entire matter in *The Cold War and the Income*

Tax (1963), which is partly an account of his tax delinquency and his subsequent Kafkaesque relationship with the Internal Revenue Service, but is mainly a polemic against bureaucracy and federal spending.

For the most part this was an ill-reviewed book. Some reviewers were awed, or pretended to be, by Wilson's willingness to risk his reputation in a diatribe against the government. Richard Gilman, one of the better reviewers, wrote in the *New Republic*: "There is nothing but the most splendid resonance to Wilson's courage and acceptance of responsibility; *The Cold War and the Income Tax* is written with a high civilized indifference to retaliation and sustained by the best kind of humanist conviction that it is the duty of articulate men to speak out against destructive tides in politics and national existence."[16] But Gilman then asserts that Wilson is naïve, that the parallel he draws between American and Russian bureaucracies is exaggerated, that his complaints against chemical warfare and the space race are marginal, and that his understanding of complex international politics is superficial. Although Gilman's complaints have some truth, he misses Wilson's intention: to write not a full analysis of the federal government and international politics but "a protest" on behalf of the intelligent citizen who is mystified by bureaucracy and angered by the way his tax money is spent. The little book is really only a broadsheet, deliberately one-sided and calculated to arouse public ire, the "kind of thing," as Wilson notes in *A Prelude*, that "I have been doing . . . periodically all my life" (*New Yorker* [May 13, 1967], 149).

The anonymous reviewer of *Time* magazine, who missed the book's significance entirely, saw *The Cold War* as a "self-righteous book," an old man's contentiousness, and a writer's special pleading: surely Wilson should have known better than to think that one needn't file an income tax return even if his income were very small.[17] Jason Epstein, however, in the *New York Review of Books*, recognized a kind of "Copperhead" rebellion in Wilson's failure to file and realized that he was really complaining about federal bureaucracy and spending, which Wilson thinks have gone to immoral lengths,[18] particularly in regard to war debts, space projects, and "defense" purposes that include not only conventional and nuclear weapons, but the more refined chemical and bacteriological ones. Nor does he want to support moon travel when worthier projects, such as education, need money.

Wilfred Sheed, writing for *Commonweal,* considered *The Cold War* "an extraordinarily disappointing book": ". . . where one had hoped for majestic indignation, one finds mostly a narrow peevishness; and where the argument needs sustained tensile strength, it tends to go slack and vague. This is Mr. Wilson the country squire, brandishing his cane at the urchins and muttering to himself, like W. C. Fields, about his ineffable woes." Sheed then resorted to Socratic wit: "If the government were to spend his tax-money on culture, instead of on germs, would he then grant its right to coerce and, if necessary, punish him to get it?"[19]— to which the answer is, No. David Bazelon suggested in *Commentary* that Wilson is out of touch with the times and has not thought the tax problem through; but Bazelon perhaps twisted the screw once too often: "He doesn't begin to understand that there is a society existing in which he makes the money on which the taxes are due *because* they are due . . . and paid . . . and spent . . . even on homicidal junk"[20]—which is mere sophistry.

Whether or not one thinks that *The Cold War* is dignified enough for a grand old man of letters, it *is* remarkable that Wilson still expends the energy to defend his social and political viewpoint and that he is willing to speak when most famous literary men of his age (now seventy-four) would have long since been content to withdraw into the shrine of the guest lecture, the symposium, or the graduate seminar to be treated with reverence by polite students. Wilson chooses to protest, and what he protests is something still simpler than the "more and more rigid because more and more mechanized federal government" (*Cold War* [1964], 51). It is, as he states in his recent book on Canadian culture, *O Canada* (1965), "the defense of individual identity against the centralized official domination that can so easily become a faceless despotism" (245).

This stand against centralization is quite opposed to Wilson's progressive position of the early 1930's when Socialism seemed the answer to poverty and to the exploitation of labor. But he learned a lesson in the 1930's about centralization, whose implications he had not understood. In "An Appeal to Progressives," he restated the position of Herbert Croly, the then late editor-in-chief of the *New Republic,* that, "if we were to save the democratic ideal, we must discard the illusion of unlimited freedom and work out a systematic curtailment of the rights of everyone in the interests of all" (*The Shores of Light*, 520). But this curtailment was to be a temporary arrangement only. In *The Cold War* Wilson candidly says that he voted for the Communist ticket in 1932 because he really believed what Lenin had written in *State and Revolution* (1917): eventually "the State, under the new regime, no longer needed by a governing class, would inevitably 'wither away' and cease to harass the individual...." The American Socialist, Wilson says, "full of old-fashioned brotherly 'democracy,'" had never imagined that a centralized, democratic government would become a despotic power (49). But the regime of Stalin soon convinced Wilson that this could happen.

Whether it is possible to remove social evils without a powerful centralized government is questionable; and Wilson's recent position is difficult to defend because it seems paradoxical, if not contradictory: on the one hand, he wants the betterment of life for poor people and the insuring of rights for minority groups; on the other, he desires the independence and individual dignity of an eighteenth-century America. Leon Edel, in the review cited above, calls Wilson, "still that queer creature, the old-fashioned tory-liberal." But even if Wilson is a queer "tory-liberal," his position is not entirely defenseless. For in the decency, stability, and order of the older America, physical and mental well-being were taken for granted: they had to underlie any stable civilization. And Wilson's ancestors worked for a living as farmers or professional people; beyond doing so, they fulfilled their obligations of citizenship and to a small extent participated in government.[21]

But American life has changed drastically, of course; and one change may be that the government has been taken away from the people. In "An Appeal to Progressives" Wilson also wrote: "Our society has finally produced in its specialized professional politicians one of the most useless and obnoxious groups which has perhaps ever disgraced human history—a group that seems unique among governing classes in having managed to be corrupt, uncultivated and incompetent all at once" (*The Shores of Light*, 529). In this most furious liberal stand, Wilson called for the amateur politician of the older America—someone who, like Cincinnatus, would leave his plow and serve. Of course, politics,

[28]

too, has changed and may be too complex for amateurs; and the kind of government that Wilson wants is probably no longer possible in America; like some of the values implied by the Talcottville house, it would be old-fashioned, impractical.

The very complexity of the federal government is what Wilson attacks today, when he maintains, as he does in the Introduction to *Patriotic Gore*, that American bureaucracy is much the same as that of the Soviet Union.[22] Wilson's readers, if one may judge from the reviews of *Patriotic Gore*, are unwilling to accept that comparison,[23] just as the reviewers of *The Cold War* either dismiss Wilson as a special pleader or wonder why he does not realize that he is living in the twentieth century.

It is difficult to estimate Wilson's influence as a commentator on American life. He seems to have been more heeded in the 1930's, when his protest took the form of fairly objective observation (see Chapter 5). One infers this from Irving Howe's careful evaluation in 1948, when he apparently thought that Wilson's important work was finished: "It is, then, as the fragmentary and undeliberate historian of the changing quality of American life that one values Wilson most."[24] On the other hand, even in the enthusiastic era of the 1930's, there were doubters. In England, for example, where Wilson has always been read seriously, Donald Culver, in an admiring review of Wilson's *Devil Take the Hindmost*, stated that Wilson had a "romantic view" of the "Man in the Street." Wilson, Culver said, would not be satisfied with the popular culture that he would establish: "Is any mass movement greatly concerned with the sensitive values which concern such a man as Mr. Wilson? . . . one thinks of Rousseau contemplating the Red Indian."[25]

Ironically enough, "the old-fashioned tory-liberal" was recently associated with a movement to end the war in Vietnam, a movement that William F. Buckley, Jr., editor of the conservative *National Review*, called a "Communist Front."[26] Wilson was one of nearly six hundred writers, editors, painters, sculptors, and theater artists who gave their names to a full-page advertisement entitled "End Your Silence" in the Sunday *New York Times* of June 27, 1965 (18x). The signers, whom *National Review* called "communists, dupes, eccentrics, and perverts," protested "the power being exercised in our names and those of all the American people" to wage "*la sale guerre*." They denied the right of the United States government to interfere in the affairs of Vietnam and the Dominican Republic. "We will not remain silent in the face of our country's shame." Wilson's name appeared with those of many other well-known figures from the intelligentsia, including Jules Feiffer, Dwight MacDonald, Lewis Mumford, Philip Roth, Muriel Rukeyser, and I. F. Stone. The list also included avowed Communists, such as Alvah Bessie, Ring Lardner, Jr., Paul Robeson, and Rockwell Kent. That Wilson should be implicated as a Communist is an amusing commentary on the vagaries of political categorizing when one remembers that Wilson was thoroughly disenchanted with Communism over thirty years ago, that he was then accused of being a Fascist, and that today he prefers a kind of Jeffersonian democracy to any other.

CHAPTER *2*

Literary Criticism

E DMUND WILSON is the best example in America of what
Northrop Frye, in *Anatomy of Criticism*, has called "the
public critic." Such a critic, according to Frye, performs a nec
essary service to the arts and does not lose himself, as the scholar
often does, in the "background" of literature, in "the growing
complication of secondary sources":

> So to "appreciate" literature and get more direct contact with it,
> we turn to the public critic, the Lamb or Hazlitt or Arnold or
> Sainte-Beuve who represents the reading public at its most expert
> and judicious. It is the task of the public critic to exemplify how a
> man of taste uses and evaluates literature, and thus show how lit-
> erature is to be absorbed into society. But here we no longer have
> the sense of an impersonal body of consolidating knowledge. The
> public critic tends to episodic forms like the lecture and the fa-
> miliar essay, and his work is not a science, but another kind of
> literary art. He has picked up his ideas from a pragmatic study
> of literature, and does not try to create or enter into a theoretical
> structure. (8)

Wilson is the "expert and judicious" reader and the critic who
employs "episodic forms." In one way, however, he differs from
Frye's description: although he is not a "theoretical" critic, as
Frye himself is, he attempts in his longer essays to make his
criticism the "science" of revealing in literature the author's personal life. In his most ambitious essays, to be discussed in this
chapter, his approach is largely "biographical" and "psychological"—not merely in bringing facts concerning the author to bear
on the analysis of the work, but in finding in the work itself
revelations about the author. Thus, to return to Frye's terms,
Wilson "evaluates" literature like the public critic, but his "use"
of it is much different. This usage is Wilson's great weakness,
and he is redeemed from it only by his discriminating taste in

evaluating a literary work, or when he becomes again the public critic. This chapter illustrates Wilson's kind of criticism and his method of analysis as observed in his four major critical books— *Axel's Castle, The Wound and the Bow, The Triple Thinkers,* and *Patriotic Gore.*

I Axel's Castle

Wilson is often and wrongly considered a "historical" critic, probably because he viewed himself as such from the first. In the dedicatory letter to Christian Gauss at the beginning of *Axel's Castle* (1931), Wilson wrote: "It was principally from you that I acquired then my idea of what literary criticism ought to be—a history of man's ideas and imaginings in the setting of the conditions which have shaped them." One notices at once that "Gauss's" definition says nothing about criticism as evaluation and nothing, in fact, about literature; rather, it implies that literature amounts to "ideas" and sugests that criticism, then, "ought to be" intellectual history.[1]

Wilson's phrase, "setting of the conditions," suggests that he wanted to record the social, religious, philosophical, and moral tones of an age and to show how literature grew from these —in other words, to do something similar perhaps to what F. O. Matthiessen accomplished later in *American Renaissance* (1941) or what Perry Miller achieved in his great two-volume study, *The New England Mind* (1953, 1954). But Wilson did not attempt that kind of book; for, as he also said in the dedication to Gauss, ". . . this book is only a very limited and a very incomplete attempt at that sort of history"—a statement as true as it is modest.

Matthiessen painstakingly studied the intellectual, social, and political "context" of Emerson, Thoreau, Hawthorne, Melville, and Whitman to account for themes and methods in their work. With Emerson, for example, he demonstrated the influence of Coleridge: in Emerson's stand against eighteenth-century rationalism, in his concern with "organic" art, in his interest in words as signs of natural facts. Emanuel Swedenborg, the eighteenth-century Swedish philosopher, had influenced Emerson, too, particularly in his idea—like Coleridge's—that language is a veil of illusion which will be withdrawn in eternity, when word and being become the same thing. But beyond these intellectual influences, which are established facts of Emerson's biography and are revealed in his own *Journals*, had been certain things typical of Jacksonian America: the concern with seeing, as expressed in photography and open-air painting (the poet, to Emerson, had been above all a *seer*); or the influence of oratory, America's one literary tradition (Emerson had been at his best in the lecture).

But Wilson's first three books of criticism do not deal with a work's "context." Indeed, in two of them—*The Wound and the Bow* and *The Triple Thinkers*—he is historical mainly in that he is biographical, an approach that is limiting and can be misleading. More precisely, he is what might be called "psychobiographical": he attempts to probe into the emotional lives of the writers. Yet his investigations into the genesis of a book are, except when he lapses, unrelated to what he thinks of the work as literature; as a result, his approach (not really historical), which tries to find out "why," usually has nothing to do with his answer as to "how good." His evaluations are frequently and strikingly sound. In fact, Wilson's criticism is inversely successful *as criticism* to the effort that he spends on the man behind the work.

Axel's Castle, then, is not historical criticism—not, at least to the extent that *American Renaissance* is. Wilson does not study the age or "the setting of the conditions" surrounding the authors. In part, however, he writes a succinct history of ideas. In the opening chapter, "Symbolism," he outlines the development of Naturalism and Symbolism from Classicism and Romanticism, respectively. In particular, Wilson points out how Flaubert and Ibsen abandoned Romanticism to take up a new kind of Classicism—Naturalism, the study of "man in relation to his particular environment and time" (9). Wilson shows that Ibsen came to feel the confinement of Naturalism and turned to a modern Romanticism, or Symbolism, for supernatural effects. Meanwhile, in America, Poe "corrected the Romantic looseness and lopped away the Romantic extravagance, at the same time that [he] aimed, not at Naturalistic, but at ultra-Romantic effects"—what Poe called "suggestive indefiniteness" (12-13).

In one of the better early studies of Wilson's criticism, Edward Fiess pointed out the influence of Alfred North Whitehead's *Science and the Modern World* on Wilson's understanding of the Romantics. Wilson apparently used Whitehead's idea that the

Romantic poet had discovered a new, subjective way of interpreting reality. Furthermore, in considering Whitehead's suggestion that the Romantic movement was a reaction against Newtonian science, Wilson saw a parallel in Symbolist poetry and nineteenth-century science.[2]

The mingling of real and imaginary experience and the deliberate confusing of different sense perceptions (Poe's *hearing* the darkness of night), as well as the attempt to approximate music with the sounds of words, was not new in English poetry, particularly since the sixteenth and seventeenth centuries. To French poets, however, who had been under Classical restraints since the Renaissance, it was a revolutionary influence. But, as Wilson points out, the counter influence of French on English literature was not recognized by most English-writing critics: "the battle of Symbolism has never properly been fought out in English . . . . the critics of the English-speaking countries have often seemed not to know how to deal with writers such as Eliot and Joyce" (23-4). Thus there was a definite need in 1930 for such a book as *Axel's Castle,* which today has been superseded by more elaborate studies of the Symbolists. But the essays on Proust and Joyce are still fine examples of literary analysis and evaluation; the Joyce essay is particularly remarkable when one considers that it was first published in 1929 when *Ulysses* was still a mystery to many literary people and *Finnegans Wake* an odd, avantgarde work-in-progress.[3]

Wilson's critical method in "James Joyce" comprises an explication of the Homeric parallels and the various "minds" in *Ulysses,* and comparisons of Proust and Flaubert in regard to psychological portrayals of characters.[4] Wilson objects to Joyce's virtuosity, his "excess of design"; but with typical fairness he also shows how even the episodes that he disapproves of on artistic grounds contribute to a "transcendent understanding" of human nature, which to Wilson is what literature should achieve. Wilson concludes the essay with a commentary on the unfinished *Finnegans Wake,* part of which had been published in *transition.*

Perhaps the best part of "James Joyce" is the discussion of the fusing of Naturalism and Symbolism:

Joyce takes us thus directly into the consiousness of his characters, and in order to do so, he has availed himself of methods of which Flaubert never dreamed—of the methods of Symbolism. He has, in "Ulysses," exploited together, as no writer had thought to do before, the resources both of Symbolism and Naturalism. Proust's novel, masterly as it is, does perhaps represent a falling over into decadence of psychological fiction: the subjective element is finally allowed to invade and to deteriorate even those aspects of the story which really ought to be kept strictly objective if one is to believe that it is actually happening. But Joyce's grasp on his objective world never slips: his work is unshakably established on Naturalistic foundations. (204)

It is obvious that so perceptive and judicious an essay—an achievement beyond the depth of most public critics and beyond the originality and scope of most academic ones—demanded a thorough analysis, not only of Joyce's work, and Homer's, but also of those writers who were artistically akin to him. Throughout *Axel's Castle* Wilson's thoroughness is rewarded by fine insights and sound judgments, such as the description of Yeats's prose as "the product of some dying loomcraft brought to perfection in the days before machinery . . . . still a garment worn in the old-fashioned personal manner with a combination of elegance and ease, at the same time that it is unmistakably of our time by virtue of a certain modern terseness and of a characteristically modern trick . . . of revealing by unexpected juxtapositions relations of which one had not been aware . . . or of effecting almost startling transitions from the particular to the general and back again" (45-6).

This kind of statement, like those on the dramatic character of Eliot's imagination and on the Symbolist poet's overthrowal of the traditional dualism of plain fact and the varying apprehension of fact, properly falls within the province of the critic. Having come from an analysis of the writings rather than of the writer, it may be examined, challenged, and used by anyone studying those writings. Sometimes, however, even this early in his career, Wilson sees literature as a kind of exposé of the author and he attempts to penetrate the work to reach and criticize the man who wrote. In his essay on Yeats, for example, he begins to speak of the voice in Yeats's poetry as if it were that of the man himself: "In the frustration of early love, apparently, he has paid the price of escaping to fairyland, and the memory of it is bitter: he still champions, he still puts above everything, the nobility and splendor of the imagination; but he must face life's hard conditions" (34-5). Wilson does not merely mean "the poet" or a persona, but obviously the man Yeats: "He finds his subjects now in the events of his own life, no longer transposed into romantic convention, and in the public affairs of Ireland" (36-7).

This divergence through the work to the author is evident in Wilson's discussion of Paul Valéry's poetry and, to some extent, T. S. Eliot's: "And I am a little tired at hearing Eliot, only in his early forties, present himself as an 'agèd eagle' who asks why he should make the effort to stretch his wings" (130). The artistic propriety of the eagle image within the poem itself does not seem to concern Wilson, who apparently did not think out his assumption that through the poetry one comes to know the man/poet and that in discussing the poetry one is really talking about the man himself.[5]

Other passages in the essay on Eliot suggest that Wilson was unsure of the object of his criticism. On the one hand, he seems to be speaking of the voice in the poetry:

> The poet of "The Waste Land" is living half the time in the real world of contemporary London and half the time in the haunted wilderness of the mediaeval legend. The water for which he longs in the twilight desert of his dream is to quench the spiritual thirst which torments him in the London dusk . . . the poet . . . making water the symbol of all freedom, all fecundity and flowering of the soul, invokes in desperate need the memory of an April shower of his youth, the song of the hermit thrush with its sound of water dripping and the vision of a drowned Phoenician sailor. . . . (106-7)

But at times Wilson identifies this voice with the poet himself: "We recognize throughout 'The Waste Land' the peculiar conflicts of the Puritan turned artist: the horror of vulgarity and the shy sympathy with the common life, the ascetic shrinking from sexual experience and the distress at the drying up of the springs of sexual emotion, with the straining after a religious emotion which may be made to take its place" (105).

It becomes increasingly apparent in *Axel's Castle*, then, that what most interests Wilson is the psychology of the author. He writes in "Marcel Proust": "The real elements, of course, of any work of fiction, are the elements of the author's personality: his imagination embodies in the images of characters, situations and scenes the fundamental conflicts of his nature or the cycle of phases through which it habitually passes. His personages are personifications of the author's various impulses and emotions: and the relations between them in his stories are really the relations between these" (176).

This kind of critical viewpoint, lying somewhere between a psychological and a biographical approach, is attacked by René Wellck (with Austin Warren) in *Theory of Literature*: "The biographical approach forgets that a work of art is not simply the embodiment of experience but [is] . . . determined, so far as it is determined at all, by literary tradition and convention. . . . [The artist sees] actual experiences . . . with a view to their use in literature . . . already partially shaped by artistic traditions and preconceptions. . . . No biographical evidence can change or influence critical evaluation" (66-8). Later, in *The Triple Thinkers* and *The Wound and the Bow*, Wilson's weakness for psychobiographical criticism leads him to indefensible extremes and occasionally even away from essential scholarship.

But in *Axel's Castle* this tendency is more than counterbalanced by two strong virtues: Wilson's ability to write a compressed, coherent survey of ideas; and his even greater adeptness in paraphrasing and summarizing the works he discusses—a skill essential for the public critic. To these a third may be added: his gift for comparative criticism. How revealing are his juxtapositions of Anatole France and Paul Valéry, T. S. Eliot and Ezra Pound, Proust and Dickens—or his deft comparisons of Tristan Corbière, Jules Laforgue, Stéphane Mallarmé, and Eliot. His remarks later in "The Historical Interpretation of Literature" (1940) on this nonhistorical kind of criticism suggest that he might have learned it from Eliot and from the English critic George Saintsbury. Paradoxically, until Wilson wrote *Patriotic Gore* (1962), he was better at comparative criticism than at historical, which he has always preferred.

II   *Marxism and Humanism*

Another tendency in *Axel's Castle* is toward social and moral criticism. By the time Wilson reaches the last chapter, "Axel and

Rimbaud," he regards Symbolism not as just a literary method or a movement in literature, but as a dangerous philosophy of renouncing the everyday world, of withdrawing like "maladjusted" *fin de siècle* poets from "general life" (268-9). If writers won't deal with contemporary society through scientific study, reform, or satire, as Wilson believes they should, he sees only two courses left to them: an isolation like that of Villiers de'Isle-Adam's Axel or a search like Arthur Rimbaud's for values in the primitive life. Malcolm Cowley, who has criticized Wilson for changing his conception of Symbolism from a method to an ideology, asserts, in *Exile's Return* (1951), the "Symbolistic *method* is less important than he believes it to be," and "the *attitude toward life* which he attributes to Yeats and Valéry and Villiers de l'Isle-Adam was also that of many writers who could not in any technical sense be regarded as Symbolists" (141).

Because Wilson became increasingly concerned with a writer's social and moral obligations, and in the late 1920's and early 1930's viewed Marxism as the hope for America, some of his readers have assumed that he was a Marxist critic. Marxism, however, has never been a significant part of his criticism, as it was so fundamentally that of Michael Gold, Granville Hicks, Joseph Freeman, and the other regular contributors to *New Masses*. Certainly Wilson has emphasized accurate social observation, which a Marxist critic would have done; certainly, too, like the Marxist—and Humanist—critic Wilson has always stressed the moral value of literature. The Marxist, however, limited art to propaganda; he based his evaluation of a literary work on how well it defined for the proletarian reader his role in the class struggle, how closely this reader could identify with the characters, and how accurately the author's point of view reflected that of the proletariat. In "Marxism and Literature" (1937) Wilson noted that Engels himself had preferred reactionary Balzac to democratic Zola because Balzac *hid* his political ideas in his novels (*The Triple Thinkers*, 205). Furthermore, as Wilson pointed out in "Communist Criticism" (1937), the Marxist belief in government control of the arts was "quite alien to the practice of Marx and Engels, who in general enjoyed art for what it was worth and pursued their political-economic analysis, even when applied to art, as something belonging to a different department" (*The Shores of Light*, 647).

[38]

For Wilson, then, literature has never been merely a social service, as he clearly states in "Marxism and Literature": "Yet the man who tries to apply Marxist principles without real understanding of literature is liable to go horribly wrong. For one thing, it is usually true in works of the highest order that the purport is not a simple message, but a complex vision of things, which itself is not explicit but implicit; and the reader who does not grasp them artistically, but is merely looking for simple social morals, is certain to be hopelessly confused" (*The Triple Thinkers*, 205). This essay, first published in the *Atlantic Monthly*, was attacked in the Marxist press. "Wilson," wrote Joseph Freeman, "gives neither the American Marxists nor *International Literature* credit for the many sensible things he learned from them; he quotes them only when they have said something which strikes him as ridiculous."[6] One of Wilson's most direct statements on literature and criticism, "Marxism and Literature" approaches literary theory more closely than anything else he has written. It stresses the social significance of literature and its moral effect, which Wilson allows may be entirely personal and something quite different from the author's moral insight. And the essay plainly deplores the "formulas" of both Marxists and Humanists.

But Marxist criticism in America was not so important as it was in Europe with Georg Lukács or in England with Christopher Caudwell. In *On Native Grounds* (1942) Alfred Kazin has said that it was "less a movement than a tendency": it "comes down to four systematic books...V. F. Calverton's *The Liberation of American Literature*, Granville Hicks's *The Great Tradition* and *Figures of Transition*, and Bernard Smith's *Forces in American Criticism.*" Kazin amusingly describes "the characteristic production of Marxist criticism in the thirties" as "a polemic written in answer to a polemic in last Saturday's *New Masses* that had in turn been written as a polemic in answer to someone's ineffable book review in the *Daily Worker* of a week before..." (408). One needs only to read *New Masses* of the 1930's to learn that Kazin does not exaggerate; it is a strange mixture of hysteria and naïveté. René Wellek in *Concepts of Criticism* (1963) has written that the Marxist approach, although it excited interest, was ineffective: "the sociological approach proved singularly unattractive to American literary scholarship and produced relatively little work of real distinction." But Wellek has also said that the lack of "genuine Marxist criticism" in the United States seems due to "ignorance or lack of interest in the kind of criticism practiced by George Lukács or T. W. Adorno with such great acclaim on the Continent" (305-6, 331).

The Humanists, or "Neo-Humanists," a much more formidable group intellectually than the Marxists, were chiefly represented by Professors Irving Babbitt (Harvard) and Paul Elmer More (Princeton), whom Wilson enjoyed attacking. They evaluated a literary work, Wilson said, by how closely it conformed to a moral and esthetic dogma which they found in the dramas of Sophocles and Euripides. In "Notes on Babbitt and More" and "Sophocles, Babbitt and Freud" (1930), Wilson underscored the truism that these "laws" were formulated not by the Greek dramatists but by Aristotle half a century after they had died (*The Shores of Light*, 451-75). The Humanists' ideal writers, Sophocles and Shakespeare, he wrote in "Marxism and Literature," like the Marxists' ideal Tolstoy, were "imaginary": "if Babbitt and More had been able to enforce against Shakespeare their moral and esthetic injunctions he would never have written a line" (*The Triple Thinkers*, 207-8).

Wilson's attack was not entirely fair—literary infighting rarely is.[7] And he oversimplified his opponents' position. The Humanists, after all, were intelligent men, and their better representatives were more learned than Wilson. In the late 1920's their most eloquent spokesman was perhaps Norman Foerster, who applied Walt Whitman's warning against the "smart and superficial modernity" of contemporary writers who had no use for "the heritage of the past." Foerster argued that, while nothing should be accepted on authority alone, ideas in the present have nevertheless issued from the past: "Nothing is more certain than the law of continuity, by virtue of which an age loosely termed revolutionary derives its formative ideas from the age previous" (*American Criticism*, 227). The then current belief that old ideas were outmoded and had no bearing on the present was based on ignorance: "If the old views rested in part upon ignorance of nature, our revolutionary views rest in part upon ignorance of the past. While romanticism has been priding itself upon its universal sympathy and understanding, and scientific realism upon its honest search for truth, both alike have failed to penetrate the essentials of the old views and to disengage them from the accidents. The modern world has been provincially intent upon its own special achievement and arrogantly indifferent to the achievement of the past. A curious consequence of this fact is a persistent confusion between the values derivable from naturism and the values inherited from humanism and religion" (234).

The doctrine and discipline of Humanism, as stated by Foerster, were, briefly, completeness ("the cultivation of every part of human nature"); proportion, or a harmony of parts with the whole (which implied a scale of values); concern for "the *normally or typically human*"; faith in reason (unlike Romanticism) and yet an attempt to transcend reason "by the use of *intuition or imagination*" (like Romanticism) in order to cope with a higher reality; and the "ultimate ethical principle" of restraint (as opposed to the excesses of both Romanticism and Naturalism (241-3).

The chief weakness in Humanism—at least the point that encouraged the most abuse—was the "central assumption ... of a dualism of man and nature." Foerster asserted that man's "world of value and quality" differentiates him from a "merely quantitative natural order" (238)—the kind of statement that elicited hoots from H. L. Mencken and others who championed the Naturalistic novel. Apart from the man-nature dualism, the Humanists seem to have made false dichotomies between content and form and, despite their belief in the law of continuity, between "ancient" and "modern." In *Theory of Literature*, Wellek points out that positivism, for example, with which the Humanists were unsympathetic, has an old history, deriving from Democritus and Lucretius in the fourth and first centuries B.C. Furthermore, the Humanists tended to view literature as more philosophical than it really is and to confuse philosophical truth with artistic value (106, 110, 112).

In accounting for the failure of the Humanist movement to take hold in the universities, Wellek has said: "... the social conservatism of the New Humanists ran counter to the temper of a nation plunged into the depression, their rigid moralism violated the nature of literature as an art, and their hostility to the contemporary arts cut them off from literature as a living institution" (*Concepts of Criticism*, 304-5). From a practical standpoint the failure of Humanism as criticism lay in the last point—its inability to deal with contemporary literature. In "Marxism and Literature" Wilson said that the only contemporary novel which even approached the specifications of the Humanists was Thornton Wilder's *The Bridge of San Luis Rey* and that they were unsure even about it (*The Triple Thinkers,* 207).

Wilson, too, has stressed the moral value of literature, but he is never so positive as the Humanists or the Marxists as to what this means exactly. His moral standard—"a complex vision of things" and "an attempt to give a meaning to our experience"[8]— is, although vague, more pliable than that of either the Marxists or the Humanists. It allows for a greater imaginative and critical achievement; and, despite Wilson's fears of the social and philosophical inferences, it made possible an understanding and appreciation of the Symbolists which the Marxists and Humanists could not share.

III The Wound and the Bow *and* The Triple Thinkers

Although it too is a collection of independent essays, *The Wound and the Bow* (1941) depends somewhat more than *Axel's Castle* upon a thesis: the creative ability of an artist is really a compensation for a psychological wound. But the thesis is less demonstrated than assumed. The six essays on authors from Jacques Casanova to Ernest Hemingway do not really show how creative ability is related to a wound, but all except one reveal that each writer was in some way "scarred." The exception and the best, in a literary sense, is "The Dream Of H. C. Earwicker," an explication of the characterization, structure, and language of *Finnegans Wake* which treats this work as efficaciously as the James Joyce essay in *Axel's Castle* did *Ulysses.* But "The Dream Of H. C. Earwicker" has virtually nothing to do with Joyce himself except to mention briefly his glaucoma, and coincidentally it escapes the damage visited upon the other essays by Wilson's psychobiographical preoccupation. (In the front matter of *Wound* Wilson quotes a passage from "Tilly" in Joyce's *Pomes Penyeach* to echo his theme: "I bleed by the black stream/For my torn bough!")

According to Wilson, the ("Freudian") idea of "superior strength as inseparable from disability" is the theme of Sophocles' *Philoctetes*, a play—discussed in the seventh and final essay—titled after the legendary archer bitten by a serpent and abandoned by the Greek army on Lemnos when his wound would not heal; ten years later his comrades beg him to come to Troy, where they cannot win without his wonderful bow, a gift from Hercules. Wilson views the theme of the obstinate exile, incurably wounded yet miraculously strong, as a significant explanation of creative ability; and he finds again in André Gide's modern treatment, *Philoctète*, the implication "that genius and disease, like strength and mutilation, may be inextricably bound up together" (287-9).

The theory raises several objections. First, regardless of its validity as an explanation of the genesis of a work of art, it is unnecessary and suspect in literary explication—and worthless in evaluation. Second, has Wilson dealt accurately with Philoctetes? Delmore Schwartz, in an essay dealing primarily with *The Wound and the Bow*, pointed out the simple fact that Philoctetes received the bow from Hercules before he was wounded; the strength, or bow, was unconnected with the disability.[9] (For Wilson, however, the artist's ability is not confined solely to talent; he sees the stricken Philoctetes as superior to his fellows in his very defiance of them.) Third, the whole concept of artistic compensation for a defect is doubtful, as Austin Warren has noted in *Theory of Literature* (69-70); and Louis Fraiberg, a student of psychoanalysis, has suggested in *Psychoanalysis and Literary Criticism* (1960) that Wilson's understanding of psychoanalysis is limited. Freud, say Fraiberg, could find no connection between talent and maladjustment:

> The most he will say is that some writers—but by no means all—suffer from neuroses of one kind or another, just as other people do. Art may be influenced by neurotic elements in the writer's personality, but it may just as readily spring from fantasies of a normal, emotionally healthy kind. Some artists are ill, but it is not at all necessary to be sick in order to be an artist; illness may even diminish the artist's power. Some works of art may be used by their creators as—among other things—curative agents, but this tells us nothing since any idea may be involved in a neurotic system and may either advance the neurosis or help to counteract it. Nor does psychoanalysis provide any support for the assumption that neurosis always finds expression in art. On the contrary, it

specifically describes a great variety of behavior patterns, neurotic in origin, which have nothing directly to do with art. (163)

"Dickens: The Two Scrooges" and "The Kipling That Nobody Read," the most ambitious essays in *The Wound and the Bow*, most represent its thesis. In both, Wilson exaggerates the importance to an artist's work of traumatic experiences in childhood—with Dickens, the blacking warehouse circumstances; with Kipling, six awful years before twelve, living with relatives in England. No doubt the Camden Town poverty made the nine-year-old Dickens wretched, and the humiliation at twelve of working for six months at six shillings a week pasting labels on bottles in a blacking warehouse while his father languished nearby in the Marshalsea debtors' prison left permanent scars and probably influenced Dickens's work. The *Leben-Kunst* approach to an author is venerable and is sometimes useful to anyone wanting to know why he chose certain subjects. But a knowledge of the misfortunes which years earlier may have originated a novel does not help us, as Wilson says, to *understand* the *work*, which has its own life. If the two main themes of the early novels are the criminal and the rebel, as Wilson says, they are discernible to the careful reader whether he knows anything about the man Dickens or not. Indeed, if the suffering of Dickens himself is unmistakable in the product of his imagination, the novel is probably defective as a self-contained work of art, whatever its merits as journalism or autobiography. Wilson's approach to Dickens the novelist was fundamentally wrong: "It is necessary to see him as a man in order to appreciate him as an artist..." (9). What *is* necessary to appreciate Dickens as an artist is a willingness to see him *primarily* as an *artist*—an imitator, a fictionalist, a more or less detached craftsman.

Bleak House and *Our Mutual Friend* are made no more comprehensible for one's knowing that Dickens, unhappy in his marriage, separated from his wife after ten children and established the eighteen-year-old actress Ellen Ternan in a house of her own as his mistress (a fact discreetly omitted by the *Dictionary of National Biography*); that he was hypersensitive about his dignity, refusing a command performance for the queen, and tormented by money problems; and that, in short, he was a manic depressive. These facts satisfy a reasonable curiosity about a

famous man; but they do not aid in comprehending the recre-
ated, and therefore imagined, experience of the novels. Again,
the reader need not know that the man Dickens was hostile to
the Victorian middle class in order to recognize that in *Martin
Chuzzlewit* and *Dombey and Son* the decline of homey values
and the rise of big business with the attendant evils of big cities
are deplored.

But, as in *Axel's Castle*, when Wilson focuses his attention on
literary analysis and explication, he writes with authority: his
discussion of the symbolism in *Dombey* and *Hard Times*, in
Bleak House, Little Dorrit, and *Our Mutual Friend*; his comparison of Dickens with Dostoevsky; his observation that a dualism of good and evil ("the two Scrooges") runs throughout Dickens' work. Wilson's perceptions are admirably clear when he
shows how the mean old men of the earlier novels—Ralph
Nickleby and Anthony Gride, Anthony and Jonas Chuzzlewit—
become the sinister, more hypocritically evil Pecksniff, Dombey,
and Murdstone; or when he points out that Dickens invented a
new genre, the novel of the social group, approximated only by
Balzac, as well as a related genre:

> He creates the detective story which is also a social fable . . . . a
> *genre* which has lapsed since Dickens. The detective story—though
> Dickens' friend Wilkie Collins preserved a certain amount of so-
> cial satire—has dropped out the Dickensian social content; and
> the continuators of the social novel have dropped the detective
> story. These continuators—Shaw, Galsworthy, Wells—have of
> course gone further than Dickens in the realistic presentation of
> emotion; but from the point of view of dramatizing social issues,
> they have hardly improved upon *Bleak House*. (36)

What is striking about Wilson's genuine criticism is that it
gains nothing from his biographical interests. If anything, his
critical acumen is dulled by his desire to learn more about
Dickens himself, as when he appears to resent *David Copperfield*
for not being more autobiographical: "But *Copperfield* is not
one of Dickens' deepest books: it is something in the nature of
a holiday. David is too candid and simple to represent Dickens
himself; and though the blacking warehouse episode is utilized,
all the other bitter circumstances of Dickens' youth were dropped out when he abandoned the autobiography" (43).

However, in the final twenty-one pages (a disproportionately large amount in an essay of 104 pages), which Wilson devotes to *Edwin Drood*, his psychobiographical approach does contribute something to one's understanding. He sets out to solve the enigma of *Drood*, to show how it continues the psychological interest of Dickens' later books and, as one expects, to account for Dickens' writing it. From a study by Howard Duffield which argued that John Jasper, the murderer, was a member of the Indian sect of Thugs, and from another by Aubrey Boyd, that Jasper was a hypnotist, as was Dickens himself, Wilson speculates fairly convincingly about what might have happened had the novel been finished. He also shows what Dickens was attempting in it—an exploitation of the entanglement of good and evil in one man. Here Wilson's approach is helpful for interpretation. But this case is unusual: the novel *is* incomplete; it falls into that category of works of art which were never finished and which therefore permit only a speculative interpretation and a qualified evaluation. In this instance it seems fair to go to the author's life for any suggestions as to what he intended—at least to do so after one has studied his total work.

Wilson apparently read the total work, including the minor non-fiction, and most of the scanty criticism of it. He also read the eighteenth-century novelists that composed much of Dickens' own reading, Dickens' contemporaries for an understanding of the intellectual "climate," and later English writers, such as John Galsworthy and H. G. Wells. In a literary sense, his preparation for Dickens, as for Joyce, was thorough. And he was a pioneer among serious students of Dickens, who in his own country, not to mention elsewhere, had been awarded "the scantiest serious attention." There had been a few good essays, such as those by George Gissing, G. B. Shaw, G. K. Chesterton and George Santayana (whom Wilson does not mention), as well as a psychological and a Marxist study. And there had been one brilliant essay— George Orwell's of 1939—which Wilson could not yet have seen. Otherwise there were many dubious memoirs, anecdotes, reminiscences, and short "lives" by a number of legend-makers, in addition to the genius-of-Dickens sort of "appreciation."

With Rudyard Kipling, too, Wilson dealt with the intellectually unfashionable. "The Kipling That Nobody Read," which concentrates on Kipling's later and least popular stories, differs from the Dickens essay in that it has a tighter order. This cohesion may be due to the facts that Kipling's illnesses, disillusion, and nervous breakdowns—particularly between the end of World War I and 1936, when he died, his reputation in "eclipse"—fall into a pattern and that his life can be conveniently laid out by the places among which he moved—India, England, America, South Africa, and so on. Another difference is that Wilson seems to have more compassion for Kipling than for Dickens. But, as in "The Two Scrooges," Wilson again commits the fallacy of explaining the work in terms of the man: "The fiction of Kipling, then, does not dramatize any fundamental conflict *because* Kipling would never face one" (126, italics added).

But once more Wilson's insights are clear, and his handling of comparative criticism is capable:

> Compare a story of the middle Kipling with a story by Stephen Crane or Joseph Conrad, who were dealing with somewhat similar subjects. Both Conrad and Crane are pursuing their independent researches into the moral life of man. Where the spy who is the hero of *Under Western Eyes* is a tormented and touching figure, confused in his allegiances by the circumstances of his birth, a secret agent in Kipling must invariably be a stout fellow, because his ruses are to the advantage of the British, or a sinister lying dog, because he is serving the enemy. Where the killing of *The Blue Hotel* is made to implicate everybody connected with it in a common human guilt, a killing in a story by Kipling must absolutely be shown to be either a dastardly or a virtuous act. (150)

"The Kipling that Nobody Read" exemplifies the problem of confusing the author's "voice" with the author, who admittedly is Wilson's major interest. To read Wilson and benefit from him, one should distinguish when he runs the two together. For example, it is acceptable for Wilson to write: "There was, as I say, a Wesleyan preacher in Kipling. The Old Testament served him as an armory of grim instances and menacing visions to drive home the imperial code; or, on occasions when the imperial masters failed to live up to this code, of scorching rhetorical language (though with more of malignancy than of grandeur) for the chastisement of a generation of vipers. But Kipling had no real religion. He exploited, in his poems and his fiction, the mythology of a number of religions" (162). As far as one can tell, Wilson is speaking about "Kipling"—the voice in the writings. This is genuine criticism, and all one has to do to determine whether or not it is valid is to place it against Kipling's poems and stories.

For the same reason it is justifiable for Wilson to say: "It is a key to the whole work of Kipling that the great celebrant of physical courage should prove in the long run to convey his most moving and convincing effects in describing moral panic. Kipling's bullyings and killings are contemptible: they are fantasies of the physically helpless. The only authentic heroism to be found in the fiction of Kipling is the heroism of moral fortitude on the edge of a nervous collapse" (167-8). But it is less acceptable, as criticism, for Wilson to say: "Something in him, something vulgar in the middleclass British way, something perhaps connected with the Methodist ministers who were his grandfathers on both sides, a tradition which understood preaching and could understand craftsmanship, but had a good deal of respect for the powers that governed the material world and never thought of putting the artist on a par with them —something of this sort at a given point prevented Kipling from playing through his part, and betrayed him into dedicating his talents to the praise of the practical man" (151). If Wilson's remarks about Kipling's grandparents are reasonable (though speculative), his pseudo-genetic conclusions about their influence on Kipling are not.

The following quotation, which illustrates as well as any other the subtle confusion between man and artist, begins and continues well enough as literary analysis; but then it is ruined by wild guessing about Kipling: "The depression described in *The House Surgeon* has been transferred, by the artifice of the story, to persons unconcerned in the tragedy through the influence from a distance of someone else; but the woman with whom the terror originates is suffering morbidly from feelings of guilt, *and the sensations are evidently based on the first-hand experience of the author*" (164, italics added). When the concern of the critic becomes Kipling and not "Kipling," it is no longer literary criticism but biography—or gossip.

The Triple Thinkers (1948) is a loose collection of twelve essays without a general thesis. Wilson selected the title from a letter that Gustave Flaubert wrote to his mistress, Louise Colet, in 1853: "In our day I believe that a thinker (and what is an artist if not a triple thinker?) should have neither religion, country, nor even social conviction."[10] Flaubert seems to have meant that an artist should possess not only imagination but a rigorous intellect, as opposed to sentimentality, cleverness, and sensuality; but Wilson's precise use of the phrase as a title is not clear.

The essays in this volume range from fairly light autobiography and reminiscence (" 'Mr. Rolfe,' " Wilson's master in Greek at Hill, and "Mr. [Paul Elmer] More and the Mithraic Bull") to serious literary reflections ("Marxism and Literature" and "The Historical Interpretation of Literature"). In between lie a number of very different pieces: a summary and explanation of Pushkin's *Evgeni Onegin* and Wilson's own translation of "The Bronze Horseman"; a revaluation of an old Wilson hero, "Bernard Shaw at Eighty"; a discussion of Flaubert's "politics" which attempts to show that his writings reveal a moral concern as strong as Karl Marx's but culminate in a Swiftian disillusionment; a fine biographical essay on John Jay Chapman inspired by and based upon the now late M. A. De Wolfe Howe's *John Jay Chapman and His Letters* (1937); and an essay showing how the concept and uses of poetry have changed in Western culture and posing the rhetorical question, "Is Verse a Dying Technique?" But the most striking and ambitious essays are "The Ambiguity of Henry James" and "Morose Ben Jonson"; in both of these Wilson's psychobiographical interests continue and, in the latter and more recent essay, intensify.

"The Ambiguity of Henry James" displays a certain ambiguity of Wilson's own. He doesn't seem to know how to take James, whose work is apparently so less realistic and topical than that of such contemporaries and early Wilson favorites as G. B. Shaw and H. G. Wells, and his approach is confused. He begins with a six-page summary of *The Turn of the Screw* and seizes upon the theory—admittedly not his own—that the narrator-governess is "a neurotic case of sex repression" (88): she is first infatuated with her employer and then with his young nephew, and she imagines that the former valet and governess have returned as ghosts and are in some way corrupting the boy and his little sister.

When Wilson first published his essay in *Hound and Horn*

(April-June, 1934), he had not yet seen James's *Notebooks*, which were not published until 1947 and which show that James intended to write simply a ghost story. Of course, despite James's intentions, *The Turn of the Screw* could be something other than a ghost story, and there is a healthy skepticism in Wilson's refusal to quite believe James's assertions in his letters and in his preface to a collection of his own stories, which dismiss the tale as a "pot-boiler" or a "fairy-tale." There is no good reason for wholly accepting an artist's claim for his own work—this fact should be a critical maxim, although it is not. Dorothea Krook, in *The Ordeal of Consciousness in Henry James* (1962), accepts James's intentions too readily, just as she accepts "the testimony to the governess's perfect normality carefully set out in the prologue to the story" (373). Miss Krook, reviewing the case advanced by a number of critics against Wilson's interpretation, concludes that Wilson was incorrect and irresponsible in arguing that the governess was sexually repressed. But she also points out very fairly that Wilson was right in noting the ambiguity— the story *can* be read in more than one way, and the governess *does* seem to be guilty of something—which depends on the fact that the governess herself tells the entire story.

To Wilson, the governess represents "a variation on one of [James's] familiar themes: the thwarted Anglo-Saxon spinster," who appears—Wilson notes—in *The Bostonians*, "The Marriages," *The Reverberator*, and *The Wings of the Dove*.[11] The counterparts to James's perverted or apathetic women are the heroes of "The Beast in the Jungle," *The Europeans*, *The Ambassadors*, and other works, who "have a way of missing out on emotional experience" (96). These hesitant figures with their "bourgeois qualities of timidity, prudence, primness" disturb Wilson (101). He wishes that James had revealed more of his characters and had directed the reader's attitude toward them more strongly: where Flaubert clearly portrays a double-crossing fool, James draws a young man who "is made wondering and wistful and is likely to turn out a pitiful victim" (102).

In the 1948 postword to his essay Wilson observes that neither does one learn very much from the characters themselves, because they are not really introspective: "What we see when we are supposed to look into their minds is something as much arranged by James to conceal, to mislead and to create suspense

as the actual events presented. These people, so far as the 'psy-
chologizing' goes, are not intimate even with themselves. They
talk to themselves about what they are doing and what is happening to them even a good deal less frankly than James talks
to himself about them, and that is already with the perfect discretion of an after-dinner conversation between two gentlemanly
diners-out" (126). Certainly much of the dialogue of James's
characters, whether with others or themselves, is a well-bred
mixture of statement and reticence. But Wilson almost resents
James, as he did Yeats, for not explaining everything and for
tending to leave the reader guessing (an old criticism held by
William Dean Howells and other early readers): ". . . his adulteries
. . . . are not always really explained, we cannot always be sure
that they are really there, that the people have been to bed together. But, on the other hand, we sometimes feel the presence,
lurking like 'the beast in the jungle,' of other emotional factors
with which the author himself does not always appear to have
reckoned" (127).

Having "reckoned" with emotional factors or not—an *ad hom-
inem* argument that is irrelevant—James nevertheless evoked
their "presence." An obvious answer to Wilson is that James op-
erates fairly consistently within the rules he has set up. When
he "conceals" characters from the reader (and the careful reader
does not find them so obscure or incredible), he thereby creates drama, as Wilson himself has suggested; and he keeps to
the narrative method he favors of restricting the "point of view"
to a single consciousness who realizes only so much and who,
for all his intelligent observing, may, like Marcher ("The Beast
in the Jungle"), delude himself or, like Strether (*The Ambassadors*), find himself bound by a Puritan conscience.[12] A more
general answer, of course, is that transparency is not everything,
that suggestion and ambiguity are present in literature more
often than not and, indeed, may even make up the "substance"
of an era's literature, as with the French Symbolists, who were
flourishing when James had mastered his craft. Finally, one
might consider the following statement by T. S. Eliot, writing on
James, J. G. Frazer, and F. H. Bradley in the February, 1924,
issue of *Vanity Fair* (and quoted by Dorothea Krook at the beginning of her book cited above): "With 'character,' in the sense
in which the portrayal of character is usually expected in the

English novel, [James] had no concern; but his critics do not understand that 'character' is only one of the ways in which it is possible to grasp at reality...."

As with other Wilson essays already discussed in this book, there are one or two points in "The Ambiguity" that stand out as incisive, if somewhat sketchy, comment: the sympathetic discussion of James's unfinished novel, *The Ivory Tower*, which seems to have fascinated Wilson as much as Dickens' *Edwin Drood* did; and, perhaps the most interesting part of the entire essay, the attempt to establish James, the homesick exile returned, as a genuinely American writer in whose work triumph "the ideals of the United States" (114)—which comes closer than anything else to being Wilson's thesis.

But as criticism Wilson's essay is not solid. First, a vagueness of plan gives it an ambiguously meandering air. Wilson seems—but only seems—to divide James's work into four parts: a nonsexual period (through *The Tragic Muse*, in 1890); a sexual, or *Awkward Age*, period (love affairs behind "thick screens") beginning after the failure of James's play *Guy Domville* in 1895 and related in some not entirely clear way to James's failure as a playwright; then, starting with *The Wings of the Dove*, what might be called the American period; and, finally, very late in James's career (*The Ivory Tower*), the period of "a new kind of realism" concerning "the poor and the old, even ... the uncouth, the grotesque" (119-20). But Wilson never troubles with the publication dates of James's novels, and he blurs the "periods" further by mixing up his discussions of certain novels. For example, in the fifth part of his essay he begins by mentioning *The Ambassadors*, *The Wings of the Dove* and *The Golden Bowl* (period three), only to jump immediately backward to period two, then suddenly to period one (*The Portrait of a Lady*), and *then* to period three again—to discuss, not the three great novels, but James's account of his trip across the United States, *The American Scene* (1907).

Carelessness is a major weakness in "The Ambiguity." In preparing his essay, Wilson did not trouble to reread the three major "social histories"—*The Bostonians, The Princess Casamassima,* and *The Tragic Muse*—which, he says, start out very well in "reporting of the surface of life" (106) only to lapse into abstractness and boredom. He is particularly annoyed by the fact that the hero never reaches the point of having sexual relations with the heroine, but admits that this is an adolescent view: "When I was writing about James, however, I did not review in this selective way the three long later novels that I had read first twenty years before; and it may be that, if I had done so, I should have given a somewhat different account. In looking into them again just now, I seemed sometimes to catch sight of qualities which I had not appreciated in my college days—at an age when James's lack of real 'love interest' is likely to prejudice one against him—and to which I feared I might not have done justice" (viii).[13] One notes in Wilson's autobiographical account of his youth, *A Prelude*, that his undergraduate opinion of James is nearly identical with that of "The Ambiguity":

> Though I won an essay prize by a paper on James—based, however, on an incomplete knowledge of his work—I did not find him entirely satisfactory. I think there was too little "love interest"— that is, sex interest—in James for a young man of my age to appreciate him. I was used to Bennett and Wells, Meredith and Thomas Hardy, and James, after these, seemed rather pale. What led me on to read him was the discovery that he was sometimes "realistically" dealing with contemporary America. It was very much in the air that our writers should write about their own country, and the passages about Albany in "The Portrait of a Lady" were a good deal more interesting to me than all the rest, which takes place in Europe. It was not till I read "What Maisie Knew"—recommended in the *Smart Set* by Mencken as a "passionless masterpiece"—that I found a work of James that I could wholly admire, though it had nothing to do with the United States, and I still think the short novels of this middle period are much better than most of his longer ones, which are likely to start off invitingly but in the second volume to run into the sands. (*New Yorker* [May 6, 1967], 87-8.)

One need not dwell on the fact than any critic who falls back on the literary opinions that he held in college is bound to undermine the strength of his opinions.

Another weakness of Wilson's essay as criticism is his biographical preoccupation—the real (hidden) Henry James. Unfortunately, Wilson did not know enough about James to make valid conclusions about him or his work: "We know so little about his personal life from any other source than himself, and even in his memoirs and letters he tells us so little about his emotions, that it is impossible to give any account of it save as it reflects itself in his writings" (105). But how is one to know when an author's life "reflects itself in his writings"?—which can't be known even about Wilson himself, for example. May one assume that an author *has* written about "himself"?—or know *which* of his selves James wrote about?

Wilson apparently must speculate about the man James; and, when he suggests that the (hidden) theme of *The Sacred Fount* is sex and not just youth, he replaces "James" with James: "Hitherto . . . it has usually been plain what James wanted us to think of his characters; but now there appears in his work a relatively morbid element which is not always handled objectively and which *seems* to have invaded the storyteller himself. It is *as if* at this point *he had taken to dramatizing the frustrations of his own life without quite being willing to confess it, without fully admitting it even to himself*" (101, italics added). Even if Wilson's conclusion were unquestionably true, it would add little to one's knowledge of James himself and nothing to an understanding of *The Sacred Fount*. But Wilson pursues James. There was something, he says, "insufficient and unexplained" about James's emotional life, and he implies that the failure of James's characters to consummate a love affair, at least in the early fiction, was due to his own lack of sexual fulfillment. Likewise their reticence was due not to their highly civilized discretion, but to James's inability to examine his own emotions. Of course, had he not really been able to examine his own emotions, his novels could yet be understood; but Leon Edel's remarkable biography has shown that James was neither so insensitive nor so timid with himself.[14]

In the psychoanalytical postword of 1948 Wilson worries about the theme of corrupted innocence (*The Turn of the Screw, What Maisie Knew, The Awkward Age*) and wonders if James did not have an unnatural attraction for little girls. Then he asks, again, whether James really meant *The Turn* to be a ghost story. By now Wilson has seen the *Notebooks;* but, instead of relying on the ambiguity of the tale for his interpretation, he accepts James's intention of writing a ghost story but argues with curious logic that James was unconsciously deceiving himself: (a) James was interested in self-deception and wrote about characters who deceive themselves; (b) therefore, James deceived himself! Miss Krook rightly criticizes Wilson for "his uncritical enthusiasm for the Freudian unconscious. . . . He plainly has no usable criteria for distinguishing between the operations of the conscious and the unconscious . . ." (380).

Why does Wilson's criticism seem to be incidental to biography that is invalid? By the mid-1930's, when he wrote "The Ambiguity," Wlson was at least as much interested in journalism as in criticism. He had already written distinguished reports on the America of the Depression and the New Deal, he had already begun work on *To the Finland Station,* and—to indulge in one's own speculations—it is probable that the young man who had been so passionately interested in literature in prep school and college may have found that literature itself and any "pure" discussions of it were not enough to sustain him psychologically during a time of crisis in the life of his country. Therefore, he exercised in both *The Wound and the Bow* and *The Triple Thinkers* what had been in *Axel's Castle* only a tendency—the search in the work for the "real" man behind it, which was perhaps more justifiable on the grounds of human interest than a merely literary discussion would have been.

"The Ambiguity of Henry James" is hardly a literary essay at all, as Wilson himself admits: "I have been occupied here with the elements that travail or contend or glow beneath the surface of his even fiction, and my argument has not given me occasion to insist, as ought to be done in any 'literary' discussion of James, on his classical equanimity in dealing wth diverse forces, on his combination, equally classical, of hard realism with formal harmony" (123). Thus, to Wilson, Henry James "is a reporter, not a prophet. With less politics even than Flaubert, *he can but chronicle the world as it passes. . . .*" (118, italics added). In this conclusion one scarcely recognizes the James of F. R. Leavis (*The Great Tradition,* 1948)—the great novelist ranking with Jane Austen, George Eliot, and Joseph Conrad.

In "Morose Ben Jonson" Wilson takes the psychobiographical approach probably as far as he can without parodying it. Although some things may be inferred about James—or Dickens or Kipling—because the temper of his age is close to one's own, very much less may be inferred about a writer of the early seventeenth century. But Wilson takes up "the problem of Jonson's unpopularity [today] ... to show that his failure as a drawing attraction, in either the theater or the study, is bound up in a peculiar way with his difficulties as an artist"—by which Wilson probably means, "difficulties as a man." In an admittedly offhand summary of Jonson's plays, he asserts that they are failures and attacks T. S. Eliot for admiring Jonson and for not warning of "the crudities and aridities, the uncertainty of artistic intention and the flat-footed dramatic incompetence ..." (215-6).

Wilson charges that Jonson lacks Shakespeare's great variety and range in characterization; that his "plots are incoherent and clumsy"; that his "impossible disguises" and "incredible practical jokes" are bad (Wilson especially dislikes practical jokes); that he has no sense of "movement or proportion"; that his puns are "sometimes of a stunning stupidity"; that "when he is dirty, he is, unlike Shakespeare, sometimes disgusting to such a degree that he makes one sympathetic with the Puritans in their efforts to clean up the theater"; that his Greek and Latin are merely an "obstructive element" or "padding"; and that he is better when he is not Classical (215-6). Furthermore, "there is no love in Jonson's plays to set against these negative values" of "envy, denial, hoarding, withholding" (222, 221); and Jonson gives Renaissance splendor "an element of the factitious as well as an element of the vulgar, which as Mr. [Harry] Levin says, have the effect of making it look ridiculous" (226).

But one makes little progress with Ben Jonson by reproaching him for being unlike Shakespeare, or *like* him, for that matter. And what Wilson's impressionistic criticism most lacks are a thorough analysis of the plays and the textual evidence to prove that Jonson was so bad a playwright. Wilson does refer briefly to four comedies—*The Alchemist, The Silent Woman, Volpone,* and *Bartholomew Fair.* Only the first of these is any good in his view, and even this one he doesn't like very much: "Yet this play, one of the funniest in English, is not really an example of high comedy as either a play of Molière's or a play of Aristophanes' is. Ben Jonson is not enough of a critic—that is, he has not enough intelligence—for either Molière's kind of interest in character and human relations or Aristophanes' kind of interest in institutions and points of view. *The Alchemist* is a picaresque farce, fundamentally not different from the Marx brothers" (217). But again no evidence is presented; "high comedy" is used inaccurately; and such phrases as "character and human relations" and "interest in institutions and points of view" do not convey very much of import. Moreover, why should the interests of Aristophanes and Molière be those of Jonson?

Having forgone textual evidence in criticizing the plays, Wilson draws inferences from them about the playwright. Jonson, he says in effect, must have been an anal erotic. For this conclusion he consulted *The Structure and Meaning of Psychoanalysis* by William Healy, A. F. Bronner, and A. M. Bowers (1930). This "handbook of psychoanalysis" characterizes the anal erotic by "(a) orderliness (bodily cleanliness, reliability, conscientiousness in performance of petty duties)—in an over-accentuated form, pedantry; (b) parsimony, which may become avarice; (c) obstinacy, which may become defiance and perhaps also include irascibility and vindictiveness" (318). Wilson says that Jonson had all three traits and that the plays—that is, certain characters in them—reveal the symptoms. *Volpone*, he says, shows a preoccupation with hoarding money; *The Alchemist*, *The Devil Is an Ass*, and *The Silent Woman*, a preoccupation with hoarding knowledge. And frequently in Jonson's plays is the type of "thoroughly disagreeable person"—such as Macilente, Morose, Surly, and Wasp—who is "the butt of deserved persecution" (220). But surely one cannot decide very much about Jonson on the basis of traits that he would share with most people, exaggerated as these may be in his plays; and to conclude seriously that Jonson was an anal erotic, one would need to know something about his defecation patterns.

Wilson of course disclaims any Freudian interpretation of Jonson: "I am not qualified to 'analyze' Jonson in the light of this Freudian conception, and I have no interest in trying to fit him into any formulation of it" (219). But, despite his lack of qualifications, he does indeed analyze Jonson and is enormously interested in the whole matter. How else could he write: "Through Morose and through the characters like him, Ben Jonson is tormenting himself for what is negative and recessive in his nature" (221)? Or, "the worthy and accomplished scholar ... who is envied by lesser men; and, on the other hand, the poor and exacerbated wit ... who envies lesser men .... are aspects of the same personality; both are identified with Jonson himself" (221)? Or, the figure of the spendthrift heir in Jonson's comedies "is obviously the creation of Jonson's own envy, stimulated, no doubt, from two sources—first, the grievance of the man of good birth unjustly deprived of his patrimony, and, second, the sulky resentment of the man who can only withhold against the man who can freely lavish" (224-5)? One more example should suffice: "Jonson is "a constipated writer well primed with sack" (226).

Not only does Wilson confuse Jonson with "Jonson" (even less pardonable in dealing with plays than with poems and novels—for in the direct mimesis of drama can "the author" always be recognized?); but he omits scholarship: he does not seem to recognize Jonson's debt to Roman comedy—rather than to a "morose" personality—for the shrewish wife, the selfish husband, the spendthrift heir, and the foolish old man. This apparent lapse is surprising in view of Wilson's educational background in the Classics. But one is probably confronted here with another collegiate antipathy; for, in A Prelude, Wilson wrote as a Princeton student: "French tragedy and Roman comedy are academic enthusiasms" (New Yorker [May 6, 1967], 119). Scholarship would also have revealed that the Renaissance audience was not embarrassed by a display of knowledge which, within limitations consistent with religious orthodoxy and Classical moderation, was always good. What was considered bad was false wit, or pretending—like Sir John Daw and La Foole in The Silent Woman—to knowledge that one had not earned and did not really possess.

Presumably, too, a very little searching would have shown that Jonson consciously intended to portray the familiar human excesses—pride, avarice, lust, duplicity. His choosing to write about vice—the choice of so many other Jacobean playwrights—may be explained more logically than by saying that he needed to work out his own neuroses. English audiences had long enjoyed the personifications of sin and the devil—a tradition which easily accommodated the trend in drama toward sensationalism. If Jonson, as a working dramatist, had an obsession besides the old Seven Deadly Sins, it was probably success.

The Jonson essay, Wilson's extreme employment of the psychobiographical method, is Wilson (or "Wilson") at his worst; but it has an air of brilliance. Generally his better pieces from this middle period of his career, when in his longer essays he became bound up in an untenable theory, are the shorter ones already mentioned and the reviews and articles collected in *The Shores of Light, Classics and Commercials,* and *The Bit Between My Teeth,* three volumes that form a "chronicle" mainly of the American literary era from the 1920's to the 1960's. These pieces, some of which are to be considered in this chapter, show his ability to digest and compress a great deal of material, although sometimes they are necessarily superficial.

IV Patriotic Gore

With *Patriotic Gore: Studies in the Literature of the American Civil War* (1962), Edmund Wilson finally wrote the kind of book that he had dedicated to Christian Gauss thirty-one years earlier: "a history of man's ideas and imaginings in the setting of the conditions which have shaped them." And, in part, he also wrote the type of study that he had described in "The Historical Interpretation of Literature": "the interpretation of literature in its social, economic and political aspects" (*The Triple Thinkers,* 257). Wilson portrayed part of American intellectual life during the last fifty years of the nineteenth century; and central to his study was the Civil War: how participants on both sides regarded it; how it affected the people at home, especially in the South; and how it influenced post-war America.

Historiographers must judge the book's value as history,[15] but even the common reader becomes aware that *Patriotic Gore* reveals an intimate aspect of the Civil War unseen in the usual history and that it introduces him to people from the past whom he seldom meets in textbooks. The diaries of three Southern ladies, aristocrats and victims, provide an impressive account of the reckless destruction of the war and a firsthand record of Southern life: Yankee threats and Negro insolence for Kate Stone; the suppression of the "bonny blue" Confederate flag and the pillaging of the family home for Sarah Morgan; and, with a shift in emphasis, the disgust of Mary Chesnut at slavery and, particularly, at white masters who kept black harems. The entire era is illustrated from a great range of people—half-legendary figures such as John Brown and people of real-life stature such as Charlotte Forten, the mulatto girl from Philadelphia who worked to advance her race. The more prominent figures also become vivid, and one's imagination is stirred by General Grant's imperturbability under fire, by General Sherman's ruthlessness, and by Colonel Mosby's bedeviling of the Union forces.

Patriotic Gore will be considered here as literary criticism, social and political criticsm, and biography. As the first, it is decidedly limited. But several features are worthy of comment. First, Wilson re-examines and appreciates "forgotten" works, such as Grant's *Personal Memoirs,* which he praises for its lucidity, terseness, and restraint: ". . . it may well rank, as Mark Twain [who published it] believed, as the most remarkable work of its kind since the *Commentaries* of Julius Caesar." Wilson even compares it with William Herndon's *Lincoln,* Henry David Thoreau's *Walden,* and Walt Whitman's *Leaves of Grass* as "a unique expression of the national character"; and he records favorable testimony to its merits from such disparate writers as Matthew Arnold and Gertrude Stein (132-3, 139-40). To a lesser degree Wilson appreciates the memoirs of William T. Sherman, Richard Taylor, and John S. Mosby. While he never asserts that they are neglected masterpieces, he presents a strong case for their literary merit.

Apparent, again, is Wilson's remarkable ability to summarize, especially books which were once popular but are now seldom read, such as Harriet Beecher Stowe's *Poganuc People* (1878), a novel of New England family life; or books which were thematically ahead of their time, such as Albion Tourgée's novel *Toinette* (1874) and George W. Cable's collection of stories, *Old Creole Days* (1879), both of which treat of miscegenation; or Kate Chopin's stories of unsatisfactory marriages.

Finally—and the book's main limitation as literary criticism— Wilson scarcely deals with major figures at all (Hawthorne, Emerson, Melville, Whitman, Dickinson, Twain, James); and, when he does, he concerns himself with a lesser work, such as Melville's *The Scout Toward Aldie,* a narrative poem about federal cavalry attempts to capture Mosby, or he treats major writing all too briefly and superficially, as in his discussion in Chapter XII of the poetry of Whitman, Poe, Crane, and the Abolitionists. Several reasons for this deficiency immediately come to mind: (1) the major figures have already received a great deal of critical and biographical attention; (2) the important political and social issues of the day interest Wilson more than the major literature and are reflected more in the writings of minor figures; and (3) Wilson's intention is to understand the decline of the old republican America and the beginnings of the powerful, centralized America—the problem which has pursued him from before "The Old Stone House" (1933) through *The Cold War and the Income Tax* (1963), and which interests him far more than literary criticism.

But, despite these limitations, he does make two contributions to literary criticsm. The chapter entitled "The Chastening of American Prose Style" succinctly explains the change in American writing from the turgid style of earlier nineteenth-century writers influenced by Sir Walter Scott to a more economical style. Wilson's reasons for the change are convincing: the rise of the "plain" man (Lincoln), the growth of journalism, the "military" writing of the Civil War, and the increasing importance of the machine and mechanical techniques. To a small extent this chapter shows Wilson's old interest in psychoanalysis, for he says that the ambiguity, prolixity, and irony in the styles of Henry Adams and Henry James, two exceptions to writers of the new style (and, one might add, two "unplain" men), "reflect a kind of lack of self-confidence, a diffidence and a mechanism of self-defense." This interpretation is dubious and so is its assigned cause: the two writers underwent the strain of the war without serving in it. Wilson prefers to regard James's mysterious ailment, which kept him out of the war, as sexual; and he implies that Leon Edel also interprets it that way (654-9). But this implication is incorrect since Edel takes pains to show that James's "wound" was a bad back which embarrassed the young man because it made him look like a malingerer (*The Untried Years,* 183).

Wilson's second contribution to literary criticism is his account of "The Myth of the Old South"—the ideal of gallantry, freedom, fine manners, and luxurious living promulgated by the poetry and fiction of Sidney Lanier. This myth, says Wilson, was purely literary in origin and, like the turgid prose which promoted it, was partly influenced by Sir Walter Scott, whom Mark Twain castigated. The myth may have begun with William Wirt's *Sketches of the Life and Character of Patrick Henry* in 1817, for Wirt overlooked the fact that Patrick Henry was a crude and not very literate man. Augmenting the myth were the

novels of William Alexander Carruthers, John Esten Cooke, John
Pendleton Kennedy (although his first novel, *Swallow Barn*
[1832], satirized it), and William Gilmore Simms, as well as
Lanier. Somewhat later, in the 1880's, Thomas Nelson Page, an
apologist for Southern sentiment against the Negro, "invented for
the popular mind Old Massa and Mistis and Meh Lady..."
(605). Antipodal to exploiters of the myth was the Tennessee
journalist, George Washington Harris, creator of the crude, sa-
distic, poor-white hero of *Sut Lovingood,* which Wilson finds
offensive and upon which he spends too much time.

But Wilson's greater interest is in comprehending the Civil
War era, which, in his view, has determined present-day political America more than any other period has. Norman Podhoretz,
in his essay on Wilson in *Doings and Undoings,* has described
Patriotic Gore as "a study in the spiritual history of American
civilization." Podhoretz notes the "wonderfully irascible assault
on the self-righteousness of the American mind in politics" in
Wilson's Introduction—which shows similarities among Lincoln,
Bismarck, and Lenin; gives a short history of the United States'
imperialism; and likens the United States and Soviet Russia to
voracious sea slugs preying upon smaller organisms. Without
keeping this introduction in mind, apparently, Podhoretz links
the great labor of Wilson in exhuming obscure writers of the past
with the "jobbist" theory of Justice Oliver Wendell Holmes, to
whom Wilson devotes a final long chapter. Holmes's conception
of the Jobbist was "one who works at his job without trying to
improve the world or to make a public impression" (Wilson,
789). Podhoretz asserts that Wilson "has now opted for the same
kind of isolation that Holmes achieved and is pursuing the same
kind of private salvation that Holmes sought in solitary dedication to his work" (51-6).

Certainly Wilson admires Holmes's aloofness, "his carapace of
impenetrable indifference to current pressures and public opinion" (782). And Wilson no longer believes, as he did in the
1930's, that writers can help solve American problems and stop
"'the triumph of the businessman'" (Podhoretz, 57). But, as the
introduction to *Patriotic Gore* and as *The Cold War and the
Income Tax* indicate, he still wages a personal war, not against
big business, but against big government which, as he warns in
O Canada, "can so easily become a faceless despotism" (245).

He retreats neither into the past nor into an obscure area of study but confronts in the present the ramifications of that era which generated federal power.

The first issue was slavery. Wilson presents a number of divergent opinions on the slave question from 1837 to the end of the century. Mrs. Stowe felt that New England was as guilty as the South in kidnapping Negroes into slavery, and even in *Uncle Tom's Cabin* (1852) she emphasized the *impracticality* of slavery. Lincoln moved from a "philosophic" attitude toward slavery to the position that it was morally wrong, but he did not like the Abolitionists and was not in favor of the political and social equality of Negroes with whites. In explaining to General Grant and General Sherman his liberal policy for the defeated South, Lincoln said that he favored giving the vote only to "'the very intelligent' Negroes or to 'those who serve our cause as soldiers'" (108, 200).

William Grayson, a Southerner, wrote a long poem in heroic couplets, *The Hireling and the Slave* (1856), which was pro-slavery and contrasted the happy lot of the slave with the misery of the Northern factory worker; yet Grayson was against resuming the slave trade. George Fitzhugh, another Southerner, insisted in two books that slavery was essential for a stable society. Still another Southerner, Hinton Helper, attacked slavery as economically unsound. Having cut through these and other opinions, Wilson accepts the position in his chapter on Alexander Stephens, the Vice President of the Confederacy, that the United States Constitution had guaranteed the right to own slaves and that this right had been reinforced by the Fugitive Slave Law of 1850. This point of view opens to the second and even more important issue, states rights.

In "Alexander H. Stephens," the focal chapter of the entire book, Wilson takes up Stephens' large, two-volume work, *A Constitutional View of the Late War Between the States* (1867, 1870). This work comprises imaginary dialogues between Stephens and three "unionists" in an attempt to justify Stephens' war policy. Stephens argued that the term "United States" had meant to the makers of the Constitution a federation of sovereign states, that state sovereignty included the right to withdraw from the union, and that the "Civil War," therefore, could not have been an insurrection or rebellion but a "War between the States."

Wilson is eventually led to conclude, "... the Southerners have a very good case for regarding the Northerners as treacherous aggressors" (414).

From the states-rights controversy came the most important issue of all—one which most concerns Wilson—the question of power. Stephens argued that Lincoln's acts after the relief of Fort Sumter were unconstitutional and despotic: "conscription, the suppression of habeas corpus, searches and seizures without warrant, the suppression of free speech"—as were also the Emancipation Proclamation and the edict of martial law. Wilson points out that even in New England there was concern over executive powers; and, for all his respect for Lincoln, he is clearly sympathetic with Stephens' fear of "'Centralism, Absolutism, Despotism!'" (415-25).

Stephens, indeed, had resisted even the "despotism" of Jefferson Davis, refusing to sacrifice state sovereignty to any central government, North or South. And Wilson, who has been careful to avoid the impression that he is advancing an argument of his own, says toward the end of the chapter: "[The issue is] the exercise of power ... the backing up of power by force, the issue of the government, the organization, as against the individual, the family group—for the South that fought the war was a family group. This issue presses hard on our time. There are moments when one may wonder today—as one's living becomes more and more hampered by the exactions of centralized bureaucracies of both the state and the federal authorities—whether it may not be true, as Stephens said, that the cause of the South is the cause of us all" (434).

Thus Wilson eventually blends his own social and political criticism with a historical analysis of federal power. It becomes clear that, although he does not agree entirely with Stephens and although he regards Stephens' assumption of Negro inferiority as absurd, he admires the courage and logic of the frail patrician—or "Roman," as he refers to both Stephens and Robert E. Lee, and by which he means a man responsible, scrupulous, and dutiful. He admires the "impossibilist" Stephens, who carried "an ideal to extremes" and raised "certain fundamental issues in a way that the more practical and prudent man could never allow himself to do" (434).

The "practical and prudent" man in *Patriotic Gore* becomes

Justice Holmes. When he was young and full of the romantic chivalry of Scott, Holmes had viewed the Civil War as a crusade for Abolition; but later, influenced by Darwin's theory of survival and by the disillusionment following the war, he came to view man as a predatory animal and to regard the law, from an historical rather than ideal point of view, as an instrument of necessity: "The law had broken down in America; the Constitution had gone to pieces. It was impossible for an honest man of Holmes's probing intelligence to pretend that the law was a sacred code, which had simply to be read correctly. He always saw it as a complex accretion, a varied assortment of rules that had been drawn up through more than a thousand years and which represented the needs and demands of people existing in particular places at particular periods of history" (765).

It is difficult to tell which of the two very different men— Stephens or Holmes—Wilson admires more; or whether he equally admires Lincoln, who told Stephens that only necessity compelled him to " 'interfere with Slavery in the States' " (430-1). Indeed, the span of *Patriotic Gore* rests on these three figures: Lincoln, the statesman, with a strong sense of mission and a feeling toward the Union of "religious mysticism," which was probably as strong for him as the Stowes' Calvinism was for them; Stephens, the logical idealist and apologist; and Holmes, the positivist and pragmatist.

These figures and many others in *Patriotic Gore* become interesting in themselves; and for most readers the major value of the book is undoubtedly biographical. Irving Howe and Alfred Kazin both compare Wilson with Plutarch.[16] It is true that Wilson employs the technique, used by Plutarch in his *Lives* and by Samuel Johnson in *The Lives of the Poets*, of reconstructing a life by its antitheses or paradoxes. Lincoln was irreligious, but came to regard himself in a religious way as the savior of the Union; he was a plain, self-taught man, yet possessed " 'intellectual arrogance and unconscious assumption of superiority' " (119). Grant was a reluctant soldier who thought the Mexican War unjust—a failure, a drunkard. But Grant was also a great general who inspired his men with self-confidence. And he was, finally, the naïve President, "the incurable sucker" (167).

Perhaps the most compact biography is that of Ambrose Bierce; it is built on the themes of death (Bierce's obsession), religion

(a personal one in which Bierce saw God revealed in the evolu-
tionary process itself), and contradicting political and social
views ("'somewhat of a socialist'" with anti-democratic tenden-
cies). Bierce was both embarrassed by his lack of formal education and pedantic about literary style; handsome and attractive
to women, yet preferring ugly ones as companions; compassion-
ate, yet destructive (627-32). The portrayal of Bierce demon-
strates Wilson's careful selection of details to give a complete
sketch of a man's personality without burdening the reader with
minutiae. This art is evident also in the chapter on General Sherman, who loved the theater and was a founder of the Players
Club, who hated "Marching Through Georgia" and was heard
to curse quietly when Negro porters sang it to him on a Pullman
car. In conjunction with Wilson's eye for striking detail is his
dramatic sense, which heightens tension through contrast and
irony. Sherman leaves Atlanta burning on a beautiful morning,
and his carefree soldiers sing "John Brown's Body" while he feels
that he alone is aware of all the forthcoming perils of the march.
Lincoln dreams of his own death.

The Radical Republicans, the villains in the drama, take revenge on Jefferson Davis, who is imprisoned and abused at Fort
Monroe for two years, until he is finally freed on bail posted by
two *Abolitionists*, Horace Greeley and Gerrit Smith. Stephens'
own isolated position of resistance to both the Northern Union
and the Southern Confederacy is a dramatic one, as is his humor-
ously melancholic attitude toward prison bedbugs: he would like
to let them alone and "'even contribute something to their support and sustenance'" (they and a discreet mouse are his only
companions for nearly five months). But, when the bedbugs
repay his broadmindedness only by feeding on him, he is forced
to kill them—"'to live and let live is not in accordance with the
laws of their existence. Hence they justly bring their death upon
themselves.'" When the sick man is released from prison, his hair
has turned white (394-5).

Wilson writes vivid biography, and his methods are sound.
Although he occasionally makes a strange, pseudo-genetic comment—"Was there something of [Helper's] lower-class German
blood in the doctrine of his later years?" (377); "It was no doubt
The New England blood which was mingled in [Cable] with that
of Virginia" (559)—he usually avoids hereditary and psychoana-

lytical inferences. And, in the case of those figures whose auto-
biographies Wilson uses for information, he is careful to check
their work against the best biographies he can find.

Patriotic Gore is Wilson's most satisfactory book—one that succeeds in portraying the literary and political life of a time when,
to Wilson's mind, commercialism and exploitation began to rule
American life. The point that needs to be stressed—in view of his
reputation as a literary critic—is that he excels when he does not
attempt criticism primarily. It is also significant that he has
tended to repudiate his role as a critic. In "The Critic Who Does
Not Exist" (1928) he had complained that America lacked
"simply serious literary criticism" occupied with "the art or ideas
of the writers" with whom it should deal (*The Shores of Light*,
367-72). Yet, soon thereafter, his main interest was to account
for a work's genesis—what kind of man was the writer, why did
he write what he did? In "A Modest Self Tribute" (1952) he was
willing to refer to himself as a "practicing critic" as opposed to
the "academic" critic, who formulates canons that "tend to keep
literature provincial." Wilson claims for himself a small contribution to the "general cross-fertilization, to make it possible for
our literate public to appreciate and understand both our own
Anglo-American culture and those of the European countries in
relation to one another. . . ."[17] But by 1959 the disavowal was
stronger: "I never think of myself . . . as a literary critic; I think
of myself simply as a writer and a journalist. . . . I'm as much
interested in history as I am in literature" ("We Don't Know
Where We Are," *New Republic* [March 30] 13-14). Wilson
seems to have become somewhat out of touch with literary criticism, at least of American literature; his statement in "Newton
Arvin's *Longfellow*" (1963) that he can think of only three first-
rate writers among scholars of American literature—Leon Edel,
Van Wyck Brooks, and Newton Arvin—suggests willful ignorance
on his part; but he is more or less correct in his view that English
departments foster indiscriminate publishing (*The Bit Between
My Teeth*, 551-5).

V   *Standards for Fiction*

At the beginning of this chapter it was pointed out that Wilson
is a "public" critic, one that (to quote Northrop Frye again)

"has picked up his ideas from a pragmatic study of literature, and does not try to create or enter into a theoretical structure." Later it was noted that Wilson dislikes—and warns against— "formula" literature. As a "public" or "working" critic Wilson is uncommitted to definitions and to a defense of premises; his criticism is mainly descriptive and impressionistic. But he *has* standards, implied by the very fact that he has taste. Since his fiction will be considered in some detail in Chapter 4, it may be appropriate to note what his standards are.

As one expects, Wilson nowhere devotes an essay to defining a novel. On the other hand, he usually explains why he likes or dislikes a novel; and, when he does not explain, his assumptions are plain enough. The short, pointed articles and reviews collected in *Classics and Commercials, The Shores of Light,* and *The Bit Between My Teeth* sometimes indicate his standards more clearly than the longer essays; and, with the longer ones, they provide ample evidence of what he thinks fiction and literature in general should be.

One of his premises is that literature is the *ordered* experience of people. In "A Dissenting Opinion on Kafka" (1947), he speaks of Joyce, Proust, and Dante as "great naturalists of personality, great organizers of human experience"; and he is critical of Kafka's novels—"ragged performances"—which he thinks are unorganized and unrepresentative of human experience: "But must we really, as his admirers pretend, accept the plights of Kafka's abject heroes as parables of the human condition?" (*Classics and Commercials,* 388). In "James Joyce" Wilson delights in Joyce's "handling of this immense material, his method of giving his book a shape" (*Axel's Castle,* 211). And he admires Joyce's use of Homeric parallels to indicate meanings in the actions and relations of the characters—for the objectivity of the narration prevents the author himself from commenting on the action—even though Wilson also feels that Joyce's construction becomes too elaborate.

There is nothing unusual about this standard, nor indeed about any of his other standards, which are, in fact, so commonplace that it would be pretentious to say that they constitute a theory of fiction. But their very ordinariness makes them difficult to understand precisely. When Wilson says "human experience," he apparently means activities and problems familiar to most people; but one cannot be sure that Wilson includes all levels of society. Fantastic experience is included as long as it is plainly related to the larger world outside. But the private world of most of Mallarmé's poetry, for example, or of Valéry's early poetry makes him uneasy. Those who withdraw from the world, one recalls from *Axel's Castle*, are "maladjusted."

The organizing of generally recognizable experience implies logic. In a passage already quoted from "Marxism and Literature," he speaks of "works of the highest order." And he uses the word "organization" at the end of "The Historical Interpretation of Literature" when he mentions "the emotion of the more highly organized man" encountering "work that is finer and more complex" in contrast to that of "crude and limited people" who are "often solaced and exhilarated by literature of the trashiest kind" (*The Triple Thinkers*, 270). The distinction between the fine and the trashy is perhaps not very clear, and Wilson obscures it further by a dairy metaphor for superior literature—"Grade A." A certain air of superiority in regard to the "highly organized man" suggests that Wilson does not have a popular art in mind —that no matter how important "human experience" is, Wilson the intellectual stands a little outside it, as do the protagonists in his novels.

The second standard narrows the first. The human experience, as Wilson writes in " 'Never Apologize, Never Explain': The Art of Evelyn Waugh," must be that of *"recognizable* human beings living in the *world we know"* (italics added, *Classics and Commercials*, 142). This standard Wilson calls "the conventions of ordinary fiction," a "norm." What "ordinary fiction" is may not be entirely clear, but in context it appears to be that dealing with man as a social being, or explicitly related to "real life." Presumably, such literature would not comprise—or at least not wholeheartedly embrace—the romances of the Middle Ages and the nineteenth century. It would include Jane Austen but perhaps not Emily Brontë.

However, Wilson's sensibilities should not be pigeonholed; for his brilliant essay "The James Branch Cabell Case Reopened" (1956) has revealed his admiration for the great modern romancer, whose work Wilson had not found congenial since the 1920's and had therefore not read during the 1930's and 1940's. And yet Wilson cannot even now accept the fanciful realm of

Poictesme except as a "criticism of life"—a phrase of Matthew Arnold's reminiscent of the Humanists which Wilson uses self-consciously. He points out that there is more to Cabell than urbanely frivolous dream painting—that the Poictesme novels are not, in other words, merely escape literature. The unreal world, unless it can be classified as "the psychology of dreams" overlaying a conflict in Cabell between a Calvinistic work ethic and a cavalier attitude toward the uses of literature, seems to make Wilson uneasy, just as he is made uneasy by the fact that Manuel of *Figures of Earth* is unworthy of becoming the legendary saint of *The Silver Stallion* and that the reader cannot identify with him (*The Bit Between My Teeth*, 291-321).

Always, Wilson implies, there must be some point to literature that is related to actual life. Accounting for Cabell's apparent preference for dreams to reality in "James Branch Cabell: 1879-1958," a memorial, Wilson ingeniously associates the dreams with "the history of the South. And his bitterness is the bitterness of the South at having had this dream proved a fiction, and then somehow having had still to live on it" (*The Bit Between My Teeth*, 322-5). Wilson's interest in Cabell's work, as he says in "The James Branch Cabell Case Reopened," is mainly "regional and historical"; and the essay is in part an apologia for the mind of the South, which views Southern traditions ironically and yet can take little interest in the affairs of the modern (and Northern) world.

Wilson touches on a difficult point for the student and teacher of literature; the temptation to explain literature by extra-literary deductions is for some reason nearly overpowering. How safe a teacher feels if he can find "psychological truth" in folk tales or can provide a volcanological explanation for the Cyclops. Doing so enables him to "get hold of" something; to reduce literature to the common denominator of information, especially facts of "human nature"; and to protect himself from the impertinent question, "What good is it?"

For Wilson, "the world we know" necessarily involves realistic observation. What most impresses him about Joyce's *Ulysses* is the naturalistic documentation: "we know precisely what the characters wore, how much they paid for things, where they were at different times of the day, what popular songs they sang and what events they read of in the papers, on June 16, 1904"

(*Axel's Castle*, 205). Likewise, Wilson admires Kipling's understanding and presentation of natives. But he does not insist upon
firsthand experience, which should be kept in mind by those who
think that his own novels must be *romans a cléf*. In "Glenway
Wescott's War Work" (1945) he is impressed by how convincing
Wescott's *Apartment in Athens* is, even though he knows that
Wescott has not been in Greece.

In "The Art of Evelyn Waugh," Wilson again states what may
be regarded as a third standard—fiction should arouse the reader's
feelings: ". . . everything in [Waugh's fiction] has grown out of
experience and everything has emotional value." Later, when
Waugh published *Brideshead Revisited,* Wilson was disappointed. For him, the book failed to become a moving experience; where there should have been a convincing spiritual experience, there was only a "Catholic tract" and no "force of
regeneration" ("Splendors and Miseries of Evelyn Waugh," *Classics and Commercials,* 298-305). In "Marcel Proust" Wilson is
impressed by the emotional impact of the relation between
Albertine and her lover, an affair which "seems to involve
neither idealism nor enjoyment"; it is most moving "precisely
when Proust seems indifferently to have neglected all the cus-
tomary apparatus for getting effects of pathos out of themes of
love and death" (*Axel's Castle,* 153-4).

But exactly what "emotional value" means to Wilson does not
really become clear until one finds it elaborated in "The Historical Interpretation of Literature," in which Wilson discusses the
"cause of this emotional reaction which is the critic's divining
rod." In attempting to explain this reaction, he launches into his
well-known definition of literature—or, more precisely, his statement regarding the *function* of literature—which one might take
as Wilson's final and most important standard: "In my view, all
our intellectual activity, in whatever field it takes place, is an
attempt to give a meaning to our experience—that is, to make
life more practicable; for by understanding things we make it
easier to survive and get around among them. . . . A drama of
Sophocles . . . indicates relations between the various human impulses, which appear so confused and dangerous, and it brings
out a certain justice of Fate—that is to say, of the way in which
the interaction of these impulses is seen in the long run to work
out—upon which we can also depend" (*The Triple Thinkers,*
268-9).

In other words, literature should enable people to outmaneuver the problems natural to living. The emotional reaction is apparently not catharsis, spontaneous delight, or what Frye calls "exuberance" so much as it is the *recognition* that a novel contains "meaning." Presumably, then, one of the more important "emotional values" would be consolation or encouragement. This attitude toward literature is very similar to Matthew Arnold's in his essay on Wordsworth: literature should teach men how to live.

Wilson's statement may be inadequate, however, because it limits the response that literature can evoke and because it omits literature that disturbs. One recalls that Wilson is unsympathetic with Kafka, that he has written little about Faulkner, and that he ignores Gide except to remark in "Marcel Proust" that Gide tries "to sell us homosexuality by making it appear attractive and respectable," as Proust does not (*Axel's Castle*, 181). In "Edmund Wilson, Then and Now," Richard Gilman, commenting on Wilson's "avoidance of the really disturbing and aberrant writers of our own time," writes: "That Wilson should not for the past twenty years have written about any of the period's significant writers except Pasternak—not about Camus, Beckett, Genet, Nabokov, Moravia, Grass, the French anovelists, Duerenmatt, the late Faulkner, the late Hesse, Bellow, I. B. Singer ... expresses the fact, I think, that *Doctor Zhivago* alone rewoke in him his early lofty hope of literature as humanizing force, as agency of social resurrection" (*New Republic* [July 2, 1966], 24). In a fairly recent self-interview (a reversion to his earlier dialogues, discussed in Chapter 3, which permits him to unload many opinions quickly without defending them), "Wilson" admits to the "Interviewer" that—except for Kingsley Amis, Lawrence Durrell, Angus Wilson, and one or two other English writers; and the Americans J. D. Salinger, Edwin O'Connor, and James Baldwin (his favorite)—he makes no attempt to keep up with current fiction ("An Interview with Edmund Wilson" (1962), *The Bit Between My Teeth*, 534-50).[18]

The omission of disturbing literature from Wilson's statement on the function of literature allows for an approach to life that seems naïve: can Fate (the way things work out in the long run) be either "just" or "unjust"? Can anyone depend upon whatever Fate "works out"? Finally, since Wilson attempts to see a practical value in literature, it is not unfair to ask whether liter-

ature really is of any use in the mundane problems of survival.
One should not overlook, however, Wilson's interest in literature as a craft, with its problems in structure, characterization,
style, symbol, rhythm, language—upon which his standards ultimately depend. He joys in one of Proust's "great technical discov-
eries": the presentation of characters "so as to show only one
aspect at a time" (*Axel's Castle*, 147), and Wilson attempts to
emulate Proust in a novel of his own, to be discussed in Chapter
4. In a number of other essays (on the Tennessee "Fugitive"
poets, *Finnegans Wake*, Katherine Anne Porter, Edna St. Vincent
Millay, for example) Wilson takes a literary interest in literature.
But he usually regards techniques as the servants of meaning,
as in his discussions of Yeats, Eliot, and Valéry in *Axel's Castle*.
In "The Politics of Flaubert," the one essay which Wilson devotes to an acclaimed master of technique, he emphasizes the
social analysis and moral intent in Flaubert's work.

Wilson's four standards—especially the realistic observation of
human behavior and the moral purpose—are based on his main
interest: the social and biographical background, the actualities
which he looks for behind all literature that engages his attention
and which motivate his own writing. If literature should teach
people how to live, it has to deal with the problems that make
living difficult or pointless. If it cannot solve people's moral problems, it should perhaps clarify them. Or perhaps it should aim at
revealing environment and the relationship of people to it. At
any rate, the highest value of literature for Wilson is ethical; in
his more ambitious critical statements the value seems unclear—
as in "Marxism and Literature," in which Wilson writes that in
literature "a sort of law of moral interchangeability prevails: we
may transpose the actions and the sentiments that move us into
terms of whatever we do or are ourselves" *The Triple Thinkers*,
205-6). But in his own fiction the value is simple.

The four articles on Thornton Wilder, which Wilson wrote for
the *New Republic* between 1928 and 1934 and which center on
a controversy regarding Wilder, provide a clearer, if general,
indication of what Wilson thinks fiction should do. In "Thornton
Wilder" (1928), Wilson discusses *The Cabala* and *The Bridge
of San Luis Rey*, and he argues that Wilder is too much influenced by Proust and not enough by "hard experience" (*The
Shores of Light*, 384-91). In "Dahlberg, Dos Passos and Wilder"

EDMUND WILSON

(1930), which reviews Wilder's *The Woman of Andros,* Edward Dahlberg's *Bottom Dogs,* and John Dos Passos' *The 42nd Parallel,* Wilson repeats that Wilder, living abroad, should come home and write about America, as the other two writers do. He admires Dahlberg for reproducing the language of the streets and for transforming the commonplace to art (Wilson does not explain this transformation). Dos Passos he praises as "the first of our writers—with the possible exception of Mark Twain—who has successfully used colloquial American for a novel of the highest artistic seriousness," and he calls *The 42nd Parallel* the most important novel yet produced by his generation (*The Shores of Light,* 442-50).

Four years later, in "Mr. Wilder in the Middle West," Wilson is more satisfied with Wilder. He says that *Heaven's My Destination* is Wilder's best novel: he has written about America and has demonstrated his "gift for social observation." The only thing that disturbs Wilson is that he is unsure of protagonist George Brush's political viewpoint at the end (*The Shores of Light,* 587-92).

But in the meantime came the most interesting of the four articles, "The Economic Interpretation of Wilder," an unsigned editorial in the *New Republic* (November 26, 1930). A month earlier, Michael Gold (Irwin Granich), editor of *New Masses,* author of *Jews Without Money,* and the leading Marxist critic, had published an attack in *The New Republic,* "Wilder: Prophet of the Genteel Christ." This article provoked so many furious letters that Wilson, a *New Republic* editor, was roused to reply. Wilson respected Gold as "one of the only American critics of any literary ability who writes books from the Marxist point of view." And of course Wilson agreed that Wilder was too much like Proust, whose pathos is "the more presentable side of the impotence, the creeping corruption, the lack of the will to live." But in his strongest argument Wilson sided with Wilder: "In dealing with a work of literature, we must consider it not only from the point of view of its significance in the social system, but also from the point of view of its craft. A Communist critic who, in reviewing a book, ignores the author's status as a craftsman is really, for purposes of propaganda, denying the dignity of human work." (*The Shores of Light,* 500-3).[19]

For Wilson fiction is, therefore, a dignified kind of social doc-

umentation *and* a personal craft. He is enough of an artist himself to appreciate artistry in itself; and perhaps, as has been
already suggested, he may not be able to view literature as a
popular art. Yet the wistful ending of "Marxism and Literature"
reveals his hope that the literary craftsman may someday pitch
his tent in the camp of the regenerated philistine: "Yet the
human imagination has already come to conceive the possibility
of re-creating human society; and how can we doubt that, as it
acquires the power, it must emerge from what will seem by comparison the revolutionary 'underground' of art as we have always
known it up to now and deal with the materials of actual life in
ways which we cannot now even foresee?"

Apart from the fact that placing Wilson's critical standards
against his fiction is interesting (one likes to see what a criticizer
of fiction can accomplish when he attempts it himself), it is also
useful—but not in the way that one would expect. His fiction
illuminates his criticism, rather than the reverse. Concerning, for
example, Wilson's most important standard—that literature should
have meaning—his fiction shows what this means more clearly
than his criticism usually does. One comes to see that "meaning"
really amounts to social criticism, which is not merely "a simple
message" or "simple social morals," but the relation of a perceptive individual to his social environment: what he perceives
in it, what he learns from it, and how he either rejects it or tries
to adjust to it.

CHAPTER 3

Poems and Plays

EDMUND WILSON's poems and plays are only briefly considered in one chapter because they are minor and, with a few exceptions, inferior parts of his work. No one should expect a successful or interesting critic, novelist, and journalist to also be an interesting poet and playwright; and Wilson's poems and plays would not justify such an expectation. Nevertheless, as lesser products of an author whose other writings demand attention, they deserve to be discussed, especially the plays.

Why Wilson tries to write poetry is a question that is answered by another: How many people in some way associated with the world of literature do *not* sooner or later attempt poetry? Why he publishes and republishes his verse is a different question, which cannot be answered here. His plays, however, seem more serious efforts than his poems and, despite their weaknesses, are more rewarding for the reader. He has said that he is "particularly susceptible to the theater" (*Five Plays* [1954], 7), but the nature of his susceptibility is less dramatic than discursive. He uses plays to discuss his ideas, which are mainly concerned with choosing the right course of conduct in a world which apparently presents a choice only between worn-out values and no values at all. In the drama Wilson can "act out" what he would report and comment on in his journalism, and what he would "observe" in his fiction. A very brief example is *Karl Marx: A Prolet Play*, included by Wilson as Appendix A in the first edition of *To the Finland Station* (1940) and undoubtedly written by him although it is "reported to have been written for the WPA theater by a member of the League of American Writers." A cynical little dialogue, *Karl Marx* depicts the author of *Das Kapital* and coauthor of *The Communist Manifesto* exterminating his early comrades after the Revolution of 1848 and then removing his beard to reveal "the smiling face of Comrade Stalin." It shows Wilson's own disillusionment with Russian Marxism in the 1930's. Marx's closing line is, "Forward to socialist inequality and democracy!"[1] But this use of drama has an inherent weakness, which I will discuss later in connection with a recent Wilson play.

I Poems

Robert Graves, in reviewing one of Wilson's travel books in 1956, said that the author has "so admirable a sense of English prose that he must surely have started as a poet."[2] Graves guessed correctly: Wilson did begin as a poet, although not exclusively; and his formally published poems date from 1916.[3] His chief detractor, Stanley Hyman, wrote that Wilson's class at Princeton voted him worst poet (*The Armed Vision* [1947], 37), a fact which Sherman Paul repeated in his book on Wilson (15). Even Wilson's early prose shows an attempt at lyricism, as does this excerpt from "Oneida County Fair," written in the early 1920's:

> Builders of strong stone houses against the crushing cold and the dark—ploughers of boulder-sown pastures—masters of the rolling waste, which the thistles and mullein-stalks bristle—scrawled across with low long stone fences that must perforce wander with the slope, yet for an acre left ruddy with buckwheat or gold with the débris of oats—drivers of black and white cattle, where the cows repose in august groves or graze high on the round bald mountains that velvet their own sides with shadow—fishers in evening ponds, when the sky leaks its last fluid yellow and the air has grown dimmer than day only as clear water is dimmer, where the heron hastes flapping off and the bullfrog throbs in the dusk. . . .
> (*Poets, Farewell!*, 41)

But Wilson's Muse was a cold mistress, and, when in 1929 he published *Poets, Farewell!*, his first volume of verse, it apparently was to have been his last: "—Poets, farewell!—O subtle and O strong!/Voices, farewell!—the silver and the brass—/I leave that speech to you who have the tongue" (75). However, like any other rejected lover, Wilson could not let matters rest there; he resumed his pursuit of the Muse's favors by publishing occasional poems in the 1930's, which he included in *Note-Books of Night* (1942), and still another collection of verse, *Night Thoughts*

(1961). This volume contains most of the earlier verse, some of it revised, in addition to new pieces and some original drawings of devils.

If Wilson's prose is good because his attempts to write poetry sharpened his sensitivity to English, the irony is that the early prose, after Wilson dropped the lyrical style, is so much better than his lyrics. It is likely that his work as a reporter and editor for the *New Republic* did more for his plain, direct prose style than his poetry did. The precision and detail of Wilson's prose are usually absent in his poetry, which is somewhat obtuse, self-conscious, and labored. His idiom is often old-fashioned, his constructions awkward, his imagery strained. He nearly always rhymes, in couplets or quatrains; but this seldom helps. The great differences between his abilities in verse and prose can be illustrated by comparing a poem from *Poets, Farewell!* with a related article that he wrote for the *New Republic* in 1925:

A Young Girl Indicted for Murder

All night the summer thunder that crashed, but never cracked
The prison of the smothered town.
Resounded, where I lay, about your prison bed,
To which one furious and drunken act
Had suddenly borne down
The spirit fierce, the stubborn copper head.

And all night, from the dull distended air,
The still unwetted empty street,
That company I kept oppressed me there:
Those praisers of the past, accepters of defeat,
The ghosts of poets—violent against God
No longer in my day; with men of thirty-odd
Fierce with the first resentment of their teens;
And those robuster captains of the age,
From brooding on some boorish heritage
Grown loud with sullen spleens.

I thought, those have foregone to carry arms;
And if these others, if a few,
Have struck, it was but drunkenly like you,
In desperate alarms—
Like you that for the butcher of your heart

Struck down your worshipper. And when have they—
So rash to shatter pain, with such swift passion wild,
Assailing lest they break—sustained a bitter part
With braver lies than you I watched to-day—
Pale, slender and a child,
Enduring without tears
The prison, the barbed "pen," the prosecutor's sneers?

—Now, all night long the summer thunder flaps
Above the town, above my bed, above
Your cramped repose of fear and festered love,
Repeating impotent claps. (9-10)

The poem contrasts a girl who has killed one lover, because of her frustrated passion for another, to the poet's evening companions: aging young men, perhaps the old college group, grown cynical and defeated, and living in the past. But one cannot be sure of what these men stood for in any specific sense ("violent against God"?) and thus cannot participate in the poet's disgust with and sorrow for them. Indeed, the poem fails where it needs to succeed most—in evoking indignation and compassion. The poetic devices, such as assonance and alliteration, are forced and obvious. The theme is undermined by bombastic and awkward phrases or silly diction: "The spirit fierce, the stubborn copper head," "The still unwetted empty street," "God/No longer in my day," and so on.

Wilson's prose account of what appears to be the same girl's indictment for murder—"The People Against Dorothy Perkins"—is easily superior although its purpose is different. Dorothy Perkins, sixteen, had shot and killed her boyfriend, probably by accident, during a drunken quarrel with him and her father over a former lover that she had continued seeing. Like the girl in the poem, she was "a pretty, quick-witted, red-haired girl, slight of figure but tense and strong-willed and reputed to have a bad temper" (*The American Earthquake* [1958], 19).

Wilson reports what he has learned in the courtroom and lets the emotional effect come naturally from the material: "In August of 1923 she began a love affair with a truckdriver of thirty-five known as Mickey Connors, who had a flat on the floor below her parents and often came to dinner with them. She used to run errands for him, and one day he asked her into his room and offered her a drink which he said was soda water but which turned out to be a highball. He appears to have threatened and maltreated her, and she seems to have loved him fiercely. He had twice done time in jail, once for robbing the mails" (19).

Eventually the judge sentences Dorothy to prison for five to fifteen years; but nowhere does Wilson belabor the reader's emotions, as he does in the poem, even though it is clear that he sympathizes with Dorothy. Pity and indignation are evoked by the seemingly plain facts of the case, not, as in the poem, by vague fustian. The restraint of the prose, which is not so objective as it might seem, helps one to decide that Dorothy received much less than justice: "But in Dorothy Perkins' case there appeared certain special elements which inevitably worked against her. For, not only is this snub-nosed gamine the sort of girl that men fall badly in love with, she has also the fiery spirit, the instinct of independence, which is equally sure to enrage them. Judge, jury and prosecutor alike were evidently agreed from the first moment they saw her that Dorothy was a 'bad' girl; not only did they strongly resent her, they were perhaps even a little frightened by her" (23-4).

The gift that Wilson lacks is for passion and song. In his verse, exaltation, tenderness, and even sensuality become merely embarrassing. An example is the poem "Copper and White," whose subject is lovemaking with another red-haired girl. The poem begins with the two lovers dreaming of sun, beach, and sea while the sounds of taxis and children filter into the New York apartment where they lie and it attempts to capture their experience:

> —But now it is for us, the smell of summer kisses,
> But now it is for us—
> With this long soft enchainment of caresses,
> Grown more precipitous—
> And now we fall—all topples—steep for fear!—
> All topples—tupping—pouring—and the pause! . . .
> Ah, let me kiss your quiet mouth, my dear—
> The room is quiet as it was!

> (*Poets, Farewell!*, 27)

Where rapture is expected, one is confronted with a jingling diction, partly archaic and unfortunately, in "tupping," suggesting the mating of sheep. And the stanza's last line, ending on an exclaimed predicate, banishes the intended ecstasy by being hilarious.

One critic who praised Wilson's verse almost extravagantly was Morton Dauwen Zabel; in reviewing *Poets, Farewell!* in 1930, he compared Wilson to other critic-poets, such as John Crowe Ransom, Allen Tate, Yvor Winters, and Malcolm Cowley. But even Zabel, in the kindest manner, admitted that Wilson was limited as a lyricist: "... so much beauty of perception and association, so much wit and pithy satire on modern life and art, and so clear an indication of a lyric gift which the pursuit of more exacting literary work did not allow to develop."[4] Zabel's review is friendly but puzzling: surely he did not really think that Wilson's verse was comparable to that of Ransom and Tate—and what literary work could be more exacting than writing lyric poetry?

The only kind of lyric that Wilson has shown some aptitude for is the epitaph, of which he has published four from World War I. In the best of them, the futility of a nurse's task and her humble gratitude for burial are emphasized by the simple diction and the precise numbers, and controlled by the narrow form:

A Hospital Nurse
I, catching fevers that I could not quench,
When twenty died for two that we could save,
Was cast with sixteen soldiers in a trench,
    Glad of no meaner grave.
                    (*Poets, Farewell!*, 65)[5]

As Zabel's statement suggests, there are two kinds of verse that Wilson can write well—satire and parody. His interest in the mechanical aspects of poetry has enabled him to compose some good burlesque verse in which the comic effects depend on a regular, forced meter and on a strict rhyme scheme. The following is an excerpt from "The New Patriotism" (1920):

Lieutenant-Colonel Roosevelt
Has unequivocally felt
That nothing less will now suffice
To purge the people's hearts of vice
And save Americans from schism
Than vigorous Americanism—

That newly-found and certain cure,
That cult incomparably pure,
But only fully understood
By people who are wise and good,
Like Major-General Leonard Wood.
                          (*Poets, Farewell!*, 67)

Still better are Wilson's parodies of other poets—T. S. Eliot,
Archibald MacLeish, E. A. Robinson—which even Stanley Hyman
admits are good. Although Wilson is not an exceptionally good
critic of poetry, he can unerringly find a poet's weakness and
construct an exaggerated "copy" of it. His most famous parody
is "The Omelet of A. MacLeish," part of which follows:

1

And the mist: and the rain on West Rock:
and the wind steady:
There were elms in that place: and graven
inflexible laws:
Men of Yale: and the shudder of Tap Day;
the need for a man to make headway

MacLeish
breaks   Winning a way through the door in the win-
an egg   dowless walls:
for his And the poems that came easy and sweet
omelet.   with a blurring of Masefield
           (The same that I later denied): a young
           man smooth but raw

Eliot alarmed me at first: but my later abase-
   ment:
And the clean sun of France: and the freak-
   ish but beautiful fashion:
Striped bathhouses bright on the sand: *Ana-*
   base and *The Waste Land:*

He puts These and the *Cantos* of Pound: O how
plovers'   they came pat!
eggs and Nimble at other men's arts how I picked up
truffles   the trick of it:
into his Rode it reposed on it drifted away on it:
omelet.   passing

                   (*Night Thoughts* [1961], 84-5)

Eventually MacLeish's omelet "becomes a national institution and gets into Fanny Farmer"; but then MacLeish "experiments with a new kind of peppercorn," and still later he "is obliged to reopen his omelet and put a little garlic in." Eventually, he "is doomed to go on doctoring his omelet." Obviously the poem is a malicious comment on MacLeish as well as an amusing parody of his "The Hamlet of A. MacLeish" (1928).

An earlier and less personal effort is "Tannhäuser," Wilson's parody of the Arthurian poems of Edwin Arlington Robinson:

> "Is this your tribute to my feast?" she said,
> "To sit apart with such sad countenance
> As makes me want to watch you every minute—
> For fear the woven tissue of our days
> (Which once could hold the passions in its woof
> Of any knight or lansquenet or minstrel)
> May suffer Time's erosion and wear thin,
> In spite of all the needle-craft of one
> Who shrinks to feel the losses that accrue
> To wives whose eyes no longer hold their husbands
> And goddesses who have no friends at court?"

> (*Poets, Farewell!*, 55)

In addition to satires and parodies, Wilson has written a few humorous verses, limericks, and other light pieces, usually addressed to his friends. Sometimes he resumes his wooing of the Muse, but she rewards him with pedantic exercises in which he experiments with backward rhymes and the elegiac meter.[6] Wilson has a large interest in poetic techniques but a small gift for poetry.

II *Plays*

Wilson's interest in writing plays appeared in college with a Triangle Club comedy, *The Evil Eye* (1915), and early in his professional career with a volume entitled, *Discordant Encounters* (1926). This book contains his first full-length play, *The Crime in the Whistler Room;* a skit, *Cronkhite's Clocks;* and four imaginary dialogues, published separately as early as 1924, in which the speakers usually present the views of actual literary figures.

The dialogues exemplify Wilson's use of the drama for presenting ideas in dramatic form—unfortunately, a use that is his main weakness as a playwright. The first dialogue, "The Poet's Return," is a debate between two critics over the value of tradition in the arts. The speaker on behalf of tradition is "Paul Rosenfeld"; opposing him is "Matthew Josephson," who argues that the past is useless and that contemporary literature should be concerned with the immediate problems of the day: old things, he says, such as Greek epigrams and the music of Chopin, "no longer represent reality" (16).[7] "Josephson" overstates his case to the point of absurdity when Wilson has him urge that the subway and the shower are more magnificent poems than anything by Schubert or Goethe—an extreme version of a similar statement by Wilson himself in *A Piece of My Mind* (61-2). "Rosenfeld" wins simply because "Josephson" argues so wildly.

The second dialogue, "The Delegate from Great Neck," is a discussion between "F. Scott Fitzgerald" and a cynical critic, "Van Wyck Brooks." "Fitzgerald" has been delegated by the "Younger Generation of American writers" to read a letter to "Brooks" expressing their concern about his lack of enthusiasm for American writers, especially contemporary ones. Wilson uses "Brooks" to make a pointed criticism of the work of Fitzgerald's (and Wilson's) generation: "In allowing your art to become a business, you have made intellectual unity impossible and have given yourselves up to the competitive anarchy of American commercial enterprise. You can at best, I fear, gain nothing but money and hollow popular reputations—each for himself—and these things for fifty years in America have brought nothing but disillusion and despair" (56-7). But the two speakers part amiably: "Fitzgerald" invites "Brooks" to a weekend party, but the latter must decline in order to work on his Henry James book.

"Mrs. Alving and Oedipus" is an encounter between a professor of fifty and a journalist of twenty-five on the subject of ancient versus contemporary literature. Similar in theme to the first two dialogues, it appears to be a precursor of Wilson's own literary battle with the Humanists (see Chapter 2); but the professor, speaking for the ancients, has better arguments.

"In the Galapagos," the fourth and longest colloquy, is a one-sided debate on progress between an eager zoologist and an iguana, who would rather doze in the sun than talk. The iguana's position is that life is a mystery; therefore, one should simply accept it as he finds it and follow his instincts. The zoologist, who favors solving life's mysteries by research, delivers an earnest but dull five-page lecture on molecules which puts the iguana to sleep. The zoologist is convinced that science alone can save the world and improve the human race, but the iguana says that a scientist is foolish to tamper with the principle of life when he does not even understand it. Eventually the bored iguana wants to crawl off to his burrow to sleep, but the zoologist captures him and will use him in research.

The iguana, however, may have been right. For the satirical skit, *Cronkhite's Clocks: A Pantomime with Captions* (for a score by Leo Ornstein), much like a silent film, showed the dehumanizing effect of the "progress" in big business and modern living. Cronkhite is a wealthy manufacturer of alarm clocks whose company's slogan is, "WE CHECK UP ON THE WORLD!" His office workers have time clocks or typewriter keys for faces and dark clothes made of tin. Telephones ring incessantly against the continual clatter of typewriters. Everyone works in a mechanical frenzy, except a Negro porter, the old stereotype of the unspoiled black who cannot be turned into a machine and who loves to dance. At lunch time his dancing becomes so infectious that various office personnel take it up; and soon the entire staff, including Cronkhite, dance with quickening abandon until all have nervous breakdowns. Cronkhite is attended to by nerve specialists, but a new office boy, Casper, dies of shock, a Horatio Alger type baffled and victimized by The Company.

Cronkhite's Clocks was a serious attempt at expressionist drama, a kind of protest-commentary that Wilson himself tended to ridicule (see Chapter 5). Another and shorter satire from this period (1926) is "The Age of Pericles," which Wilson has included in *The American Earthquake*. It deals with a cocktail party in New York's Grand Central Station, where everyone rushes about impulsively and is very confused. The worst that can happen to anyone is that he should feel inferior. This little play is both a spoof of heavy expressionist drama and a summation of Wilson's attitude toward the years 1923-28, which in *Earthquake* he has labeled "the follies."

The Crime in the Whistler Room (1924) is the first of three plays representing what Wilson, in the preface to *Five Plays*

(1954), calls "three successive stages of the artistic and moral revolt which had its headquarters in New York after the [First World] War." His next two plays are *This Room and This Gin and These Sandwiches* and *Beppo and Beth,* from the mid-1930's. Wilson thinks that the three have "a certain historical and critical interest as attempts to dramatize the mentality, the characteristic types and the various milieux of the twenties and the early thirties." Even *The Little Blue Light,* a much later play (1950), is "another instalment of the same historical chronicle . . . since it deals with the same sort of people in a later and even more desperate phase. . . ." (7-8). What one may infer from these statements turns out to be true of the plays: they are usually topical and dated; and, because they deal more with types than with individuals, they are superficial as commentaries on human nature.

The Crime in the Whistler Room (produced by the Provincetown Players on October 9, 1924, in Greenwich Village) deals with a gawky young girl from Pittsburgh called "Bill" (for Elizabeth); her mother is dead, and her father is a well-meaning but pathetic ne'er-do-well. Bill has been informally adopted by Miss Streetfield, a wealthy and socially prominent patroness of the YWCA. The Streetfields, a snobbish "old-money" family who live on Long Island, concern themselves over such matters as whether a table in a room with a Whistler painting (of a cockney girl) looks better against the wall or farther out in the room. They enjoy playing bridge and reading Trollope aloud in the evenings; they take conventional religion and morality for granted; they are fond of quoting Browning.

Bill is in love with, and pregnant by, a brash young writer named Simon Delacy, who likes to speed in roadsters. Delacy is brilliant, supposedly, but unstable, and is too obviously a representation of F. Scott Fitzgerald. The play's theme—a favorite of the young Wilson—is the stifling morality of pre-war American society as opposed to the spontaneous, rebellious, and sincere approach to life of the new generation, silly as it may sometimes be. After a great deal of mental suffering over her inability to fit into polite society, Bill leaves the Streetfields to their charming Whistler cockney girl and elopes with Delacy.

The play's main fault is its tediousness. Two-thirds of it comprise scenes from Bill's dreams: nightmares of being hounded and despised by the Streetfields and of her denouncing them all, and then, by Act III, happy dreams of herself and Delacy in lavish surroundings, possessing things which in real life only the moneyed set can have. The social protest attempted in the fantasy fails because it lacks the force of actuality. Getting even with someone in a dream amounts to very little, even in a personal sense. Although the dream technique can provide insight into a character and allow him to express what he is not allowed to in the everyday world, in Wilson's play this convenience is overdone; furthermore, it is unnecessary: Bill's frustration and protest can be subtly conveyed without dreams, which were probably the easiest way out of the problem of representing externally an internal dramatic problem. Likewise, there is little subtlety in the presentation of characters, which for the most part represent good or bad. Miss Streetfield is more interesting than any other character; she honestly wants to like and help Bill, but can approach her only with platitudes.

Wilson's second play in point of time setting was *This Room and This Gin and These Sandwiches* (published in 1937 but written, according to Sherman Paul, in 1934-35; original title, *A Winter in Beech Street*). *This Room* is much better than *The Crime* because it does not resort to dreams, its characters are more complete, and it does not preach so openly. It shows, as Wilson says in his preface to *Five Plays,* that phase of the artistic and moral revolt "consolidated and concentrated in the Greenwich Village section of New York" in the mid-1920's. The play's main theme is the struggle to maintain integrity and independence and yet survive in a society whose values are commercial.

This theme is exemplified by a small theater group (like the Provincetown Players) that attempts to stay together and to produce worthwhile plays despite not making enough money to pay its members. The play focuses on the personal struggle of Sally Voight, the star of the group, who passionately wants to be free of men, but who cannot afford to live independently without working in the well-paying theaters uptown. (Sally was probably based on Edna St. Vincent Millay.) She is tirelessly pursued by Arthur Fiske, a prudish and partonizing, yet sensitive, young architect. But the man she really loves is Tom ("Bugs") Brophy, a married newspaperman, who resigns from his job because his newspaper changed his factual account of a strike-breaking incident to exonerate the police and the company "goons" of brutal-ity in breaking up a picket line. Bugs has shown some talent for writing social-protest drama, but he can never quite bring himself to renounce wife, children, and comfort in order to join the Village movement. Eventually he becomes a writer for a weekly paper owned by a Detroit automotive tycoon (obviously, Henry Ford and his *Dearborn Independent*).

While the theater group is struggling to stay together—one faction wants to put on popular plays uptown while the other wants to stay in the Village and eke out a living—Sally has an abortion, apparently of Bugs's baby. By the end of the play, the group is breaking up; and Sally's own future is unsure. Half-heartedly she agrees to marry Arthur, but she plans to have dinner with Bugs that evening.

The play is full of different types of people: Dan, an idealistic and impractical producer; Sophie, his cast-off and spiteful mistress, who tries to undermine the group; Harry Greenaway, formerly a second-rate drama critic and now the group's business manager, who has become Sophie's new lover and who also wants to make money uptown; Fred, an alcoholic ex-poet and ex-lover of Sally, full of plans and reminiscences but undependable; Tracy, who has provided for himself by arranging a marriage with a rich lesbian; and others. In the play these people are not the trite caricatures that they may seem in this discussion, and Wilson presents them sympathetically and amusingly. They represent different political points of view—Anarchist, Socialist, Communist—and it is not surprising that in the preface to *Five Plays* Wilson called this play a *"tableau de moeurs,* almost encyclopaedic."

Beppo and Beth, published in 1937 although written in 1932, is a somber comedy about a cartoonist named Beppo Miles and his ex-wife Beth Badger, who finally decide to resolve their lonely aimlessness by remarrying and going to live in Mexico. Both are sophisticated New Yorkers who have undergone the Crash, a number of love affairs, and a loss of values; he has been divorced three times and she twice; and both have been "psyched." The setting is a dinner party in Beppo's lavish apartment, during which his daughter, Mimi, runs off with Jack Payne, a bootlegger to whom she has been secretly married for two weeks; Beppo's landlord is shot three separate times by a small-time gangster; his ex-wife Beth is jilted by a buck-toothed, impecunious English nobleman (named Longbroke) who has mistakenly thought that she is wealthy; and Beppo is told by his current mistress—a girl of Polish peasant stock who plays the piano in a nightclub (and who says, "like-um," "love-um," "want-um")—that the only big love in her life was the gangster who shot the landlord. This basic cast is supported by a Chinese houseboy spouting Communist "dialectic"; a foolish psychiatrist; another of Beth's former husbands—a stuttering artist, Chet Chives—and his current wife, Charlotte; and assorted inept policemen. A powerful newspaper owner and potential employer of Beppo—whose specialty is drawing cynical tigers which he will have to make cheerful if he takes the job—is expected at any moment but never appears; when the doorbell rings at the end, Beppo and Beth ignore it.

Although Beppo and Beth begin the evening by freely telling each other about their love affairs, they are both disillusioned and lonely. Beppo attempts to put a brave face on his unhappiness with several aphorisms, such as," Politics is a dirty game—amusing, if you like low comedy, but not a thing in which a civilized person can take the faintest interest." Nevertheless, Beppo finally confesses that his own life is "Just a crazy party with everybody talking about themselves. . . . I have to keep myself going with things that are so infinitely little!—a cocktail before dinner, the opening of a new revue, seeing an amusing friend, buying a new picture. . . ." (*Five Plays*, 325, 391, 406).

At the end of the evening Beppo is alone with Beth, who is recovering from a non-lethal dose of iodine that she took in a moment of despair. Beppo attacks the America of Prohibition, bad bonds, popular gangsters, and a general lack of principles: "Well, why should we be ashamed of our Puritanism, now that we've broken the rules and only feel glummer than ever? Our Puritan tradition of protest is perhaps the one sound thing we've got. Why, in God's name, *don't* we protest instead of trying to drug ourselves . . . ?" He suggests, somewhat vaguely, that he and Beth protest "against ourselves!". They decide to remarry and to "take the first boat to Mexico!" (412-14).

The play seems an odd but earnest effort. Wilson sets up a moral dilemma: what can one believe in, when no one else believes in anything? But Beppo has such a hazy grasp of the social and political issues, and the protest-solution he proposes is so absurd, that he becomes more ridiculous than the two main objects of satire, the psychiatrist and the houseboy—and the latter is really more tiresome than ridiculous. Beppo is neither pitiful nor admirable, and his intelligence is doubtful. In other words, he is uninteresting.

The only theme of real promise is struck accidentally during a comic scene and is never developed. The police are searching the apartment while Mimi's bootlegger husband (who defends hoodlums by equating them with big businessmen) hides in a grandfather clock, which keeps chiming. To spare Mimi's feelings, Beppo's guests pretend that nothing is wrong with the clock; and, in harboring a criminal, they unwittingly become as guilty as he. But Wilson does not exploit this situation, and the viewer's attention is turned again to Beppo's half-articulated moral pain.

Unlike *Beppo and Beth, The Little Blue Light* (1950) is not serious comedy but allegorical melodrama. The play is set in the near future at a large country house not far from New York. The background is political: the American two party system has died, and a number of groups have been struggling for control of the United States. At the far right are the Reds, who, like a religious faction called the Children of Peter, want government by an oligarchy and favor keeping the working class uneducated and powerless. At the far left are the Constitutionalists, who favor returning to the principles of the United States Constitution. In the middle are the New Federalists, representing big business and usually supported by the Fascist Yankee Elitists. The largest and supposedly strongest party is Labor. But all of these groups are corrupt and fumbling; and the real strength, carefully disguised, lies with a large employment agency, the Luke Teniakis Relief Bureau, operated by a Greek immigrant who has no political credo at all but simply wants power for its own sake. His secret slogan is "Rule by the Uncommon Man in the Interest of the Common Man."

Placed against this confusing political background are the personal and professional problems of Frank Brock, the editor and publisher of a liberal magazine, *Spotlight*. Frank runs his magazine on the idealistic premise "that everybody's got a right to look at the world from the corner he's sitting in—and to yell about anything he doesn't like." But Frank's wife, Judith, who also edits the magazine, is bored with her husband and his belief in the magazine and with sitting in the big country house reading copy. She goes to live in the city, where she has several love affairs and writes articles for *Spotlight* on New York nightlife. Part of her dissatisfaction with her husband is due to his new secretary, a popular mystery-writer named Gandersheim, who owns their house; she hints that Gandersheim has a homosexual interest in Frank.

Gandersheim, a fawning, morbid mystic, cherishes the theory that a "hideous subhuman power [is] wreaking havoc all over the world"; his stories are always about "the demiurge that's running amuck, devouring civilization" (440, 427). He calls this "Monster God" Shidnats Slyme (Gandersheim's own given name, Miles Standish, spelled backwards for reasons having to do with his unhappy childhood). The monster god, Shidnats, has never been described in Gandersheim's books; but for a new horror story, Gandersheim imagines Shidnats as a little blue light "quietly and steadily shining, but with devilish deadly intensity—with a ray like an old-fashioned hatpin that will stick you right through the brain" (489).

Frank wants to include an article in the next issue of *Spotlight* on Luke Teniakis: "He's not an important figure, but he's a hell of an admirable guy. . . . Here's a little Greek delicatessen dealer who comes over here without a cent and who builds up something unique: an employment agency that sticks by its clients— just because he remembered his own hard times" (486). But Frank gets a threatening letter ordering him not to print the article, and Judith, who has picked up a great deal of information in her nightlife reporting, warns Frank that Teniakis is really the mastermind behind an immense political machine that controls even the White House and has spies everywhere. Teniakis, she says, "doesn't want publicity. He wants to be known as just head of a relief bureau. That's why he's trying to stop your article" (496). She has also learned that Teniakis has a new device for electrocuting people who get in his way—an electronic gun enclosed in a flashlight and triggered by the victim's own emotions of hatred, fear, or grief; for the device will not respond to pleasant emotions. It was used in an unsolved crime to kill Cardinal Keenan, a prominent leader of the Children of Peter.

Frank stubbornly insists that he will print the article anyway. Indeed, he will take an airplane and drop leaflets exposing

Teniakis all over Manhattan. Before he can, he is killed, along with Judith and Gandersheim, by a little blue light from a flashlight planted in the living room by Ellis, Frank's former secretary and Judith's former lover, who is now a Teniakis agent. The flashlight is set off by a quarrel between Judith and Gandersheim over Frank.

The Little Blue Light is partly a morality play on the danger of political apathy and the importance of individual interest in government. It is also an appeal for brotherhood, a homily on selfishness, and a warning against replacing human relationships with material and mechanical values. Men must be human, or subhuman forces will destroy them. Acting as a kind of chorus at the end is a mysterious old gardener who has appeared throughout the play, speaking in a variety of accents—Italian, Irish, Scotch, Hebrew, and Russian. Aside from adding an element of suspicion, the gardener has had little to do with the action; but at the very end he identifies himself as Ahasuerus, the Wandering Jew, who mocked Christ on the way to Golgotha. In a long monologue he reproaches the audience for not recognizing "the sign of God," not fighting "at the command of the spirit," and not serving "the vision of Justice that has gleamed for our secular leaders." The audience, who he says has never heeded him, trusts in "merely the brute vitality that animates the universe. . . ." Mankind is faltering on the "precipice-edge," but the Wandering Jew will continue to bear God's light "to show where the abyss drops" (540-1).

The Little Blue Light was neither a popular nor a critical success. It had two brief appearances—at the Cambridge (Massachusetts) Summer Playhouse in 1950 and at the American National Theater and Academy (ANTA) Playhouse in New York City in 1951, where it ran for eight performances. The critics generally did not understand it. Wolcott Gibbs wrote in *The New Yorker* that it had enough ideas for five or six plays.[8] In the *Nation* Margaret Marshall called it a "satirical commentary on sex, politics, and religion"; she enjoyed the evening but wished that the play had had a happy ending.[9] Walter Kerr in *Commonweal* was annoyed by it, partly because he felt that Wilson was attacking Catholics.[10] Brooks Atkinson, of the *New York Times*, didn't know what to make of it: "Mr. Wilson has a full mind and he has emptied it with abandon. His drama involves feminism, psychiatry, the obsolescence of education, sexual aberration, a new method of murder by remote control and the Wandering Jew...."[11]

The only critic who saw some sense in the play was Harold Clurman, who reviewed it both off and on Broadway for the *New Republic*. In his comment on the Cambridge production, Clurman wrote that the play was "the voice of our disquiet," a dramatization of "the sense that the self has almost no right to exist and the fear that man—whatever he may be—is being crowded out, denied, done away with and destroyed altogether, not only as a fact but as an idea."[12] When he reviewed *The Little Blue Light* a second time, Clurman's comments were similar to those in his first review: "...it is tonic to have a man voice his terror and throw the little blue light of his despair upon us"; the play is "one of those partially unrealized artistic efforts which hold us whether or not we 'like' it."[13]

The reviewers who did not understand the play were more outspoken than Clurman about the lack of stagecraft. Walter Kerr, whose criticism in this instance is suspect because of his apparently Catholic bias, called it "devoid of meaningful characterization" and "moth-eaten" in language. Wolcott Gibbs criticized a "toplofty and cliché-ridden idiom" and an "almost wholly unmotivated behavior suggesting that [Wilson] regards physical movement and emotional conflict on the stage as no more than tiresome interruptions to the main business of conversation." And Brooks Atkinson wrote: "...we might as well face the fact that Mr. Wilson's ideas are disembodied and that he has no more talent for the stage than Henry James." Atkinson, however, praised the actors (Martin Gabel, Arlene Francis, Burgess Meredith, Melvyn Douglas, and Peter Cookson), but the comments of the other reviewers about the acting were mixed.

Wilson's plays are decidedly dated, as he himself recognizes; but in defense of this fact, Max Cosman wrote in *Theatre Arts*, "...the datedness does not invalidate his indictment of the hedonist's answer to the problem of right."[14] While allowing that this statement may be true, one must nevertheless admit that the datedness prevents the audience from paying the indictment much attention.

Wilson's lack of success on the stage is probably due not only to his use of the drama as a forum or to a lack of ability, but also to the fact that the wrong plays were staged. *The Crime in the Whistler Room* and *The Little Blue Light* are probably his weakest plays, although *Beppo and Beth* may be just as weak. But *This Room and This Gin and These Sandwiches* and the much more recent *Cyprian's Prayer* (1954) are superior to the others and undoubtedly would have made better "theater." *Cyprian's Prayer,* the one play of the five without a contemporary setting, seems the least dated. It also took longer to write than any of the others; Wilson began it in a hospital in Odessa, where he was quarantined with scarlet fever in 1935, and did not publish it until nineteen years later. To this play he brought not only an interest in demonology, literature, and history, but also his mature thought about human reform.

The action, set in France during the 1460's, is worth viewing in some detail. A twenty-year-old peasant youth named Cyprian, who has mastered the unique feat of reading French and Latin, is supposedly studying for the priesthood. But his reading has acquainted him with black magic and with revolutionary ideas concerning individual human dignity. Angered at his family's brutal landlord, Tancarville, who rides through their garden on a hunt and deliberately shoots their poultry and sheep, Cyprian commits himself to the unprecedented cause of freedom for the peasant. Tancarville's possessions extend to Cyprian's coquettish mother, Lottie, who visits the manor upon demand and who yielded the landlord his *droit de seigneur* on her wedding night; indeed, Cyprian's older brother, Cyrus, is probably Tancarville's son. Although Cyprian's father has long since resigned himself to humiliation, Cyprian decides to become an apprentice of the magician Merlin, for he believes that black magic is the only kind of power that can work for the peasants ("Jesus Christ is not on our side"); he refers to Black Sabbath's as "People's Rallies" (21).

When Cyprian tells Merlin that he wants to study magic because "it gives knowledge and power," Merlin tries to discourage him. Indeed, Merlin himself seldom practices real magic, but attempts to promote a practical goodness with false magic. He is actually a pharmacist who is very careful about dispensing drugs. He makes sure, for example, that an apparently anemic woman, actually a vampire, is not given a sleeping potion.

Merlin dies of heart failure after an unpleasant encounter with

Tancarville, who is enraged because an aphrodisiac that Merlin prepared has not worked on the Lady Elinor. Cyprian stays on in Merlin's tower with Janet, the magician's daughter, and Claude, a priggish former assistant to Merlin and now his successor. Claude resents the skeptical newcomer, especially because Cyprian does not believe in bat's blood, skeletons, and other items of fakery.

With the assistance of a devil disguised as an Italian, Cyprian succeeds in making a pact with Satan granting the latter six months control over his body and soul in return for the power "to work wonders" and to take revenge "against the oppressions of the earth" (69-70). Satan also agrees to keep the envy of Claude and the charms of Janet from interfering with Cyprian's work. But Cyprian does not know that this guarantee will result temporarily in Claude's decapitation and in Janet's transformation to a Jezebel. Furthermore, Cyprian suffers a continual meddling in his work by the Italian devil, three mischievous imps, and his brother Cyrus, who appears as an agent of the king and who wants Cyprian and his magic on the side of the king against the nobles. Cyprian's only friend is Mr. B (for Beelzebub), who rejected Satan and thereby made an enemy not only of Satan but of God, too, in that he upset the established universal order. Mr. B wants to renounce the devil's ways and join the race of human beings because of "the germ of some new power in them" (98). However, he has problems of his own: God has punished him by killing his human wife with the plague, and the local priest will not allow him to bury her because she is rumored to have been a vampire.

Cyprian complicates the disorder in the tower by freeing a Mohammedan genie to hold Satan in check. But it does not take the genie long to obtain control of the tower himself, and he wants Cyprian to go to Venice and join the Sultan, who is plotting the overthrow of Europe. When his frustration is highest, Cyprian is tempted by a charming idler, the Moonlight Drunkard, to while away his life in soaking up moonbeams and doing nothing at all. Eventually Mr. B instills in Cyprian the courage to confront the genie and return him to his bottle. He tells Cyprian to use his intellectual freedom, "the light of your mind," and "never appeal again to a power outside yourself!" (118, 121). Human beings, says Mr. B, should drop both Satan and Savior and depend on themselves.

After restoring Janet's personality and Claude's head, Mr. B leaves earth for human beings to remake and decides to harass heaven again. Cyprian last sees him in the distance, falling through space, apparently knocked from the sky back to the bottomless pit. The play ends with Cyprian and Janet returning to the use of Merlin's bogus magical equipment as a professional cover behind which they hope to extend slowly "the kingdom of thought and art." Their immediate problem is to pacify their liege lord, who thinks that Cyprian is responsible for his steward's defecting to the king's party. Old Merlin was right, after all, in working for the good of mankind in a small way rather than in attempting sweeping reforms for human dignity.

The questions of the sources and uses of power, which provide so much of the interest in *Patriotic Gore*, form an interesting discussion within the action of the play. Cyprian learns that, whenever he looks outside himself for power, he always becomes embroiled in political machinations which pervert his search for truth. He also learns that, if he tries to act according to a set of principles, he is paralyzed. The moral of human self-reliance, along with the necessity of compromising with earthly authority and ignorance (a clearly deliberate coupling), is more closely knit into the action than the more topical messages of Wilson's other plays; it follows naturally from Cyprian's thirst for knowledge and freedom and is not forced onto the drama. Still more remarkable are the characters, who are too individualized to be mere types, and the dialogue, which is supple and conversational. Perhaps Tancarville, with his loud vulgarity and profanity (which Wilson wisely renders in a modern idom instead of attempting to approximate fifteenth-century speech) is the most vivid character; but Mr. B. and Cyprian himself— who is earnest and candid, yet never priggish—are also memorable.

Cyprian's Prayer suggested that Wilson could be a good playwright. He has always been an able critic of plays and has always been aware of the especial importance of characterization and language. In *"The Pilgrimage of Henry James"* (1925), a review of a book by Van Wyck Brooks, he wrote: "The dramatist makes no attempt to decide between competing interests: he is content to understand his characters and to put their behavior before us" (*The Shores of Light*, 221). Yet at least in *The Crime in the Whistler Room* and in *The Little Blue Light* the playwright has certainly made the decision for his audience, and in *Beppo and Beth* he has failed to reveal much understanding of character. Wilson's criticism of Eugene O'Neill's inability to write convincing dialogue, "the language of the people" (*Shores*, 104), could also be made of most of his own attempts; but this defect is not nearly so serious as his tendency to preach.

One trouble with preaching is that not all ideas are worth a sermon, at least not in narrative form—a fact unintentionally illustrated by Wilson's recent play, *The Lamentable Tragedy of the Duke of Palermo, By Henry Chettle and William Shakespeare, Now First Discovered and Transcribed by Homer R. Winslow, M. A. Hillsdale, Ph.D. Harvard.* First published in the *New York Review of Books* of January 12, 1967, this droll little farce lampoons the teaching of English literature: on the one hand is the arcane, "explicatory" approach to literature (that is, a kind of New Criticism without discrimination and with the worst features of psychological and biographical criticism); on the other, the older philological approach, with its heavy emphasis on determining authenticity and establishing a text. Both extremes neglect the delight and edification of literature—both, in other words, are "anti-humanistic."[15]

The plot concerns an aging Shakespearean, Homer Winslow, who is close to being reduced to teaching Freshman English at Hillsdale, a small New England college, because his younger chairman, a professional climber, despises Winslow's flamboyant methods of "selling" literature to his classes. The chairman, Ned ("Spooky") Simms, thinks that Winslow's courses in Shakespeare should be taught by someone more "explicatory." Simms himself represents this "Talmudic" approach, which he of course takes very seriously; and one of the funniest exchanges in the play concerns his interpretation of Yeats:

> SPOOKY: I've cracked *The Wild Swans at Coole*!
> WINSLOW (*smiling*): Not irreparably, I hope.

In unwittingly reducing biographical criticism to absurdity, Spooky, completely serious, continues: "The poem is crammed with homosexual allusions. The wild swans—Wilde—remember that Yeats knew Oscar—we don't know how well. And swans—that refers to Proust. *Swann's Way* had come out in 1919—just six years before the poem."

Professor Winslow has discovered in England a lost revenge-tragedy by the minor Elizabethan dramatist Henry Chettle in collaboration with Shakespeare. He stages the play at Hillsdale, stocking the cast with members of the academic community, including Chairman Simms (in a villainous role), the chairman's mother, the college president, Winslow's own daughter Fran, and various other students and instructors. The lost play is of course a forgery by Winslow and is publicly denounced by the world's leading authority on Elizabethan dramatic texts, Dr. Edgar J. Creech, of Pratt College in California. But Winslow's intention has been only to awaken an interest in Elizabethan literature; he says in his play's epilogue: "We needs must live the poets that we cherish;/ We needs must nurse their spirits lest they perish—/ Nor peer at them from scholarly removes./ Each man perhaps must forge the book he loves . . . I can aim no higher/ Than dimly to communicate, forsooth,/ Some spark of splendor to our groping youth" (21). This is the moral of the entire action, which ends well: "Spooky" Simms is fired for homosexuality and will take a position at Pratt, in "a climate more relaxed"; Fran Winslow will marry a young M.A. in English whose real interest is the unfashionable Classics and who has been offered a position at Harvard following an amazing revolution there against the Ph.D. and the attitude of "publish or perish"; and Professor Winslow will stay at Hillsdale teaching Shakespeare.

The play is a strange, jocular comment on the profession of teaching English by someone obviously not on the inside. Although the dialogue is plausible and although the characters and their problems are somewhat interesting, the framework play (the story of the friction in the Hillsdale English department) is on the whole implausible and dull—at times amusing, but otherwise slight. The attacks on both explication and pedantry seem strained; and the alternative, the appreciation of literature for the humanistic values it expresses, has an ambiguous proponent in Professor Winslow, who teaches Shelley's "Skylark" to football louts by flapping his arms like a bird. Perhaps, to Wilson, all English professors are ridiculous. The essential difficulty for this play, as for any narrative of ideas, is that, while all human experience is worth dramatic treatment, all ideas are not. If a storyteller is interested in the "life" of his characters—what happens to them and why—their attitudes and opinions do not matter except as aspects of their personalities. But, if the teller is primarily interested in his characters as embodiments of intellectual positions and seeks frankly to moralize or propagandize through them, his "ideas" need to be worth the narrative vehicle; and he should not bother writing a play when an article or even a letter to the editor would do. Frankly, the controversy, such as it is, of *The Lamentable Tragedy* is scarcely worth the trouble. The teacher-scholar imbroglio, despite the brassy publicity from the Berkeley riots of 1964 and the firing of teachers at several universities, really represents a false dichotomy. "Publish or perish," for instance, has been as faked an issue as ancient or modern, Humanist or Naturalist, or "Red or dead." Good departments of English seek neither the Creeches nor the Winslows, but scholar-teachers.

The inner play, the "lamentable tragedy" that Winslow "discovered," is a fairly competent imitation of Elizabethan drama—an imitation, however, which would be far more interesting than it is as mere humor if, as in Wilson's satirical poems, it were useful as literary criticism. For Wilson's strength lies in parody, which is absent from *The Lamentable Tragedy* despite the clever imitation of the Elizabethan style—why, after all, should one ridicule the Elizabethans? An early example of Wilson's parodic gifts, "A Greenwich Village Production" (1923), again shows how Wilson can put parody to work as literary criticism:

I unfortunately missed the first act of *Sandro Botticelli* but from the program and what I saw afterwards, I know it must have gone much like this:

LEONARDO DA VINCI. What ails our friend Botticelli? He seems silent and distracted to-day—this day of all days, the birthday of Lorenzo the Magnificent, when the people are dancing in the streets like cicadas after rain.

FRA LIPPO LIPPI. They say he is enamored of Giuliano's mistress, the beautiful Simonetta. But look, here comes Lorenzo himself with the learned Poliziano!

LORENZO DE' MEDICI. Ha, our incomparable Leonardo! How goes the Mona Lisa and what are your latest experiments in engineering?

POLIZIANO. Gentlemen, I must confess it. I have turned another little canzone to Simonetta. *Per Bacco*, I cannot find it in my heart to keep away from the subject. (*All laugh.*)

FRA LIPPO LIPPI. No more can our friend Botticelli! (*All laugh.*)

BOTTICELLI. (*joining them*). Greeting, good master Leonardo and Your Most Excellent Highness Lord Lorenzo. Is it not a day for men and for angels, for music, for flowers—

LEONARDO. And for lovers? (*All laugh.*)

POLIZIANO. All Florence is laughing in the sun. Come, let us taste some of our host's good wine.

Exeunt omnes—except Botticelli, who hides behind a potted rosebush to watch Eva Le Gallienne make her entrance.

(The American Earthquake, 53-4)

CHAPTER 4

Fiction

WILSON'S FICTION comprises only two novels and four-
teen stories, five of which are reserved for the discussion in
Chapter 5 of Wilson's use of fact to make fiction. His narrative
ability continually improves. *Memoirs of Hecate County* (1946),
his last sustained work of fiction, justifies his surprising little complaint at the front of the revised edition (1959): "*Hecate County*
is my favorite among my books—I have never understood why
the people who interest themselves in my work never pay any attention to it. . . ." In this chapter Wilson's fiction is considered as
narrative art, successful or not, rather than as the autobiographical pastime of a critic—a common attitude toward it. His own
standards for fiction, outlined in Chapter 2, become clearer, especially his conviction that fiction should analyze social ills and
depict the individual's reconciliation to social responsibility; and
these standards are then applied to an evaluation of his fiction.

I *Early Fiction*

Wilson's earliest stories as a professional writer concern World
War I. "The Oppressor" (*The Liberator* [May, 1921], 25-6, 28)
concentrates on two incidents in the life of an American sergeant.
In the first, which takes place one night at a military encamp-
ment in France, the sergeant is berated and kicked by his captain
for not following orders quickly enough during a mustard-gas
bombardment. He vows to avenge his humiliation. In the second,
back home after the war, the sergeant, a good Legionnaire and
Red-baiter, participates with a mob of police and army veterans
in breaking into an International Workers of the World headquarters and beating up the few "wobblies" inside (cf. F. Scott Fitzgerald's "May Day"). Later he and fellow Legionnaires attend
a radical meeting and throw garbage at the speaker. But when

the sergeant recognizes the man next to him as his former captain, he slinks off, his evening's fun spoiled.

The story denounces the military sadist who is fundamentally a coward and it argues that the oppressor is always the person with authority on his side. The sergeant's cowardice is as vividly shown as the earlier gassing incident. But the story is weakened by its partisan emphasis; Wilson's anger against the Red-baiters dominates the action. This weakness characterizes most of Wilson's early fiction; the young writer wants to "say" something, but cannot write a story strong enough as narrative to bear the burden of pronouncement.

Or he may take promising material and ruin it. An example is "The Hero," published in *The Liberator* of February, 1922 (12): "I remember a curious patient who came to the hospital in France. He had a small undeveloped head left naked by close cropping, and his screwed-up features were as fixed as a face carved out of peach-stone." The man has bayoneted a young German and cannot forget it; he shakes all the time—can he be a brave American? The final paragraph is an outright harangue: "Now will you be convinced, romantic Americans... that there can be no real triumph of greatness in war for the civilized human spirit, when the deeds of heroism are too hideous for the heroes themselves to endure?" Hemingway would have shaped this material into "In another Country" or "A Way You'll Never Be," with emphasis on the hero's psychological conflict rather than on a moral application.[1]

But in Wilson's next story, "The Death of a Soldier" also published in *The Liberator*, September, 1921 (13-17), as well as in *The Undertaker's Garland* (1922), he more successfully keeps himself in the background. A boy just out of high school has enlisted in the army because of the chauvinistic fervor wrought by a commencement speech and a sermon in his home town. Sent to France, Henry is shocked by the language and thrilled by the squalor of the barracks. He has caught a bad cold from sleeping on the ground at Southampton; and, as he and his comrades are shipped from Le Havre to the front in boxcars, his cold gets worse: his head and throat ache, his legs are cold, and breathing is difficult. His noisy companions and the jouncing boxcar make him more uncomfortable and keep him from sleeping. He is tantalized by memories of the warm comforts of home.

Finally, someone notices him and at one of the stops tells the lieutenant, who, after examining Henry cursorily, tells the men to make space for Henry to lie down and says that he'll give him something "when we get there." By this time Henry is very sick. When another lieutenant examines Henry and notifies the major of his condition, he replies, "They've all got colds."

The next day, Henry is finally taken off the train and put into an ambulance, but is conscious of scarcely more than "a little piece of cotton in his throat; he thought that if he could only get that out he would be all right." At the base hospital he dies of pneumonia. " 'He put up a pretty good fight there at the last,' remarked the doctor, noting the death in a register. . . . The orderly assembled in a khaki handkerchief all the things in the pockets of the uniform. There were a pipe, a crushed bag of tobacco, photographs of Henry's mother and sister, half-a-dozen obscene post-cards bought from a man who had been to Paris and a little brown leather pocket-book stained dark with sweat" (119-20). It is appropriate that the youth should die prosaically without having experienced any of the glamour that had been promised him for "bearing arms" against the "Antichrist." The reader's position is simply that of watching the inexorable work itself out. Henry is a very ordinary, inexperienced youth, who gets sicker and sicker and, at the end, automatically struggles like any animal to live. He has no insight into his plight; he apparently never considers the significance of what happens to him and could happen to the others; certainly he has no time to generalize. He merely becomes ill, suffers, and dies. Nor does the author sentimentalize Henry or openly moralize from his predicament.

The narration, too, is matter-of-fact. The style is drab, like the rainy French countryside, even in an exciting scene: "The next day, it was their turn to leave at four in the morning. He could hardly go to sleep for thinking how he would have to jump up quickly and get into his pack; he kept waking up and thinking the Sergeant had called and when the Sergeant did call, it found him nervously awake. He tore himself out of his blankets, buttoned his breeches hurriedly and put on his blouse and coat, then spread out the blankets on the muddy floor where the men had been spitting all night" (103-4). This sound, descriptive style has none of the rhythms of Hemingway or the striking detail

of Orwell, and only some of the vivid imagery of Scott Fitzgerald: "The country consisted mostly of barren fields and dismal
woods, inhabited by unfamiliar birds, and there were endless
lines of poplar skeletons in whose fishbone-like branches the
mistletoe clumps were lodged like enormous nests" (106). To the
limited imagination of Henry's mind, the trees are only skeletons
and fishbones, images which become somewhat confused by
mistletoe "nests."[2]

The Undertaker's Garland (1922), in which "The Death of a
Soldier" appeared, was written in collaboration with John Peale
Bishop, a friend and former classmate of Wilson's at Princeton.
Wilson contributed the preface, two stories, and four poems;
Bishop, five poems, one very short play, and a story. The theme
of *Garland* is death, a subject with which the two young authors
became familiar during the war, even though "we were neither of
us ever in much danger of getting killed ourselves." Upon their
return home, they faced a different kind of death; and Wilson
wrote bitterly in the preface that America seemed dreary in
spirit and sterile in culture, its values established by the mer-
chant, its laborers sacrificed to business interests, its dissenters
harassed by authority:

> We were confronted with a colossal strike in which citizens were
> terrorised and murdered for believing that twelve hours a day
> was too long to work in a blast-furnace. A revolt against the
> intolerable life of the steel mills and the mines was punished
> with a repression and a blackguardism which we thought had
> been exorcised forever when the Czar's knout was broken. And it
> was not only among labourers that free speech and free assem-
> blage was done away with: so panic-stricken had the employers
> become for fear they should be made to lose money that they
> arrested citizens without a warrant, deported aliens without trial
> and were finally able to revoke elections to one of the state as-
> semblies by refusing to admit the representatives whom the
> people had legally chosen. (20)

As the emblem of freedom, hope, and justice, America was moribund; and, "in a spirit which we honestly hope is one of loyal
Americanism," the young men decided that they could "best
interpret our country in a book devoted to death" (22).

"The Death of a Soldier" comments implicitly on the stupidity
of bearing arms for an absurd death in war. But war is no less

stupid than home, a point made in Wilson's second story in *Garland*. "Emily in Hades" is a jejune attempt at moral fantasy, a kind of fiction which Wilson later, in *Memoirs of Hecate County*, combines more successfully with realism. This early attempt details the post-mortem adventures of a young, frigid wife who has been killed by influenza. In Hades she discovers that people behave as they did on earth: they stay with their own group and make no efforts to try anything new. The main apparent difference between the dead and the living is that the dead no longer have sensory perceptions; but, by implication, neither in a full sense do the living.

As Emily wanders around meeting people whom she knew in life, she recognizes her former school mistress and reproaches her for having falsely represented love to the girls as "something impious and unclean," for having planted in Emily "a fear and distaste she had never quite got over" (140). The old teacher explains that she was religious and believed in the hope of something better after death that could be earned by purity. When Emily sees her mother, grandmother, and aunts, she also blames them for her sexual repressions. Then she meets a boy who courted her, went to war, and, as a member of the military police, was shot and killed by a resentful soldier. In life he wanted to make love to her but refrained because of his ideal of chivalry. They now try to make love but, as spirits, cannot grasp one another. Understandably, she is frustrated.

Eventually Emily meets Sappho, the great love poetess of ancient Greece, and desperately asks her why she has never known love, whether she is incapable of it, and what she must do to obtain it: "Was there once another sort of love less clumsy and unkind than now? Is love cooling off like the sun? Did it die with the ancient world?" (162-3). But Sappho, whose lyre is broken and whose superb body is now useless, can only weep for Emily and embrace her in a ghostly way, without contact or comfort.

The story is a youthful manifesto against conventional American attitudes and ideals, as well as Christian beliefs: Charon, the ferryman, says, "How could man, who lives so short a time, hope to make a God who would be deathless?" It preaches the unfettered, free-loving life, and represents what was probably the typical reaction of "informed" youth in the 1920's to the prewar generation. Against the fundamentalist view of sex as sin, it upholds sex as beauty.[3] Sappho knew that mutability is life's great truth; therefore, people should fulfill their passions while they still have them, even though Sappho had found small enough satisfaction through hers. Whether they do or not, desire will fade; and only the memory of beauty will remain.

However, the cynicism is not pointed enough; the message is not very well thought out. If, indeed, one should vigorously exercise his desires in life because he will be haunted after death by memories of unfulfillment, why are the Sapphists also frustrated after death? But probably the story cannot be questioned too closely for satisfactory answers. The main point is simply that love should be spontaneous and free, but that it is spoiled by an untenable system of morality.

Because Wilson's realism is superior to his fantasy, most of "Emily" is tedious; the beginning, however, is promising: "Emily had died of influenza in the stiff and rather barren bed-room which no longer than a year before she had fitted up with wedding presents. Her husband sat dry-eyed and dazed, aghast before the prospect of his future; it was not that a great passion had united them; it was not that the contrast was so great between Emily lying beside him living and Emily lying beside him dead; but he had really been fond of Emily and had grown completely accustomed to her, and having worked very hard to support her in the bondselling business, now found himself at a ghastly loss as to why he should go on selling bonds" (129).

The theme of American intolerance and mediocrity continues, but with more restraint and without the sexual emphasis, in three stories published between 1925 and 1927 and later included in *The American Earthquake* (1958). All three deal with people who attended college or prep school together. The first, "After the Game," is a surprisingly funny, if somewhat juvenile, monologue concerning two Princeton boys who have gone to the 1915 Princeton-Yale game at New Haven and have stopped afterwards in the rooms of Arthur, a priggish, scholarly lad whom they knew at St. Matthew's prep school. He and the narrator get into an argument about modern writers versus the ancient: are Hardy and Ibsen better than Sophocles? The debate is interrupted by the arrival of Arthur's irresponsible roommate, Ed Haynes, whose wildness worries Arthur. The two visitors and Ed go to a variety show at the "Hype," where they/join an unruly audience of students and alumni. After Ed causes the human-pyramid act to collapse by yelling "Hup!" at the most delicate moment of balance, he takes over the stage to do "the Transformation Scene from *Dr. Jekyll and Mr. Hyde.*" This precipitates a melee; when the police come, the theater is a shambles. Later that evening, when Arthur hears about the riot, he is very disturbed: "Arthur was afraid that Ed had gummed his chances for Bones or something." Eventually Ed feels sorry, and the two visitors, trying to sleep in the sitting room, hear him go into Arthur's room and apologize. "It was sort of embarrassing. If it had taken place at Princeton, we would just have yelled to tuck it in; but there was something sort of religious about it" (*Earthquake,* 143-4).

After the grimness of *The Undertaker's Garland* and, indeed, the sobriety of Wilson's writings generally, the humor in this story is refreshing. Just after the game, when all four boys are together, Ed impersonates "Weeping Fred" Hotchkiss of St. Matthew's School (cf. the YMCA speaker in the essay "Mr. Rolfe" of *The Triple Thinkers* and in the story "Galahad," which is discussed later in this chapter):

> I see a bare and unlighted room on the topmost story of a tenement. I see a man and a woman huddled there about a guttering candle. Their seventeen children—all under the age of three—are clamoring for food. A package has arrived. What is in it? They carry it to the failing light. At first, they think there must be a mistake. It must have come to the wrong address. But no! there is a card: it says, "From the students of St. Matthew's School—bought by voluntary contributions." And inside is a ripe grape. And I see the joy that fills that humble room—I see the smile that lights the mother's face as she turns to the children about her . . . and says, "Children, the boys—of St. Matthew's School have sent you this ripe grape!" (141)

In all its obviousness the humor perfectly suggests the silliness and hilarity of college boys. Viewed in the context of Wilson's work dealing with the disillusionment of the 1920's, the story becomes a piece of nostalgia. In 1925 the irresponsible college world is long since dead, as remote and strange as the world of poverty was in 1915, when it elicited the contribution of a grape. But there is a more serious element in the story, understated though it is. Irrepressible Ed is gradually made to feel guilty by Arthur. Little by little he is shamed into conforming, in the interest of Arthur's being elected to important campus positions. He is taught that "running out the string" is bad form and, therefore, bad.⁴

In "Reunion" (1927), a more sophisticated and profound story than "After the Game," the narrator is now a college graduate who goes to a class reunion. Drowsy with gin, he dozes in his chair and then wakes to find an old classmate, Newt Graves, sitting beside him. He is glad, for he has not seen Newt since the war:

> He began to ask me questions at once, with an eagerness I thought slightly unnatural, about what I had been doing since the War. . . . "In the Army," he said, "I used to yearn terribly for quiet and leisure to work. I could almost have wept about it." I thought he was a little drunk, too. "Just to get up in the morning and to know that you'd be there till evening! I bought a copy of Dürer's St. Jerome in a printshop in Nancy, and I used to carry it around with me. It would never have occcurred to me to envy St. Jerome before I was in the Army, but the sight of that solid old man sitting there in that clean solid room, with its thick walls and heavy beams, while the sun of a whole long day was moving the panes of light across his desk and the floor, and with a lion, which apparently he kept as a pet, contentedly dozing beside him, used really to affect me deeply." (146-7)

Newt continues speaking about the madness, the lack of privacy and peace, during the war. The narrator is puzzled: "his tone was not the tone of disillusionment, but had the accents of the freshest enthusiasm, and I hardly knew how to meet it. I tried to find out what had happened to him, but all his answers baffled me." Newt seems to be a little out of touch with things—"in his mouth the word 'humanity' seemed dated"—and he talks hopefully about the post-war world. The narrator replies with a long speech about the exhausting war, which destroyed his ideals and stifled his revolutionary urges for making the world better. In contrast to Newt's optimism, he says that he has now become simply a reactionary. Newt smiles a little disappointedly and says, "there are certain compensations, it seems, about being in my situation." After the narrator's attention has been diverted by a drunken classmate, he notices that Newt has disappeared and, when he inquires, is told that Newt is dead—blown up in the war by a shell.

"Reunion" is a good ghost story. Wilson has planted a number of hints throughout about the true state of Newt Graves, whose very name suggests the cemetery. The dramatic irony of the narrator's unawareness of the truth is successful. By his oblique handling of death, Wilson creates a story more interesting and poignant than "Emily in Hades"; later, in "Ellen Terhune," he employs the same technique still more skillfully.

Both characters emerge distinctly, if somewhat narrowly, through the views they represent: Newt with his hope; the narrator with his cynicism. But the story also has psychological and even historical interest. The man blown out of life in the midst of battle has had a cause to the end, but he who survives to the bitter peace sees his beliefs die. And the narrator's point of view is undoubtedly the same as that of many intelligent young men who returned from the war. The story's point is that World War I exhausted and demoralized its fighters and thus left them useless for making a new world.

The ruminative dialogue is perhaps implausible for a university club, even before the era of higher education for all. The narrator doesn't converse, he lectures: "To learn to think ill of oneself is to learn to think ill of the world. It's no wonder if, since the war, we find we have lost our faith in the theories of perfectibility which assume a natural goodness and a natural common sense on the part of the ordinary person—if, indeed, we become reactionaries and read pessimistic classical writers instead of hopeful romantic ones and, taking refuge in such battered old fortresses as our race has been able to defend, unexpectedly align ourselves on the side of tradition and authority!" (150). Of course, the narrator is a little drunk, which may justify his ponderous eloquence. But Wilson's fiction is generally less concerned with recreating human experience, where plausible dialogue is essential, than with *discussing* human experience, where clarity and logic are most important.

Up to this point the social concern in his fiction has been fairly general, sometimes commonplace, even when, as in the *Liberator* stories, he has been most angry. But in "The Men from Rumpelmayer's" (1927) the concern is more intense and specific. The story takes place on the day that the Massachusetts Supreme Court rules on one of Nicola Sacco's appeals of his conviction for the murder and robbery of a payroll guard in South Braintree on

EDMUND WILSON

April 15, 1920.[5] Throughout the narrative the plight of Sacco
and Bartolomeo Vanzetti is a gloomy motif contrasted to superficial, failing gaiety. The story line itself is slight: the narrator
spends a day in and near Boston with an old college acquaintance
named Ralph, Ralph's wife Lynn, and her sister Julia. Apparently
he has spent several days with them, and today is the last. Ralph
is boring; Lynn and Julia are lovely, charming, and a little ironic.
Ralph thinks that Sacco and Vanzetti should have a new trial,
but that they won't get one; he prefers not to talk about it, afraid
that someone will take issue with him. Lynn and Julia are sure
that Sacco and Vanzetti are innocent, because anyone who could
say, as Vanzetti did, "I am innocent of these two harms!," could
not be guilty. The narrator is entirely for Sacco and Vanzetti, but
he, too, refrains from "this explosive subject."

In a Boston apartment the four young people eat a lobster
supper that Ralph has prepared. Returning to a summer camp on
the train, the narrator, "cocktail-dazed," learns from a newspaper
that the Supreme Court has refused on technical grounds to accept the appeal. The next day he receives two telegrams: one
from the girls, who want him to come back; the other from a
friend on the Sacco-Vanzetti Defense Committee who wants him
to picket and speak on behalf of the doomed men. "But I had
used up my extra money, so I couldn't answer either summons."

The point of the story is summarized by the narrator after the
lobster supper: "Ralph rather bored us by singing all the stanzas
of 'Oh, landlord, fill the flowing bowl Until it doth run over!'
Before I reached the point of not caring, I was beginning to
wonder whether college wasn't going on a little too long" (160).
The unreal college world with its songs, escapades, and fraternal
ties dissolves in the one in which two men have been condemned
to die on a dubious conviction of murder. This point is underscored by Julia's telling of the breakup of the marriage of two
old college sweethearts. The narrator feels divorced from the
youthful world that was once so witty, daring, and important.
But neither is he anxious to join the larger, grimmer world—his
extra money used up, he wants to think that there is nothing he
can do.

"Rumpelmayer's" evinces more skill than any of Wilson's previous stories. It is constructed on the contrast of jollity and gloom:
a forced cheerfulness always interrupted by reminders of Sacco

and Vanzetti. Moreover, the freshness of the girls is contrasted
with the narrator's "old world" weariness and melancholy. The
merriment trails off awkardly. When they are driving into the
city and chattering about the drinks they had the evening before,
they pass a stinking beach. Lynn says that the smell is caused by
condemned clams, but Ralph says that the water always smells
that way in summer. The girls try to joke about it: " 'There are
two people clamming,' said Lynn, indicating two distant figures.
'Two condemned people clamming for condemned clams.' 'Only
condemned people are allowed to go clamming here,' supple-
mented Julia. We didn't, however, pursue this joke" (156). Even
the prospect of a lobster supper is somewhat marred by having
to kill the lobsters: " 'Do they boil them alive?' asked Julia. 'Yes:
I guess so,' I answered. 'Oh, how awful!' she said," The grimmer
feelings are only undercurrents in the chatter; the condemned
clams and lobsters are not symbols but reminders of the condemned men. Thus Wilson comments more powerfully with suggestion than he did in his earliest stories with invective.

The puzzling title is taken from a phrase in an English novel
that Julia has read: "Have the men from Rumpelmayer's come?"
Rumpelmayer's could refer to the famous cafes in Berlin and
Vienna which flourished during the 1920's and were especially
patronized by successful artists and writers. In this sense the
phrase suggests the vanishing world of leisure, where perhaps
the only social problems are someone's bad manners. The two
young men, at least, make a gesture toward repossessing this
world, to which they may have been introduced on pre-war trips
to the Continent. The girls' telegram to the narrator says, "Come
back at once. The men from Rumpelmayer's are draining the old
oaken bucket." Earlier the old oaken bucket has been referred
to as a jug of gin that Ralph manages to have filled every morning and it obviously implies the sentimental past. Even as a jug
of gin, it is a memento of more carefree, frivolous days—now
unsatisfying and embarrassing.

Although the dialogue is better than in previous stories, the
characterization is weak. Ralph takes shape fairly well, with his
"insistent, even-tempered," and "neat careful" ways, and his
"usual self-satisfaction"; so does the bored, troubled narrator. But
the girls hardly emerge at all, and the one false note in the story
is the narrator's incredible rhapsodizing on them: "the voices of

those young girls, with their dear American clearness, their American freedom and gaiety"; "how darling the girls were: their humanity and generosity; they were scarcely even jealous of one another!" (156, 159). Perhaps this gushing seems odd after Wilson's denunciation of America as a boneyard. But he did have another, fonder concept of his country: spaciousness, freshness, and vitality—qualities usually associated with the past and, in this story, with the West. Even in "Night Thoughts in Paris: A Rhapsody," where Wilson so bitterly writes, "Among us ... a decent novel takes on the air of a miracle," he comes back to his ideal of America and sees "our poets and saints" as pioneer heroes because they struggled against the enormous odds of a barbarous background (*New Republic* [March 15, 1922], 75-7). What he abhors is the meretricious, powerful America from the Civil War onward, which he examines in *Patriotic Gore* and in the essays discussed in the first chapter of this book.

Wilson's best piece of fiction before 1929 was a long story published in *The American Caravan* (1927), an anthology of new writing edited by Van Wyck Brooks and others. Entitled "Galahad," the story concerns a prep-school boy's heroic victory over his sexual urges despite a great temptation and his subsequent loss of the girl he has treated so virtuously. Hart Foster, of the Fifth Form, is secretary of the YMCA of St. Matthew's School and a promising candidate for president next year. But Hart is troubled by the ambiguous state of his faith, the lack of exaltation in his prayers, and the erotic daydreams that catch him off guard.

The pre-Christmas YMCA meeting, which is presided over by Hart's roommate, "Boards" Borden, features the renowned YMCA leader, Mr. Hotchkiss, and, as a special attraction, an ex-debauchee named Bergen. "Weeping Fred" Hotchkiss harangues the boys against abusing their bodies and souls during the Christmas vacation—"the most dangerous period of the whole year!" With particular relish Hotchkiss dwells on the horrors of a boy's dragging some poor innocent girl into the mire. He distributes before-and-after pictures of a girl who had given up an honest, decent living as a worker in a soap factory to become a prostitute. Then he invents a lurid tale about a "St. Matthew's fellow" who might seduce a simple girl and commit her to the same fate. The audience "sat stunned and gaping, petrified before the abyss. It had never occurred to most of them to think what they could do to that girl. Even Hart, who, in his present mood, had tended at first to sit through this classical set-piece with the composure of a conjuror's assistant looking on at a levitation act, found himself both stimulated and scared by this imaginary seduction. But the description of venereal disease which followed quickly disinfected his imaginings" (*Caravan*, 228-9).

Bergen, "a bloated red-faced man with a wild alcoholic eye," follows with pictures of skid-row bums who had once been great athletes. Then, in depicting his former state of dissipation, he unwittingly describes his present condition: "with bleary eyes and a sodden face.... You couldn'ta told me from the tramps and bums that you see laying around in the street." There follows a fine little scene of "short prayers," in which individuals in the audience are encouraged to pray aloud: "little jets of prayer, lifted sometimes in plaintive trebles, were heard rising one by one. Thus they had been taught to feel the stirring of the Spirit." Part one of the three-part story ends with Hart's consecrating himself to the YMCA ideal of remaining "clinically ascetic and pure" and renouncing a life of "prostitution, syphilis, shame."

In part two Hart spends the Christmas holidays at the palatial home of his roommate, whose sister he meets. Barbara Borden is a bold, outspoken, reckless young woman—Hart has never met anyone so outrageously careless. But enchanted, he imagines her as his wife, sharing his work in the service of Christ. One night she visits him after he has gone to bed. He is terrified; but, before he quite realizes it, he is kissing her passionately and insisting that he loves her. Suddenly she slips off her kimono and shocks Hart into feeble protests, which she easily overcomes. The kissing continues. "But, as they lay, he felt the waking of desire.... In horror, he drew away. How base that that should have happened! How dreadful if she should have noticed!" He protests again, saying that they should wait until they are married. She in turn is shocked and says that she never wants to get married, that girls who stay pure do so "just to get themselves married! They just hang on to their old purity so that the man'll still want something from them" (243-4). Finally, she becomes extremely annoyed with Hart for not being "a good sport" and slams out of the room.

In part three, back at school, Hart is nervous and irritable. He finds himself taking issue with Mr. Hotchkiss on the latter's favorite theme of how young men corrupt girls. His surroundings now seem to him unspeakably trite: "His school fellows were children! the masters were fogeys and pedants. He was a mighty and tragic figure, humiliated by these pygmies. He strode among them like a god. . . ." He indulges in fantasies about Barbara: "He saw in his imagination a fresh young woman in a kimono, with brown hair unloosed about her shoulders, who sat happy, before a fire, with a clean-cut young man at her side" (249-51).

Worried by Barbara's failure to answer his letters, he determines to see her again. At three o'clock one morning he sneaks down the fire escape and takes a milk train to the village near the Borden estate. He finally arrives at Barbara's house in time for tea that afternoon, only to despair at finding her with "Runt" McGuffy, the celebrated Princeton tackle. When Hart obtains a moment alone with her, he feels utterly childish. He apologizes for having been a prig and desperately declares his love:

"Lots of people are in love with me," she replied.

"But you don't know how *I* love you! I love you the way Lancelot loved Guinevere! I could stand with you against the whole world! I don't care about—about public opinion. I want to be with you—to face life with you! I want to be with you—for ever!"

She smiled at him mockingly. "I think you better go and get some nice little girl that won't scare you."

Sick at heart, he asks her why she has not answered his letters:

"I never write letters," said Barbara.

"I don't think that's fair!" he replied—"I wish you still liked me," he went on.

"You reminded me of a boy I like who's away in Canada."

He was dazed as by a cannon's loudness.

A pair of wool-lined slippers that he had worn in sneaking down the school fire escape falls from his coat pocket, and his humiliation is complete. In a final burst of desperation that mockingly parallels the "little jets of prayer" in the YMCA meeting, he invites her to New York for Easter; but she says that she's going to Toronto. "He pulled open the big door and strode off down the night of the drive—burning face against the cold—as if with the energy of some sturdy errand. But the further he plunged among the bare black trees and the shapeless bush-masses of the grounds, the more he felt like some captured sea-man marching bravely toward the end of the plank. He was advancing into emptiness, into a universe divested of meaning; and all about him, in the winter desert, the darkness seemed to ache" (259-61).

"Galahad" moralizes on the fatuity, frustration, and misery of adhering to conventional ideals simply as a matter of principle. Like "Emily in Hades," it protests against American morals and to this extent is a period piece: a Horatio Alger type of idealist is baffled and destroyed by a "world" which mocks his virtue. The American Dream, in which a boy by honesty, pluck, and clean living could become a railroad tycoon, if not President of the United States, was dispelled in the post-war era by the new cynicism, expressed early in *The Undertaker's Garland* and summarized a dozen years later in Nathanael West's satire, *A Cool Million.*

Hart takes his place in at least two American literary traditions. A number of romances and novels from Nathaniel Hawthorne's *The Blithedale Romance* to John Updike's *Rabbit, Run* expatiate on "the unlived life" or "the defaulting male," with Henry James supreme as the most inventive with this theme. Hart, however, is less a defaulter than a loser. Like Theodore Dreiser's Clyde Griffiths, F. Scott Fitzgerald's Jay Gatsby, and Philip Roth's Neil Klugman, he comes to want something which he is not prepared to have.

But actually his antecedents appear in literature from all over the world, ancient as well as modern. In attempting to act upon moral standards that are inadequate to the demands of his dilemma, he is a little Greek tragic hero—an Agamemnon believing that he is doing the right thing by following the priest's advice and sacrificing Iphigenia, or a Pentheus insisting on traditional patterns of order and decency and slain for not accepting the new god, Dionysus. He is, like Parzival, "a brave man slowly wise"; but he is not, like that bumbling knight who failed to ask the right questions, ultimately victorious.

The Galahad motif is of course ironic. At the YMCA meeting one of the hymns is "Onward, Christian Soldiers." Fancying himself a Christian soldier armed with shining ideals, Hart sees his weapons become absurd and ineffectual toys when he meets a woman who ridicules his "reverence for womanhood" and intimidates him with "the awful prestige of her sexual experience." What especially confuses him is the betrayal of his ideals by his own awakened sensuality. After he returns to school, the Galahad image in his mind becomes overlaid with one of Lancelot, just as the chaste Christian girls of his visions become mixed up with the wanton ladies of Boccaccio. Thought of Galahad is unable to defend Hart against the memory of what Barbara said when she took off her kimono, "It's better that way." He is a confused knight, indeed, with no heart for his vows; and there is nothing left for him but to take a thorough beating. In a "universe divested of meaning," what he has stood for is bitterly embarrassing.

In his preface to *Five Plays,* Wilson has said that his stories take shape in dramatic form: he envisions them scenically, each scene built on conflicting themes. "Galahad," much like a "well-made" play, has three tightly constructed "acts" and a rising and falling action. Each act has an emotional high point and is a little drama in itself: Hart's discomfort at the YMCA meeting, followed by a temporary resolution as he rededicates himself to purity; his encounter with Barbara in bed and the mockery of his standards; his renunciation of his values for Barbara's sake and his complete rout. Certainly the scenic arrangement is commonplace in the short story form since fiction has taken over much that once belonged to drama. In "Galahad," for instance, there are also dramatic irony, the hero's internal conflicts, and even a "fatal flaw"—his righteousness.

In summary, the central theme of Wilson's apprentice fiction is an unsystematic social criticism which becomes increasingly less harsh but more pointed. The shrill stories in *The Liberator* and in *The Undertaker's Garland* tend to overgeneralize about the stupidity of war and the intolerance and oppression of America. It is likely that Wilson was influenced by H. L. Mencken but lacked his gift for the flamboyant, devastating phrase. Today one sometimes comes across a surprising and mistaken notion that Wilson is a grand old man of letters who has somehow kept aloof from feeling lost in his own environment, who has lived snugly in the world of books. An example of this misleading opinion appeared in a biographical article, "Wilson," in *Esquire* (July, 1963) by Eleanor Perényi, who wrote: "Having had no illusions, he had no disillusions, and when he emerged into the New York of the Twenties it was with no sense of belonging to a lost generation" (84).

As Wilson apparently came to observe America more closely, he more clearly defined the objects of his social criticism—the refusal by the old college set to recognize fully the extra-mural environment and to commit itself to a position in it and, again, the falseness of the old morality; and he also treated his characters with more compassion or, at least, understanding. Furthermore, he came to appreciate what seemed to him typically American values of energy and candor although he tends to sentimentalize these.

From the beginning of his career, the young Edmund Wilson seemed to view fiction as another way of commenting on his environment. What fiction lacked in trenchancy, it perhaps made up for in suggestion. But most of Wilson's early fiction preaches too much. When, as in "Galahad," more attention is paid to developing the story, the commentary becomes more effective because of the reader's involvement. What best served Wilson's use of fiction for comment, either directly or indirectly, was plain diction and a reflective style. Wilson's apprentice fiction reinforces the approach implied in his criticism: fiction should be useful for discussing human nature and society in the most articulate way.

II   I Thought of Daisy

The structure of Wilson's first novel, *I Thought of Daisy* (1929), is the most important factor in understanding the main theme, which concerns the attempt of a young intellectual to merge his life with the lives of non-intellectual people. In his foreword to the 1953 edition Wilson wrote: "This novel, first published in 1929 and written much under the influence of Proust and Joyce, was intended, like *Ulysses* and *A la Recherche du Temps Perdu,* to be a sort of symphonic arrangement. ... *I Thought of Daisy* is thus very schematic, and the scheme does not always succeed, for it is sometimes at odds with the story. In rereading the book for the first time since I wrote it, I have sometimes been rather appalled by the rigor with which I sacrificed to my plan of five symphonic movements what would nor-

mally have been the line of the story." The five "movements"
reflect different attitudes and moods: the central character, who
is also the narrator, keeps changing his mind about people and
ideas in a bemused attempt at understanding them, and his vacil-
lation has a development that might be called "symphonic."

The terminology of music should be applied to literature with
caution, not only because any specialized vocabulary loses its
precise meanings when removed from its own area, but also because, when it *is* used in another sense, it tends to mean nothing
at all: a concert-goer, for instance, has been heard to remark that
an orchestral performance lacks "metabolism." Nevertheless, discussing any of the arts without borrowing familiar terms from the
others, as well as from various sciences, is nearly impossible;
thus, in discussions of literature the nomenclatures of music,
painting, architecture, and sculpture are common, if often imprecise. By "symphonic" Wilson probably means what he indicated
in his essay on Proust in *Axel's Castle*: in *A la recherche du
temps perdu* the characters, scenes, moods, actions, and ideas
vary, intertwine, and recur like motifs in a symphony; there are
also intense situations connected with brooding reflections by
more tranquil narrative.

But *I Thought of Daisy* is not as structurally complex as either
Proust's or Joyce's great novels; indeed, it seems to be patterned
more on Joyce's *A Portrait of the Artist as a Young Man*, which
also has five "movements" and which also deals with the intellectual growth of a literary young man. Of course, the time span
of *Portrait*, which begins in Stephen Dedalus' infancy, is much
longer than that of *Daisy*, whose unnamed protagonist, fully
grown when the story opens, requires only two years to find his
purpose in life.

Regardless of influence, the structure of *Daisy* is well suited to
reveal the narrator's development. The first chapter shows his
innocence: a näive young man in love with poetry, he is much
impressed by the intellectuals he finds at a Greenwich Village
party, particularly by his cynical friend the novelist Hugo Bamman and by the young poetess Rita Cavanagh, whom he meets
for the first time. He also meets the hostess, Daisy, a chorus girl
whose candor and beauty charm him, and he glimpses her life
as the mistress of tabloid journalist Ray Coleman, who watches
her jealously. At the end of the evening he takes Rita to his

Bank Street rooms, where they passionately discuss poetry until dawn. Later, after he has escorted her home and has returned to his rooms to sleep, he interrupts the story with an eighteen-page meditation on Hugo, his family and education, his court-martial and imprisonment in France, and now his lonely life as a social revolutionist.

The second chapter mainly concerns the narrator's involvement with Rita. They share a love for poetry (he, too, is a poet, but not a good one) and apparently have become very close in other ways, although the exact nature of their friendship is unclear. There is a hint that it is sexual: " 'You know very well,' she replied . . . 'that I know what sort of person I am—but if I wasn't that sort of person, I shouldn't be the sort of person who would do what I did with you. . . . I was cruel to other people then' " (73). However, it is also likely that their relationship has little to do with sex and that this troubles him; he speaks later of his "exacerbated passion," and, moreover, he is the kind of man who would be proud enough of his sexual exploits to tell the reader about them. He resents Rita's other male friends, and by the time she leaves to return to her childhood home in upstate New York, his admiration and ardor seem to have cooled. But then there is a tender and grateful ten-page reflection on Rita, similar to the previous one on Hugo. He seeks out Daisy, who has left Ray Coleman, and begins to fall in love with her.

In Chapter III the the nameless hero is embittered. After a stay of several weeks in the country, he returns to New York to find Daisy looking dissipated. Her companions are unsavory, and she has lost her job in the *Frolics* for missing rehearsals. To him the typical Village party is now a bore. At one of these he sees Rita with Ray Coleman and assumes a sardonic view of his own relationship with her. He ruminates on Dostoevsky and the wellspring of art in suffering, and on the harshness in Sophocles.

Although his thoughts keep returning to Rita, he and Daisy appear to renew their relationship and they leave the party with plans to meet later and go to some nightclubs. But when he arrives at her apartment, he discovers that Pete Bird, an ineffectual little "twirp" of a poet, has taken charge of her. Daisy has slashed one of her wrists in attempted suicide, but the hero is willing to believe her story of an accident with a tin-can lid. He returns to the party, only to be knocked out after a while by an

Italian nightclub proprietor whom he has been berating for
bringing prostitutes to "work" the party.

Chapter IV presents the hero's renewal. In November, half
a year or more after his nadir and the unfortunate party, he
visits the tranquil home of a professor who befriended him in
college. He is surprised that Professor Grosbeake, whom he has
always considered withdrawn into metaphysics, should be so
much in touch with current affairs; and he is even more surprised when the professor defends Rotarians, whom Sinclair
Lewis attacked in *Babbitt*, which the professor has been reading.
The gentle professor's humane attitudes do much to soothe the
hero's bitterness and allow him to reexamine his own harsh snob-
bishness. When he leaves the professor's house, it is beginning
to snow, and the world looks a good deal lovelier.

He takes a train far into the country to visit Daisy and Pete,
who are barely surviving in an old house on the little money that
Pete can earn by restoring antique furniture. The hero, who considers their existence noble, overlooks Daisy's anxiety about their
poverty. He is moved by "what seemed to me their pioneering
heroism . . . this core of civilization!" Indeed, he now thinks well
of the entire human race and believes that life can be lived
worthily: "How had I ever been taken in by that foolish and
shallow philosophy of living only for the moment?" (236-7).
Actually neither the narrator nor anyone else has articulated a
carpe diem attitude, but the narrator is nevertheless disillusioned
with the New York literati.

The fifth and last chapter is meant to show the central character's acceptance of the robustness of life. On a hot August day in
New York he seems to see things clearly for the first time: what
he took to be a celebrity's statue in Abingdon Square, on
the night when he first met Rita, turns out to be a monument
to the soldiers of the ward who had died in the war; what
appeared to be a temple or a tomb is merely a disused band-
stand. Daisy is in New York—Pete has gone to Boston to look
for a job. She does not love Pete and no longer wants to live with
him, but she stays simply because she is tired of leaving people.
The narrator takes her to Coney Island, where they win a baby
doll, a miniature roulette wheel, a harmonica, an atomizer, and
a pistol that shoots out a snake. The pistol and snake most fasci-
nate Daisy. Later, in the fun-house, the narrator falls on the

roulette wheel and breaks it; still later, he leaves the mouth-organ in a taxi.[6]

He tries to learn everything about Daisy: her girlhood in Pittsburgh; her elopement on a motorcycle; and her marriage, forced by her father, who, with a priest and a policeman, surprised the lovers in a Coney Island hotel room. At the same time, he cannot fully comprehend her; he does not understand why she shies away from a fat woman in a souvenir shop who tries to be friendly, and why she does not want to see the freaks; he also seems somewhat surprised that the wax museum makes her think of death. Daisy gets sick from the clams they eat (she and Pete had only dry cornflakes during most of their last week in the country). While he waits for her outside the washroom, he sees a ridiculous-looking man standing opposite in a doorway and then realizes that it is his own reflection from a trick mirror. He listens to "Mamie Rose," a favorite song of Daisy's, sung over a radio, and for the first time hears a line that he had never quite caught: "She tells me, Fireman, do your duty!" Speculations about the composition of "Mamie Rose" lead him back to meditations on the origins of literature. He decides now that there is a sweetness, as well as a sting, in Sophocles, the "Attic Bee":

> I saw it now, not merely in the nightingales and the ivy of that chorus at Colunus [sic] for which the jury had applauded Sophocles, when his competence to dispose of his property had been called in question by his son; but in the passionate frankness of Antigone, even in the asperity of Oedipus, even in the guile of Odysseus . . . in the case of Dostoevsky, I remembered, no longer the contention and the horror, but the brightness of the high comic sense which interpenetrates all that is turbid, which flowers constantly in such charming passages as that in *The Idiot*, for example, where the young girl buys the hedgehog from the boys and sends it to the Prince for a peace-offering, and which makes even of *Crime and Punishment* a comedy rather than a tragedy. (293)

He comes to regard Daisy more as a simple American girl than as a creature from Broadway or the Village; after all, she "had grown up in an American town like other towns, lived in a house like other houses, gone to a school like other schools. I seemed to have been given a new vision of the fluidity of manners in America, the plasticity of social position—of the swiftness and adventitiousness of the way in which such things changed" (301).

He takes Daisy to his rooms, where they drink bootleg Scotch and finally make love. He thinks then that he wants to write "sketches of Daisy, as I remembered her at different times and places—if I could only hit off, in prose, her attitudes, her gestures, her expressions, the intonations of her voice . . . as Degas had done for his dancers—as Toulouse-Lautrec had done for the women of cabarets" (307-8). This attempt, he thinks, would allow him to apply his talent to everyday actualities rather than to private literary matters: "So I would perhaps save myself at last from that dreadful isolation of the artist which had appalled me in Hugo and Rita . . . so, by the way of literature itself, I should break through into the real world . . . when one came right down to it, there was really no difference in kind between carpentry and literature" (308).

Thus, the novel's structure, which in one way resembles a series of impressionistic pictures, is very useful for showing the hero's stages of intellectual and social growth from Innocence and Isolation, to Involvement, to Despair, to Renewal, to Active Acceptance—stages indicated by his changing apprehensions of people and ideas: Rita and Hugo, Daisy and Ray, Pete Bird, Professor Grosbeake, and the origins and significance of literature.

But, more subtly, the pattern is one of collision among the characters. The novel opens with a party; people meet one another and some pair off. Daisy has already been paired with Ray, and the narrator with his friend and idol Hugo. Then the narrator links with Rita, and Daisy is attracted to Pete and later to Hugo, who then drops out of the pattern. Rita and the narrator separate, she to link briefly with Ray, and he with Daisy. But Pete collides with the narrator and goes off with Daisy. Rita drops out of the pattern. The narrator, now alone, links briefly with Grosbeake, who checks his despair before leaving the pattern himself. The only ones left are Pete, Daisy, and the narrator; then, finally, the narrator and Daisy. With each collision the narrator gains a new impression which changes or cancels an old one. He is most "alone" and unsure when there are many people around; when he has eventually accepted American life and is going to write about it, he is without any companions at all—his is a solitary "merging."

There are thematic similarities, also, with *A Portrait of the*

Artist as a Young Man. The first "movement" of *Portrait* shows Stephen's innocence and loneliness; but his innocence is tempered, and his loneliness sharpened, by his increasing sentience of the world's bitterness and injustice (the family quarrel over Parnell, the pandybatting at school). Chapter II portrays Stephen's closer involvement with the mortal world's sadness (his pathetic father) and pleasure (the prostitute). In Chapter III he has a burst of religious feeling, common among sensitive teenagers, and plummets into the despair of believing that his sins have cast him from the grace of the Church; but through penitence and confession he attains a temporary peace (by contrast, the despair in Wilson's third chapter keeps increasing right up to the end). Chapter IV at first finds Stephen in a delusive religious renewal, then he deliberately refuses to study for the priesthood and begins a genuine renewal as he turns to the freedom of art (he has no Professor Grosbeake to help him). Finally, in Chapter V, he completely rejects religion and Dublin, and dedicates himself to art: "I will try to express myself in some mode of life or art as freely as I can and as wholly as I can." Unlike the narrator of *Daisy,* Stephen turns inward upon himself to perceive a secret kind of loveliness.

Joyce's hero is always surer of what he thinks about people and ideas than Wilson's. Even with Stephen's sliding for a time into religious despair and conviction, his education is accumulative. The education of Wilson's hero is more impressionistic: his ideas and acquaintances differ with his moods, circumstances, and apprehensions until he eventually arrives at what seems to him to be the truth—at a reconciliation of his love for literature with his feelings that he must live with, understand, and write about ordinary people. The organization of *Daisy* serves this trial-and-error education.

Nor is the organization too elaborate for the narrative. When Wilson speaks in the 1953 foreword of having sacrificed the story line to the five movements, one cannot wholly agree with him since it is easily apparent. Each of the five parts consists mainly of two or more fairly static tableaux, and the parts themselves are separated by rather wide gaps in time which do not really interfere with the story. But the story does not have much motion; it is something like a medieval painting of a saint's martyrdom: enclosed within one border is the series of scenes of the prominent incidents from the saint's life, with the main scene being the martyrdom itself. In *Daisy*, the biggest scene is the day at Coney Island.

Interspersed among, or interrupting, the tableaux are the hero's long dialogues with himself on people and literature, which perhaps slow the story's movement more than the five-part arrangement does. For example, in Chapter III he ruminates on Dostoevsky's sense of guilt and elaborates a theme that Rita had suggested earlier. She had started his serious thought "that any great strength or excellence of character must be, by its very nature, incompatible with qualities of other kinds—that it carries with it weaknesses and ignominies inseparable from excellence and strength" (87)—the wound-and-bow theme which fascinated Wilson in critical essays which he began to write about the same time that he wrote *Daisy*. The narrator mulls over this theme rather gloomily: "What were literature and art but the by-products of these collisions with the uncomprehended reality—collisions whose repercussions, when we had withdrawn into the shelter of ourselves, we attempted to palliate, to harmonize, to account for, to subdue to a smoother rhythm in the current of our thought, now resuming, which for a moment had been troubled or torn? . . . the instinct to produce a work of art was merely a self-protective reflex like another" (174-5). He continues at some length on the imposture of art: the artist, having recognized chaos instead of harmony or logic in the universe, foists upon the public a comforting but false diagram of life as ordered and harmonious.

By Chapter V the narrator is more optimistic; without fully replying to his former despair, he allows for a certain healthfulness in art—in "good" art—which repays one for the harshness of life: "And so every sort of good literature, so every sort of good art, provided an aliment, a stimulant, as natural and necessary as food and drink themselves! Even the tannic tincture of Poe, which seemed to turn the throat to leather and to petrify the taste, had its own peculiar tonic value, and even from the coarse, used mash of Byron it was possible to extract a strong brandy" (294). But he is a little unsure of his esthetic position, and he drops the subject without having faced the question: palliative, tonic, or whatever, is art nevertheless false? Or, how should it be concerned with truth? Or, what *is* art? And it is doubtful that

Wilson himself satisfactorily answers these questions later in "The Historical Interpretation of Literature," in which, as has been noted, the highest value of literature is "an attempt to give a meaning to our experience—that is, to make life more practicable."

The mingling of story and soliloquy is undoubtedly part of Proust's influence on Wilson. In *Axel's Castle* he sees this interminging as the basic structure of *A la recherche du temps perdu*: "Proust has made of these social episodes ... enormous solid blocks, cemented by, or rather embedded in, a dense medium of introspective revery and commentary mingled with incidents treated dramatically on a smaller scale. Proust's handling of these complex social scenes is masterly: it is only in the intermediate sections that we feel he has blurred his effects by allowing the outline of the action to become obscured by the profusion of the hero's reflections on it. We also become aware that these main scenes follow a regular progression" (139). Wilson's novel also progresses; however, in comparison with *Portrait*, whose five parts flow naturally into one another, *Daisy* is static, like the episodic form of Wilson's literary and social criticism. Or, to take up the music metaphor again, his "symphony," with its sharp breaks between sections, is, like a symphony by Haydn or Mozart, more classical than organic in form.

Again in his 1953 foreword Wilson apparently thinks that keeping Rita's role from expanding, as one might expect, is the fault of his rigorous scheme: "There is no satisfactory account of the narrator's relations with Rita, though the reader must have been led to expect it—since, though Rita is more interesting than Daisy, her role had to be kept to proportions that would not prevent Daisy from playing the central role; nor could I, for similar reasons, allow her to be too sympathetic." But Daisy is not, after all, the central character; the narrator is. The novel focuses on *his* involvement, *his* despair, *his* acceptance; it is he whose education one is forced to watch, whose musings one is forced to hear—he is never absent. Daisy, the most vivid character, is what he lusts after. By the end, she comes to represent the reality that he seeks to merge himself with.

His relationship with her is worth tracing. In Chapter I she appears as a kittenish girl, not at all intellectual, yet not dull—one sympathizes with her putting "Mamie Rose" on the phono-

graph while Rita is reciting her poems because the poetry *is* out
of place at Daisy's party and because there is something stagey
about Rita which Daisy apparently cannot abide. Then the reader
learns nothing about Daisy until some thirty pages later, in
Chapter II, when Rita annoys the narrator by being eager to
leave the city and by saying goodbye to her various male friends.
In a jealous mood he thinks about Daisy ("I thought of Daisy"
occurs three times) as someone to fall in love with, now that his
relationship with Rita has soured. As soon as Rita leaves, he goes
looking for Daisy, who is no longer living with Ray. They have
dinner and go to a movie, but he continually thinks about Rita,
as well as Hugo. Later that evening, with Rita so strongly in
mind, he does not try to make love to Daisy, who is too tired
anyway; and he seems somewhat disappointed that her figure is
not as statuesque as Rita's.

In Chapter III, the despair chapter, he is smitten by memories
of Rita; but he "resolutely thought of Daisy" as if he were insisting on loving her. Later, when he and she attend a party, all of
his old pangs return when he sees Rita with Ray; he tries to be
critical of her, but "now my need to love and believe in Rita,
even stronger than my impulse to reject her, reasserted itself."
When Daisy leads him upstairs to a bedroom, he is slow to respond sexually: "I became aware of the succession of my kisses
as something tediously mechanical and repetitive" (154-7).
After her suicide attempt later that night, he sees her in a way
different from before: "She looked like a wounded owlet: I was
astonished to observe that her nose . . . could appear like a little
beak. She had through suffering and fatigue reached one of those
moments when women seem completely dispossessed of their
sex, and it occurs to us as a surprise that they probably resemble
their fathers" (186-7).

When he visits her and Pete in the country (Chapter IV), he
is attracted by her new appearance of health, freshness, and
cleanliness—she is once again different from his earlier views of
her as first glamorous and then debauched. But the narrator is
sentimentalizing Daisy and deluding himself, like the narrator in
"The Men from Rumpelmayer's" and his theme of "dear American girls." Daisy is a little crude even though she strikes him
as charming, as when she proudly has him feel her biceps. And
it is difficult to believe that even a disillusioned man of culture

could see the "core of civilization" in the meager life of Daisy and Pete. If the central character is indeed fooling himself, if he is as ridiculous as the image he sees in the trick mirror, the main theme of the novel becomes suspect, as will be argued later.

It is clear that even in the country, whose seemingly noble simplicity so enchants him, his thoughts are still with Rita, now in Paris; he imagines her to be lonely and is sorry for having treated her coldly at Sue's party. He thinks that Daisy is like Rita and himself in having felt that "life without honor was horrible" (254). Her attempted suicide strikes him as proof of this conclusion, rather than as a compulsive act of hopelessness, which seems more likely. At Coney Island with Daisy, in Chapter V, he still feels the tug of Rita, although less strongly. He still seems to be fooling himself when he thinks of Daisy as the inspiration for literary projects which are less interesting than he realizes. When the reader turns back and examines these, he finds that one was the beginning of a sentimental short story, treated ironically by the narrator himself; and the other, a confused, half-drunken notion of a sonnet (19, 110). Also, the narrator well knows that with Daisy he cannot have "those drunken nocturnal conversations which seemed to mean so much!—which did, no doubt, mean so much" that he had with Rita. It is really Rita whom he loves and with whom he "had found" what he "had come for" (275, 44). He can scarcely ever act or decide upon something without considering what Rita would have thought of it, and he is obviously vexed by his inability to keep her. He never entirely gets over her.

Central to his relationship with Daisy are his impressions of her, not herself as she "really is": "On each of the occasions when I had met her, I had seen in her something different, as my own mind had been differently disposed by my personal situation at the time and by the influences by which I had been affected. . . . And I could see how she herself had taken the color of each of the men with whom she had lived since she left Pittsburgh . . ." (301). She is important for him mainly insofar as he is able to formulate attitudes toward her. Not that she is entirely uninteresting: she is pathetic and winsome; she has never really been happy, as she tells him toward the end; she has withstood a great many hardships to become, so far as one can tell, a practical woman who knows far more about life than the narrator. Limited by the narrator's consciousness, however, the reader can see no development in Daisy, but only a change in the impressions of her.

The central character, then, is the narrator himself, who presumably changes enough to reach an understanding of life wider than that attainable by an exclusive devotion to books. His final impression of Daisy is supposedly the correct one: "But she seemed now to have taken her place in a world which I had always known. She was no longer of a different race—of an exotic glamor or guile: she was simply an American girl, who had grown up in an American town like other American towns, lived in a house like other houses, gone to a school like other schools" (301). Later it will be shown that one needs to be wary of the narrator on this point. To a certain extent he has invented Daisy to represent the Simple American Life, the Reality of Our Nation —but is he qualified to recognize American reality? What, after all, is "simply an American girl"? Rita, too, the upstate New York girl, should be included. At any rate, the main theme is the shifting of relationships between the narrator and almost everyone he knows.

In addition to the arrangement of scenes and the alternation of narrative with reflective or informative passages (such as Rita's and Hugo's backgrounds), the impressions themselves become a structural principle of contrast. For example, at the party which opens the book, the narrator becomes very much annoyed with the bullying host, Ray Coleman, for his treating Daisy like a naughty child. But in Chapter III, when he and Daisy have left the party, he in turn becomes irritated with Daisy in the taxi and now sees her as he imagines Coleman had; and he excoriates himself for having treated Rita harshly:

Hadn't [Daisy] behaved like a little fiend?—Hadn't she turned on a phonograph record in the middle of Rita's poems? Hadn't she humiliated Ray by leaving the party with Pete Bird? I found that I forgave Ray more easily for his violent scene with Daisy, which Rita and I had overheard.

But, when I remembered that detestable scene, it was no longer as it had seemed to me that evening. That night I had been a spectator looking on at a melodramatic tableau of jealousy: Ray pointing at Pete's broken cane; Daisy abashed among the ruins of the party; and I complacently and gallantly helping

Rita on with her wrap. Now I myself had played Ray Coleman's part. I remembered that spiteful scene which I myself had provoked with Rita, in the taxi, and the scenes which for weeks had preceded it . . . now it was I who was the jealous blackguard and Ray Coleman who was the solid decent citizen! (167-8)

The reader, who has witnessed both scenes—between Ray and Daisy and between the narrator and Rita—understands that the moody narrator simply longs for Rita and is shaping his memories to exonerate her (she had, in fact, been a trial to him because she shared herself with several men) so that he may blame himself and thereby intensify his desire. The scene with Rita was actually rather mild, and the reader never saw the other ones alluded to.

Things, as well as people, are contrasted. When the narrator first hears "Mamie Rose," it is only a "popular fox-trot" at the first party. He next hears it in Daisy's messy apartment, where he is waiting for her. Tired and bored, he cranks up a small victrola and puts the record on. But the needles are worn out; the best he can get is a "kind of fiendish jig, running itself off at impossible speed: too fast, too nasal, too shrill" (91). However, when he hears it the third time, at Coney Island, he likes it enough to launch into five pages of (unconsciously comic) musings, which culminate eventually in the "Attic Bee":

> . . . I now thought it quite good: there was something rather unexpected, something even quite original about the manipulation of the tune: what was original and unexpected was the repetition, in some sort of minor, of the pattern which had just gone before—recommencing, with "She's proud and snooty," what one had thought was entirely finished—and recommencing it agreeably and queerly, so that for the moment one always paused to listen. . . . Where had [the composer] got it?—from the sounds of the streets? the taxis creaking to a stop? the interrogatory squeak of a street-car? Some distant and obscure city-sound. . . . Or had he got it from Schoenberg or Stravinsky?—or simply from his own nostalgia . . . . (290-2)

The line he was unable to understand before—"She tells me, Fireman, do your duty!"—becomes significant; he makes love to Daisy that evening and presumably merges with American reality.

Thus the design and construction of this novel have been very thoroughly thought out. In addition, there are some less complex merits which distinguish it, such as an occasional sharp scene which the reader can immediately visualize. Toward the end of Chapter I, for example, Hugo and his father—a distinguished lawyer, political theorist and former solicitor general—having lunched at a university club, are putting on their coats when the elder Bamman is jostled by a hurrying young man: "Mr. Bamman was broad-shouldered and well set-up, and he still wore a fine Olympian beard and one of those flat-crowned derbies which were fashionable in the eighties . . . but, at the moment of the impact, as Mr. Bamman looked dazedly around, Hugo had caught on his father's face the shadow of feebleness and pain. And he had realized then . . . that his father had no longer the prestige of an acknowledged leader of the community, nor even of a distinguished person: he was a figure of isolation, bewilderment and fatigue" (60).

The simple descriptive passages are also graphic, even though they are marked by some over-writing. Wilson the *New Republic* reporter is recognizable as the narrator ambles around New York, describing what he sees:

> In that asphalt sky of August, the summer sun burnt a blunt point of light, like the blinding violet-livid torch with which a worker on city mains gashes through a tough piece of pipe. A gray haze blurred the vistas of Fifth Avenue and dulled the too full-blown bushes and trees which one saw beyond Washington Arch, as if the buildings and pavements themselves, under the action of the terrible heat were vaporizing and fogging the air.
>
> Down a side-street, an old white truck-horse stood sleeping and stupefied, its head lowered like a lizard's and its eyelids closed, while the driver, sluggish and sweating, piled a mountain of boxes on the dray. And farther over, on Seventh Avenue, I saw a barefoot ragged boy, who had flung himself down on his stomach above the grating that ventilates the subway, and whose coat was blown up violently behind him, like the streamers of an electric fan, by the warm, sudden gust from the trains. (261)

This description leads to a consideration of *Daisy* as social history. A recent review of the book grants it "historical value and piquancy, a sense of both how much and how little things have changed."[7] In 1929 one reviewer praised the book as "an honest record of the philosophy of a bewildered generation."[8] And Granville Hicks in an article cited in Chapter I said that

Daisy is Wilson's "farewell to Bohemianism." By the early 1920's—
the period of *Daisy*—the Bohemian Village, which had begun
with the conversion of stables to studios in the 1890's, was disap-
pearing. The old Village, actually composed of poor artists and
radicals, was the home of the original *Masses*, edited between
1912 and 1917 by Max Eastman, who took it over from a Dutch
restaurateur. Eventually the *Masses* was forced out of business
by the government, mainly because of its anti-war views. In
January, 1916, it was removed from the subway and elevated
railway newsstands of New York; in August, 1917, it was barred
from the mails. Its successors, the *Liberator* in 1918 and especially the *New Masses* in 1926, were not so iconoclastic and
radical in tone; but, of course, they did not have to be since
attacks on capitalism were increasingly common.

After World War I, the Village became "commercialized." For
middle-class people with money, living there was exciting and
fashionable; Albert Parry, in *Garrets and Pretenders* (1960), calls
this phase the "invasion of the Village by Babbittry." Since most
of the poets and artists could no longer afford to stay in the
Village, they either went "west to Chelsea, and east to Avenue A
and Avenue B" or they left New York entirely and went to other
colonies: Carmel, California; Taos, New Mexico; and, for a
while, even Hoboken, New Jersey, the Bohemia of Christopher
Morley. The boom in Greenwich Village lasted from 1923 to the
Crash, but the Depression partly restored it to indigent artists
and prophets.

In *Daisy* Wilson catches the passing of the Village into commercialism. With the exception of Hugo Bamman and Rita Cavanagh, the characters are almost all middle-class "new Village":
Ray Coleman, the tabloid journalist, and Daisy, the chorus girl;
Larry Mickler, an advertiser, and Bobby McIlvaine, a Broadway
stage designer. The narrator himself works for a publisher: "beyond publishing a few satiric verses in a radical magazine, I had
never myself struck any blow in the war for humanity" (6). It is
difficult to tell whether Pete Bird, the hapless poet, belongs to
the new Village or the old since he is misplaced in either. Sue
Borglum, the society woman who belongs to both, is still trying
by her frequent parties in the new to carry on the old. Rita and
the old revolutionist Hugo find the middle-class Village stifling
and both leave it.[9]

Wilson himself was never a Bohemian, although he had associations in the Village, where his first stories were published and his first play was produced after the war. But his acquaintance with it came late: he did not come to New York until the late summer of 1916 and he stayed there sharing an apartment with three Yale friends on West Eighth Street between Fifth and Sixth Avenues, only a year before enlisting in the army. Moreover it is doubtful that he ever could have become a Bohemian type.[10] Edna St. Vincent Millay came to the Village around 1917 and for a time lived and wrote in a cold room on Waverly Place (the room of *This Room and This Gin and These Sandwiches* and also Rita's room in *Daisy*). Albert Parry, however, considered her not a Bohemian but a New England girl: "The rigid beauty of her verse and feelings had nothing in common with the gay pretensions and social protest of the Village" (*Garrets and Pretenders*, 298.)

Yet, apart from the book's historical interest and despite its careful structure, *Daisy* is finally unsatisfactory as a novel because it is weak in characterization and narration. The characters are simply unrealized. Although Rita, for example, is well described, she never seems alive. A somewhat shabby-looking girl with mouse-colored hair, she has "eyes of a greenish uncertain color, a curious alert intent look, as of a fox peering out from covert." She is serious, poor, popular, and near exhaustion. And yet her reality is not felt. The narrator says that she is intense, but nothing that she says or her manner of saying it indicates intensity. Some "unexplained disturbing reality... underlay everything she did" (12, 38), but this statement is not felt to mean anything more than that she is preoccupied. Her tremendous appeal to the narrator and to men in general is understood by the reader but, like the narrator's esteem for Hugo, never sensed.

This deficiency of character was noted by Herbert Gorman, reviewing the book for *Century* (Autumn, 1929, 152-3), who suggested that Wilson was really interested in his characters as ideas. But they do not seem to be ideas so much as attitudes toward life. The "essays" on Hugo and Rita, on Hugo's father and Rita's aunt introduce the characters without ever making them seem familiar. This deficiency is particularly regrettable because the narrator is sometimes very perceptive, as when he remarks that Rita had "the faculty of endowing her admirers with qualities which they themselves may hardly have hoped to possess" or that the vitality in people she knew was really her own. Yet Rita still fails to "live."

One "biographical" reason for her inadequate characterization is that she was too closely modeled on Edna St. Vincent Millay for Wilson to "imagine" her. But the narrator, too, is unrevealed, guarded: on the one hand, he is a serious, intelligent young man who can discourse at length—only to himself—on art and literature; on the other, he is too naïve to be entirely plausible and too self-centered to be sympathetic. These two groups of traits do not necessarily exclude each other, and no one expects a well-drawn character not to be both agreeable and disagreeable. The problem is that, while he seems to be taking his audience into his confidence, he is not really being honest. At times a little condescension peeps through what has been posed as a questing openmindedness, as in his attitude toward women: "[Rita] had read extraordinarily widely for a woman, and she talked about the poets as only a master can talk of the masters of his craft and with the fierceness with which only a woman, *when women's narrow concentration has been displaced from its ordinary objects, can concern itself with art...*" (41, italics added). Or he betrays a discomforting priggishness while he seems to believe that he is the spokesman for human values. At the end of Chapter IV Daisy plainly wants to leave Pete; the narrator toys with the idea of taking her with him, but decides that this would not be fair to Pete. His decision seems laudable, but he must cap it with a little homily: "I spoke to Daisy of the sad imperfection inherent in all human relations, and of the necessity for loyalty and faith in a world where love was sure to fail us" (258). The very seriousness of his platitude makes him absurd.

An academic young man should be granted some license to be unworldly, but Wilson's hero is somewhat too unworldly at the same time that he would have the reader think that he is sophisticated. Occasionally he is even a little dense. At the party which opens the book, Ray Coleman offends several guests by telling with relish how the police beat up a West Indian boy who had been caught in the basement of the apartment building and who was suspected of thievery. Hugo and Rita are incensed; but the narrator, unruffled, says pleasantly and with a prissy irony that redounds to his own cautious noncommitment, "I perceived that, although Ray Coleman enjoyed entertaining poets and radical journalists, he was far from sharing the humanitarian feeling which at that epoch pervaded the Village" (19). And there are other examples of his completely serious naïveté. He is surprised at the end of Chapter II that one of Daisy's breasts is "low and lapsed a little"; and, in Chapter III, by the fact that a prostitute has a bold look and is uninterested in just being friends with him. At the end of the novel, while Daisy is reclining and staring at him passionately, he describes his esthetic revelations at great length, getting as far as the Attic Bee.

Of course, some of the hero's pomposity, timidity, and ignorance may be deliberate—he is supposedly learning what life is all about. During the night that he spends with Pete and Daisy in the country, the three of them have gone to bed in the same room —Pete and Daisy in their bed and the narrator on a couch. They talk and sing for a while; then:

> I rendered, with what I felt at the time was an impressive solemnity and resonance, *Oh God, Our Help in Ages Past,* and *The Starry Firmament on High.*—But the second of these was met by silence—I received no response from the bed. And when Pete and Daisy replied to my good-night, it was plain they had been asleep.
>
> Those magnificent hymns! I went on thinking. What a first-rate poet Watts had been! And that grandeur of the universe, of the moral principle it implied—did one not feel it, also, even, in the calm complacent firmament of Addison? (239)

The narrator looks a little foolish here, as when he and Daisy are on their way to Coney Island in a steamer, he remembers—and must tell her—his sensations upon returning home from the war: the smell of New York, the sight of a street lamp, a train, a tugboat, a sailor at the tiller of a motorboat. All of these impressions were very significant to him, and he assumes that they will be to her, too, but she says, "You'd be very good-looking if it wasn't for your nose" (270).

How ridiculous should the narrator be? Obviously he is not meant to be a buffoon, which would at the end invalidate his declaration to merge art and reality; but one cannot be sure when he is intended to be foolish and when not. However, there is at least one time when the author is unmistakably having fun with him: "I regretted now that I had never had the foresight to study physics and biology at college. And in an attempt to exercise, at least, that gift of scientific observation upon which I had rather prided myself, I asked the taxidriver, as I was paying him, whether he had not been born in Alabama. But he replied that he had been born in New York, and had lived there all his life" (187-8).

The novel could have been a wonderful comedy with a hero who grimly theorizes about literature and his sensations while he continually falls into ludicrous situations. But clearly *Daisy* was intended to be "serious," with a message about the purpose of art; and the narrator's ambiguity cannot be explained except as due to the author's reticence, if not his ineptness. It is quite possible, of course, to mix comedy with high seriousness; but the reader must be allowed to see into the main character more. In *Daisy* the narrator almost never thinks intimately; he always ruminates grandiosely and—quite unlike Stephen Dedalus, another intellectual—without ever a private, mundane thought.

The lack of familiarity with the hero is unfortunate. For at the end, when, aglow from making love to Daisy, he resolves to merge his literary ability with the "real world," he is not wholly credible. He wants to save himself from "the dreadful isolation of the artist"—but how? What will he do? Because he has been to bed with a girl, how can he think that she epitomizes or even represents reality? It is true that he sees her more clearly than he did in the country, when she was an all-American girl of the type which might appear in soft-drink advertisements. He will write a series of impressionistic sketches of Daisy, but how will these be useful to anyone ("there was really no difference in kind between carpentry and literature"), least of all to Daisy? "Real life" in any broadly representative sense is nearly as remote from him as ever. But in one respect he is right: whatever snobbery, fear, prejudice, and disgust would reject is interesting and valuable to the artist. Daisy, however, is not an object of rejection. Thus one cannot know how effective the lesson will be or how the narrator has reached his conclusion.

The details of his life are also not very conclusive. The description of the furnishings of his apartment is both suggestive and puzzling: "There were a large and comfortable couch, sets of books in glass-doored bookcases, Whistler's 'Battersea Bridge,' and a drawing by Leonardo ... a small mahogany desk, a green carpet and a French clock" (36). This formal presentation implies that the narrator is neat, enjoys comfort, and treats his books carefully, but not much else. Or does it? The pairing of Whistler and Leonardo is ambiguous: the pictures may indicate a conventional esthetic cultivation, although Whistler was no longer fashionable in the 1920's; or they may suggest an inability to appreciate contemporary art and an honesty in not pretending to. But whatever the objects say about the narrator is imprecise. Why is the carpet green or the clock French?

By contrast, from a similar description in Nathanael West's *Miss Lonelyhearts* (1933), the characterization of the hero is instantaneous because of details that "say" a great deal: "He lived by himself in a room that was as full of shadows as an old steel engraving. It held a bed, a table and two chairs. The walls were bare except for an ivory Christ that hung opposite the foot of the bed. He had removed the figure from the cross to which it had been fastened and had nailed it to the wall with large spikes. But the desired effect had not been obtained. Instead of writhing, the Christ remained calmly decorative" (*The Complete Works of Nathanael West*, 74-5).

But what may ultimately best reveal character in realistic fiction is the way people talk. Beyond Wilson's rather obvious device of having Daisy say "um" for "him," there are few distinguishing elements in the speech of his characters. Scott Fitzgerald, on the other hand, could sketch Tom Buchanan's domineering and oafish character in *The Great Gatsby* (1925) with just a few words of conversation:

"What you doing, Nick?"
"I'm a bond man."
"Who with?"
I told him.
"Never heard of them. . . ."

These comparisons are of course unfair to Wilson, for they match a first novel with two mature works. But the better novels show what *Daisy* lacks. And one might add that Wilson writes dialogue much more skillfully later in *Memoirs of Hecate County*.

Finally, there is the problem of narration: first-person narration in *Daisy* was a mistake. The "I" narrator has been very popular in modern literature, chiefly because credibility is inherent in it; and for short pieces of fiction, it is probably the easiest of all narrative techniques. But for long works of fiction it is a trap because it can destroy the very sense of immediacy that it is designed to create by putting the story at one more remove from the reader. A very skillful writer, such as Hawthorne or James can use it to attain a dimension beyond that of the surface story, so that the reader can see through the narrator to the real but implied story.

Daisy's narrator never implies another story, and yet he constantly reminds one of his presence, which, without any dramatic irony, merely becomes tiresome. He would be less noticeable if *Daisy* were a less reflective novel: not only does he muse too much, but he constantly points out that he does: "I reflected," "I was thinking," "I remembered." This establishes the impression that the narrator has a prodigious memory, and credibility and spontaneity are thus defeated. Furthermore, his insistence on talking all the time leads him to emphasize rather trivial things, as if he were trying to keep our attention: "But now I could stave it off no longer; I could talk no longer against time: I had to think about Rita and Ray!" (154). Because the hero cannot be taken very seriously, his lesson—that literature should help one to understand and accept real people—is not very effective.

III   Memoirs of Hecate County

On first impression, *Memoirs of Hecate County* (1946) is not a novel but a collection of six separate stories. Of the perhaps twenty important characters, only two besides the narrator appear in more than one story and then only in two. The situations and plots are different, and the somewhat vague spans of time are overlapping but not sequential: "The Man Who Shot Snapping Turtles" apparently takes place sometime in the 1920's; "Ellen Terhune" is framed in 1926, but is carried back to the 1880's; "Glimpses of Wilbur Flick" extends from around 1915 to the late 1930's; "The Princess with the Golden Hair," from 1929 to 1931; "The Milhollands and Their Damned Soul," from the early 1930's to the mid-1940's; and "Mr. and Mrs. Blackburn at Home" takes place in the summer of 1934. In plot, time, and cast of characters the book is, therefore, not the conventional continuum, although Wilson, unlike Joyce, Faulkner, or Alain Robbe-Grillet, cannot be regarded as an innovator or even an experimenter in technique. However, a sustained progression in mood, which—as will be pointed out again later—reaches a climax in the last tale, provides a unity that makes the book more than a group of stories.

The book reviewers in 1946 tended not to regard *Memoirs* as a novel although some of them did not distinguish between "novel" and "story," rather carelessly interchanging the terms in referring to the separate tales. Among the better reviewers, Diana Trilling in the *Nation* considered the book a "volume of stories." The *Saturday Review of Literature*'s Harrison Smith erroneously thought that it was three short novels prefaced by three short sketches. But Malcolm Cowley, who wrote for the *New Republic* perhaps the soundest review of any, thought that *Memoirs*, while not a novel, was a story collection of a peculiar kind.[11] He pointed out that, although "one physical and social and moral frame" unified the book, it was really a grouping of "novella." Cowley also pointed out that this grouping of long stories into cycles is an American phenomenon; and certainly one is reminded of Sherwood Anderson's *Winesburg, Ohio,* John O'Hara's *Sermons and Soda Water,* and, pre-eminently, William Faulkner's *Go Down, Moses.*

Despite the disregard for some of the conventions, *Memoirs* can be considered as one piece of long fiction. First, as Cowley says, the main location, Hecate County, gives the book some continuity. It is a suburban/rural area near New York City, inhabited mostly by summer dwellers. Except for several houses in it, it is never as specifically mapped as O'Hara's Gibbsville, Pennsylvania, or Faulkner's Yoknapatawpha County, Mississippi. Cowley regarded it as a combination of Monmouth County, New Jersey, and Fairfield County, Connecticut, with several features from Cape Cod. But the true Hecate County is not geographical but psychological, and its oppressive "atmosphere" sometimes drives the narrator to the "freedom" of the city.

The narrator, who is also the main character, is the same person throughout the book and, of course, helps to unify it. One gradually learns a great deal about him (as in *Daisy,* he is never named): he is too young to have served in World War I; he studies economics in college, but has given that up for art history; and he is writing a book called *Nineteenth Century Painting* from a social-economic viewpoint. Politically liberal, he scarcely ever associates with other liberals; he is lonely, impatient, critical, egotistical, and somewhat irascible.

But the novel is unified primarily by the recurrent theme of diabolism, although this is seldom, if ever, direct. The devil himself never appears, except in the last tale in the puzzling figure of Blackburn, who has a chameleonic identity. People know almost nothing about him, or their stories conflict; and with different groups of people his name—as well as his accent, manner, and even looks—differs: with Italians he is Mr. Malatesta, with Russians Mr. Chernokhvostov, and with Germans Swarzkopf. He seems to belong "to some remote time and place." He strikes the narrator as highly cultivated yet gross, as charming yet irritating. He converses in French and German as easily as he does in English. He has prophetic powers; he foretells Stalin's purges and Hitler's terrorism of Europe. He says that he is the devil, but that the world has become so cruel that he is no longer considered important. He hopes to start a religious revival in America just so a few people will take him seriously again. What complicates his identity is that, by the time the increasingly disturbed narrator relates the last tale, Blackburn may be an illusion. In the next to the last tale, "The Milhollands and Their Damned Soul," pacts seem to be made with the devil; but one cannot know with certainty since this is the opinion of Si Banks, a drunken, sly wit, and since the reported devil never appears before the reader.

For the most part, then, the diabolism is indirect; it is simply neurosis, the modern form of the devil. In "The Man Who Shot Snapping Turtles," the neurosis is first the anxiety of Asa Stryker and then the paranoia of Clarence Latouche, a clever advertising agent who suddenly from envy and fear murders Stryker, whom he has helped to become a wealthy manufacturer of turtle soup. In "Ellen Terhune," it is the guilt which Ellen, a musician and composer, has been made to feel from childhood by a mother who never wanted her, and which manifests itself in melancholy and in something like epileptic seizures. "Wilbur Flick" has delusions of grandeur with the accompanying sense of inferiority. Imogen, the "Princess with the Golden Hair," imagines that her back is crippled by Pott's disease, but she is actually a "neuromimetic" and becomes hysterical when she thinks that the narrator wants to humiliate her. The Milhollands are ruthless publishers who seem to make pacts with the devil to keep them on top of their trade at the expense of an *âme damnée*, or scapegoat. They reveal emotional disturbances: in the oldest of the three brothers, by lechery and suicide; in the other two, by semantic aphasia at moments of duress.

The most prolonged neurosis (incidentally, none is cured) is that of the narrator himself, who is a depressive; he broods and is willing to blame others when he cannot concentrate on his work, he tells people that they bore him, he is too much upset by commonplace disturbances, he feels sorry for himself. At one point, in "Ellen Terhune," he candidly examines his mental state:

> One of the symptoms of certain neurotic states is an irrational drop of morale, a depression that may suddenly descend on you and absolutely flatten you out, from some stimulus that seems irrelevant or trifling—a passing sarcasm in conversation directed at someone else, a child ducking a cat in the gutter, a memory drifting into your head of something clumsy you once did in your childhood. I had had a touch of this at one time, and I found that my visits to Ellen's renewed it. . . . I would feel suddenly after lunch or dinner that living in the country was hopeless, that I had no communication with other people, and that nothing I was doing meant anything; yet on the other hand I could not see any hope in living in the city or traveling: I knew what human beings were—they might be more or less picturesque in their various environments and climates, and to the young this was a source of excitement; but to me, on the verge of thirty, it was desolatingly, incontrovertibly evident that people under any conditions were the same wry pathetic freaks, and why should I go to the trouble of moving about among them in order to observe the shapes which their defects and distortions could take?

> (*Memoirs* [1959], 48-9)

The entire account of Ellen Terhune—Wilson's answer in a "ghost" story to the ambiguity of Henry James—is based upon the narrator's frightening hallucinations, in which, on successive visits to Ellen's house, he experiences a regression through time. He sees her first as she is in 1926, distraught over the breaking up of her marriage; then as a merry and talented young woman early in the century; and, on his third visit, as a precocious thirteen- or fourteen-year-old girl in the 1890's. When he pays a fourth visit, he meets a young woman of the 1880's whom he comes to realize is Ellen's mother, pregnant with Ellen. She thinks that he is a gynecologist and wants him to recommend a legal abortion. The last time back, he meets a still younger, unmarried woman, who takes him as a family friend and asks his advice as to whether she should marry Fred Terhune.

Throughout "Glimpses of Wilbur Flick," "The Princess with the Golden Hair," and "The Milhollands and Their Damned Soul," the narrator's neurosis increasingly manifests itself in sudden changes of mood—depression, impatience, petulance, disgust, torment, sentimentality, joy, love. Behind this shifting, which he watches and analyzes, at once fascinated and detached, is the steadily growing pressure of completing his book on nineteenth-century painting. Finally, in the last tale, he has another hallucination—a frantic climax to the whole book—in which he imagines himself to be Blackburn and Mrs. Blackburn to be his girlfriend, Jo Gates. When he eventually regains enough of his senses to escape to his little stone house in the woods, he experiences a maudlin tenderness—perhaps imaginary, perhaps drunken—with Si Banks, a writer who has published nothing but who has given up wife and child for the art he believes in and who, like the narrator himself, is "honest."

Hecate County, then, is a place of despair, delusion, anxiety, ennui, and futility. It is noteworthy that at the end of the last tale when Jo Gates coaxes her distraught lover to come to the Southwest with her for a cure in the sunshine and fresh air, they take Hecate County with them: "... we were to find that the hangover by the cold mountain stream made it hard for us to see the bright morning; that the space of the gigantic pastures turned to boredom before we had crossed them; that the tall intimidating presence of the forests of aspen and pine, with their alien life that excluded ours, only left us the more alone with the strain of our wrong relation. We were to find the fears and suffocations, the drugged energies, of Hecate County; I had packed my bad nights with my baggage. ..." (447).

Even though very few characters appear in more than one story—the exceptions are Jo Gates, in "Princess" and "Blackburn," and Si Banks, in "The Milhollands" and "Blackburn"—the recurring Hecate County types help to unify the book. These are, first,

either those who, like Asa Stryker and Wilbur Flick, are economic opportunists and moral drifters, respectively; or those who
bargain with the devil—the three Milhollands. The second group
comprises more or less decent people who are, or who become,
deranged: Clarence Latouche, Ellen Terhune, Imogen Loomis,
and the narrator. Wilbur Flick perhaps belongs in this group,
too, although he is less decent than pathetic. Imogen herself is
not really innocent—at the root of her neurosis is a desire to spite
her father, whom she has hated since childhood. The third type
is those who manage to preserve their sanity and their integrity.
In this smallest group, Anna Lenihan, the Ukrainian working girl
who becomes the narrator's mistress in "Princess," and Jo Gates,
his mistress of six years, are emotionally the healthiest. Si Banks,
also a member of this group, barely manages to preserve his sanity. Anna and Jo escape the malaise because they are not really
Hecate County people, especially Anna, who lives in Brooklyn
and never even visits the county.

The people composing these three types can also be grouped
by occupation. Five belong to the artistic professions: Ellen,
a composer; Si, a writer; Lydia Moffat, a painter (of small
ability); Reggie da Luze a song writer; and the narrator, an
art historian and critic. Most are in business, as manufacturers
(Stryker), advertising agents (Ralph Loomis and Clarence
Latouche), publishers (the Milhollands and their "damned
soul," Flagler Haynes). Mrs. Blackburn is a politician; and
Anna, the novel's heroine, represents the proletariat. Others—
Imogen, her friend Edna Forbes, and Wilbur Flick—have no oc-
cupations; and it is not clear what Mr. Blackburn does for a living. This cross section through social strata suggests American
society in miniature, but omitted are the "white-collar" worker,
the teacher, and the clergyman. The novel's social commentary,
to be discussed later in this chapter, is apparently intended to
apply widely. Certainly one learns from Jo, a divorcée who
spends six months of every year in Southern California with her
children, that the Pacific Coast is just as frantic and pointless as
Hecate County.

What else is *Memoirs* besides a novel or a collection of stories?
Is it an account of the pangs of bringing forth a book? Is it the
history of a nervous breakdown? Certainly it contains close parallels with Wilson's own life that suggest these things. *Axel's Castle,*

published in 1931 and begun six years before then, was probably a severe strain on its author, as undoubtedly *Finland Station* was in the 1930's, although Wilson has not yet written of any struggles with either. He does say in *A Piece of My Mind* (1956) that he had a nervous breakdown in his mid-thirties, and from a letter of Wilson's to Christian Gauss one learns that it happened early in 1929.[12] But these speculations are beyond the role of the literary critic, who ascertains from the novel itself that it includes satire, social protest, and esthetic theory.

The most common satire in *Memoirs* is that on Hecate County life: the loud cocktail parties, the vapid conversation, the boredom of suntanned people who have a lot of money. The narrator finds it all distasteful and strained; he describes the dessert at a dinner party given by the Loomises as "a compote of cut-up peaches, raspberries and smooth white almonds—the whole washed down, as they say, with bootleg red Chianti in blue and green glass Mexican bottles. These bottles were effigies of the Virgin, and they provoked a good deal of amusement of a violently sophisticated kind" (122-3). Unlike Nick in *The Great Gatsby*, who is impressed by Gatsby's lavish parties even though he feels alienated from the people there, the narrator in *Memoirs* has a critical eye. And yet he feels sorry for Wilbur Flick, whose entire pursuit of nothing so epitomizes Hecate County and who finally, after narcotics addiction and a nervous breakdown, achieves a short triumph as an amateur magician; the narrator, indeed, is the only person who rather likes Wilbur and feels compassion for him.

But despite the narrator's discomfort in Hecate County and his contempt for its values, he is finally forced to admit in "Princess" that he is more at home there than he would be with the immigrants in Anna's Brooklyn. And—despite his admiration, fondness, and even love for Anna—marrying her, when he has to face the question, seems unwise. " 'So you're done with me,' she said. . . . 'I'll always love you—you know that,' I insisted . . ." (306). At the end of the tale, he is at another party, and he does indeed miss Anna: ". . . as Bess Filsinger came over to me, protesting that I was snooting them by myself in a corner, I was felled by a sudden glumness as I knew, and found it bitter to know, that I was back now in Hecate County and we should never make love again" (313).

Within the general satire on Hecate County are sharper attacks on specific aspects of the entire United States. Big business is dealt some of the more trenchant blows. At one point in "Princess," the narrator reflects on the General Tires Corporation in Detroit, where his father works as a "management engineer": ". . . conflicts were to be carefully worked out through a system of interdepartmental committees, so as to save needless effort and cost. Everything was taken care of in this system except the interests of the public and the worker, who had never been considered at all. But when I tried to make my father see this, it only became hopelessly apparent that he regarded the depression as an act of God like an earthquake, a drouth or a flood" (207).

But most of the narrator's gibes at business are directed at advertising and publishing. In "Snapping Turtles," the most amusing story of the six, Clarence Latouche cynically tells Asa Stryker how to persuade the public to buy his product: "You know, the truth is that a great big proportion of the canned turtle soup that's sold is made out of snapping turtles, but that isn't the way they advertize it. If you advertize it frankly as snapper, it will look like something brand-new, and all you'll need is the snob appeal to put it over on the can-opening public. . . . convince them that there's some kind of social prestige attached to it . . . create the impression that a good ole white-haired darky with a beaming smile used to serve turtle soup to Old Massa" (10-11).

"The Milhollands and Their Damned Soul" is more than anything else a satire on the ruthless, fraudulent aspects of the publishing industry, which, interested only in selling books, aims knowingly, in the words of Si Banks, "to feed back to the public its own ignorance and cheap tastes," especially through book clubs, one of whose monthly offerings the narrator parodies at some length:

"She [the female possum] watched him with half-closed but unblinking green eyes. Who was this bearded intruder striding into the comfortable fastnesses where her family had dwelt for centuries, which had been sacred to untold generations of South Carolina possums since before those upstarts, the humans, had come with their heavy boots that crashed through the underbrush instead of slipping daintily through the twigs, with their harsh shrill voices that frightened the wood folk and caused them to shrink into their green retreats? But she did not shrink now, she stood her ground. Merely signaling to her babies with an invisible twitch, the quick unobtrusive warning of the patrician Southern mother, to lighten their hold on her tail, she tensed her muscles for instant flight. . . ." (354-5)

Even more damaging is an account of how Warren Milholland's publishing house puts out a historical novel. Flagler Haynes says, "It's one of those long historical rigmaroles . . . that takes typical American characters through every goddam war and national event from the Revolution on" (379). Supposedly the triumph of one man, the historical novel is actually a hodge-podge of plagiarism and invention put together by several people and falsely advertised as having an advance sale of three hundred thousand copies.

Other things also are treated satirically, although none so extensively as business. In "Wilbur Flick," they are Fascism and anti-Semitism, prevalent in the early 1930's: "He complained that when one went to the theater, one ran into too many Jews in the lavatory" (91)—and then a more fashionable Communism in the late 1930's. In "Blackburn," Hollywood gets a share of scorn. Reggie da Luze says, "You know what they mean by culture in Hollywood: Scriabin's Golden Poem in the Hollywood Bowl— they think that Scriabin's some kind of big orange!" (433). And apparently Wilson does not spare even his own theme of the wound and the bow; a loud "literary" woman in "The Milhollands" makes the idea seem vulgar: "You stutter, I notice. . . . Whenever I hear a stutter, I know there's a psychic defect. I don't mean to be invidious, of course—all great literature grows out of defects—like Somerset Maugham's club foot.—And that's where your 'sprung rhythm' comes in—didn't Hopkins have a stutter!" (367).

Although the satire in *Memoirs* establishes an opprobrious attitude toward Hecate County values and emphasizes the narrator's critical personality, it also leads to another theme: the narrator's (and, one recognizes from other writings, Wilson's own) attitude toward some of the larger social problems. The sufferings of the poor are taken up in "Princess," the most ambitious tale and the one in which the narrator comes to know Anna, a member of the poor, who strikingly contrasts to the people of the upper middle class in Hecate County. The narrator had already become disenchanted with capitalists: "I had, however, been affected by the radical wind that had blown at the end of the war ... and had come to be repelled by the indifference of my father and the employers' world that he served to the human need of labor. I had called myself a socialist at college, and had found myself more and more at odds with the college Economics Department, where the professors were mainly apologists for the bankers on the board of trustees or people of the dry-goods and grocery type who had a sympathetic interest in business without the competence to be businessmen" (136-7).

During his evening walks past the little shops on New York's Fourteenth Street, he reflects on the plight of the workers who made the garments and shoes he sees in the shop windows and who have to picket, now in 1929, in an attempt to get a minimum wage: "I had a vision of the economic system as a pitiful and disgusting fiasco" (141). But not until he meets Anna, a dance-hall girl, are the poor more than a vague group of people that someone ought to do something for. From her unaffected accounts of home life in Brooklyn and of jobs in Manhattan as a dance-hall girl and, later, as a waitress—all of which he carefully notes in a journal—he learns what wife-beating, frustration, malnutrition, sickness, and bone-weariness mean. He comes to feel, much as Wilson himself did, that Marx was also right for America; that people are divided into the bourgeoisie and the proletariat, the haves and the have-nots—and for the latter, even staying alive is harsh: "... somebody [in Detroit] had told with enthusiasm of having been present at the Fords' Christmas party, where a hunchbacked and jolly Ford worker, dressed up as Santa Claus, had handed around the gifts. I felt that Karl Marx and Anna had given me the right to be bitter" (208). He is surprised, however, that Anna never complains; and, when he tries to talk to her about a workers' revolution, he finds that he merely embarrasses her by consigning her to the "working class":

> To tell her that the fur workers like her mother, the garment workers like her cousins, and the waitresses at Field's like herself were expected to dislodge their employers and the big figures she read about in the papers and to make themselves the rulers of society—must seem to her, I could see by her silence, to be thrusting on herself and her people a rôle for which she knew

they were not fitted and for which I must know they were not—so that I soon began to feel silly and insincere; and my Marxist way of talking seemed at the same time to imply that Anna and her family were at present such "underprivileged" beings as to have been practically outlawed from humanity, when the fact was that she and I, in our manners with one another and in the freedom with which we had both bound ourselves, as it were, by emotional contract, were meeting on equal terms. . . . (220)

Later, when Anna is suffering in the hospital from the after-effects of a hysterectomy, he reads a Communist newspaper in Washington Square and finds it "rather false in tone." Anna arouses in him both compassion and the knowledge that ready-made answers for alleviating misery are simply political catch-words. At the end of "Princess," when he sits dolefully back in Hecate County, he realizes how much he owes Anna: ". . . it was Anna who had made it possible for *me* to recreate the actuality; who had given me that life of the people which had before been but prices and wages, legislation and technical progress, that new Europe of the East Side and Brooklyn for which there was pro-vided no guidebook" (312-3). What he can contribute for the poor is apparently what the hero of *I Thought of Daisy* hopes to do: to write about them as they "really are."

This development of the narrator's social thinking influences his esthetic principles. At the beginning of his relationship with Anna, he discovers one day, when he is brooding about his "aesthetic problems," just what it is that has been bothering him:

I had just been rereading Clive Bell, whose doctrine of "signifi-cant form" as opposed to illustrational value had become so much a part of my thinking that I had never got my quarrel with it clear. But I saw now how impossible it was for me to accept his Platonic idealism which made art represent a reality independent of the vicissitudes of life; and I could never work out the relation between his theory of the history of art and my social-economic one. For Clive Bell, the school of painting that began with Cézanne was the herald of a great rebirth; to me, it seemed already to reflect the human decadence and the mechanical tyr-anny of a dying social system. Though I admired many abstract paintings, I tended to find in them the savage self-loathing, the helpless splintering, the self-immolation, of urban man in the modern world. . . . if I were myself an artist, I should want to leave explicit in any painting of Anna some evidence of her tar-nished prettiness. (145)

One recalls Wilson's increasing concern in *Axel's Castle* over writers who withdraw from the world of social reality, or his criticism of Marcel Proust and Thornton Wilder in "The Economic Interpretation of Wilder": "the presentable side of the impotence, the creeping corruption, the lack of the will to live" (*New Republic*, November 26, 1930).

Anna's situation, which comes to be truer to the narrator than anything in Hecate County, strongly affects the narrator's book:

> I had been trying to show in my book how the painting of the nineteenth century had been influenced by the Industrial Revolution; and now I saw that the union of Imogen and Ralph was a striking dramatic symbol of the queer combination, under capitalism, of a disgraceful economic reality and a dissembling romantic screen. Ralph made the money in advertising—that is, in hiring himself out to glorify whatever the industrialists were hoping to manufacture with profit; and Imogen spent the money on domestic settings and panoramas of travel abroad that made it possible for her always to fancy, and for Ralph part of the time to pretend, that their situation was other than it was. But the world of Anna was the real world, the base on which everything rested; she was the worker who gave all that he could give and who got for it as little as he could live on. I listened to her reports of Field's restaurant with the same kindling indignation with which I had been reading in *Das Kapital* the hideous industrial chapters. (209)

His thoughts on the relationship of painting and money—and the laborers who get very little of the latter—coalesce into definite opinions on the outstanding painters; and these opinions, despite the prevalence of non-representational art, favor the contemporaries. He hotly argues with a friend who prefers Whistler to Braque and Picasso: "I declared that Whistler's famous passage about the Thames clothed with poetry by the evening mist and the chimneys becoming campanili, was one of the most pathetic, if not one of the most ignoble admissions ever made by a modern artist, because it showed that he was absolutely incapable of dealing with his environment as it actually was" (229). As he says later to Blackburn, the narrator sees cubism as a reflection of contemporary life.

It may be that "Princess" comprises Edmund Wilson's own statement of the nature and purpose of art, which should define people in terms of their social and economic liabilities. This obligation is directly opposed to the Romantic idea of the artist's robing what he sees in the veils of his imagination and is obliquely opposed to the Humanistic idea of his illustrating the great moral truths. In Wilson's view, the artist is an emphasizer or accentuator, pointing out the harsher elements which were always present, but which less perceptive people had never noticed or thought about. The artist should reflect the problems of his time, whether they are the plight of the proletariat in the 1930's or bureaucracy and the loss of individuality in the 1960's.

This concept of the usefulness of art is a common one which yet would eliminate much that is ordinarily considered art. But the standard is pliable, as is apparent in "Blackburn," in the narrator's conversation with Blackburn about an article taken from his forthcoming book:

> "What interests me particularly," he said, "is your idea that the methods of the Impressionists were essentially the result of their unwillingness to look the contemporary world in the face. They created a veil between themselves and it. They couldn't come to grips with it, in fact—so that their work was unreal and worthless." This was not precisely what I had said; and he spoke, I thought, a little too dogmatically: as if *he* were telling *me*. I explained that, though it was true that the Impressionists had sometimes been repelled by their century, their work could not be said to be worthless: they had made their own kind of beauty though they had had to create special conventions under which it could be realized. "And eventually, of course," I went on, "it did come to present a reflection of the world from which it had tried to withdraw. When crystals began to form in the saturated solutions of the atmospheres of painters like Monet and Seurat, they made the abstract designs of angles that you get in a modern city and the accidental patterns that you find in machines. You have Cubism, in other words." "I have always been assured that Cubism," said Blackburn ... "was an experiment in pure and fundamental form, and now you explain it quite comprehensibly as the product of historical necessity." (406-7)

With regard to literature, Wilson's curiosity and intelligence are too great—despite certain blind spots—and his discrimination too fine to allow him to rely on a formula. In *Axel's Castle* he is impatient with the French Symbolists though he admires them; but he also defends Romantic poetry in the first chapter: "a

Romantic poet like Wordsworth ... has perceived that the world is an organism, that nature includes planets, mountains, vegetation and people alike, that what we are and what we see, what we hear, what we feel and what we smell, are inextricably related, that all are involved in the same great entity.... The Romantic poet, then, with his turbid or opalescent language, his sympathies and passions which cause him to seem to merge with his surroundings, is the prophet of a new insight into nature: he is describing things as they really are...." (5). One might only add "things as they really are" to *him*.

Besides satire, social protest, and esthetic theory, another notable element in *Memoirs* is humor. There are riffles of comedy blended with the grimmer aspects; indeed, Wilson's characters are often most amusing when they are serious. For example, in "The Man Who Shot Snapping Turtles," Asa Stryker has been brooding over the destruction of his ducklings by turtles. The problem takes on a sinister significance for him:

> "If God has created the mallard," he said, "a thing of beauty and grace, how can He allow these dirty filthy mud-turtles to prey upon His handiwork and destroy it?" "He created the mud-turtles first," I said. "The reptiles came before the birds. And they survive with the strength God gave them. There is no instance on record of God's intervention in the affairs of any animal species lower in the scale than man." "But if Evil triumphs there," said Stryker, "it may triumph everywhere, and we must fight it with every weapon in our power!" "That's the Manichaean heresy," I replied. "It is an error to assume that the Devil is contending on equal terms with God and that the fate of the world is in doubt." "I'm not sure of that sometimes," said Stryker.... "How do we know that some of His lowest creations aren't beginning to get out of hand and clean up on the higher ones?" (6)

Stryker tries everything to get rid of the turtles; he shoots them, drains the pond, pollutes the water with chemicals, installs elaborate fences—but nothing seems to work: "One day, as Asa M. Stryker was walking around his estate, he encountered a female snapping turtle unashamedly crawling in the direction of the pond. She had obviously just been laying her eggs" (7).

But as "Snapping Turtles" continues, one realizes that it is not just amusing. The humor is sharply set off by the theme of derangement and chaos (what I have referred to as diabolism). In "desperate moral anxiety," Stryker talks to Clarence Latouche about his problem with the turtles and, thus, the universe. Latouche tries to calm him by pointing out that, if God cannot keep evil out of the universe, how can mere human beings do any better with Hecate County. He reasonably suggests that, since Stryker cannot get rid of the turtles, he ought to capitalize on them by starting a turtle farm and a soup factory. Before the somewhat unhinged Stryker, who knows that "Right is Right and Wrong is Wrong," can accept that point of view, there is a horrible, superbly written scene in which Stryker confronts one of his tormentors:

> He would scoop them up with a net, and this morning he paused over the first one he caught before he cut off its head. He scrutinized it with a new curiosity, and its appearance enraged him afresh: he detested its blunt sullen visage, its thick legs with their outspread claws, and its thick and thorny-toothed tail that it could not even pull into its shell as other turtles did. It was not even a genuine turtle: *Chelydra serpentina* they called it, because it resembled a snake, and it crawled like a huge lizard. He baited it with a stick: it snapped with a sharp popping sound. As he held the beast up in his net, in the limpid morning air which was brimming the world like a tide, it looked, with its feet dripping slime, its dull shell that resembled a sunken log, as fetid, as cold and as dark as the bottom of the pond itself; and he was almost surprised at the gush of blood when he sawed away the head. What good purpose, he asked himself in horror, could such a creature serve? Subterranean, ugly and brutal—with only one idea in its head, or rather one instinct in its nature: to seize and hold down its prey. The turtle had snapped at the hoop of the net, and even now that its head was severed, its jaws were still holding on. (9-10)

This incident, more than any other, suggests a kind of underlying malignancy in Hecate County, which infects the people. After Stryker does accept Clarence's suggestion and become a Hecate County opportunist, the "demon" that troubled him seems to pass from him into Clarence, who becomes morbid and then deranged enough to kill Stryker—only to fear later in California that "Stryker" may still get him: if an innocent man is accused of the murder, Clarence, "the soul of honor," will have to confess.

The longest and most complex memoir is "The Princess with

the Golden Hair," which combines two extremes in fiction—the Naturalistic novel and the fairy tale. This dualism is important because the structure of the tale, the full characterization of the narrator, and his final concept of the nature and purpose of art depend on it. The Naturalistic aspect is the story of Anna and her struggles to live decently. With a scientist's fascination, the narrator learns and chronicles all he can about her: her background, her upbringing, her occupation, home, relatives, worries, pleasures—everything. Life is very hard for her; but, unlike a Frank Norris or an Émile Zola character, she is indomitable. She refuses to pity herself or be pitied; she surprises the narrator by her strength of character without coarseness. There is something noble and courageous about her which he is at a loss to define, unused as he is to observing it in Hecate County. She becomes more to him than the subject of a sociological study and much more than a diversion: he eventually comes to love her and her "fine little humor, her clear little sense of things, her gentleness, her appetite for love" far more than he has ever been able to love anyone else. It is almost her diminutiveness that he loves, that he finds cunning and precious against the forces threatening to overwhelm it.

The golden princess of the fairy tale is Imogen Loomis. Dressed always in stunning clothes which are out of fashion and seem to belong to a past time and another place, she becomes the beguiling enchantress whose beauty and chastity madden the narrator. Both ravished and famished by her beauty, when he voluptuously describes the food at a huge party, he is really describing, as Gottfried von Strassburg might do, his sensations of her. His entrapment is largely his own doing, for she does little to encourage him. Presumably she is happily married to a successful advertising man and is not looking for a courtly lover in the full sense. Rather foolishly, he views her aloofness as the "danger" which he, the knight, must overcome. He attempts to make himself worthy of her by getting a job in the Metropolitan Museum to supplement his small annuity and by moving his New York lodgings from a room to an expensive apartment.

Intellectually she is below him—a porcelain princess with an earthenware mind—but he is so taken with her beauty and his own desire that he almost deliberately chooses not to notice this difference: " 'I feel as if we were going to see the Glamis Horror,'

[152]

I remarked as we climbed the steps [of a small staircase outside her house]. 'I'm afraid we haven't got any ghosts,' she replied, after a moment's silence. I imagined she had stopped to think and did not know what the Glamis Horror was. It was supposed to be a monster, not a ghost, but I did not correct her. . . ." (128). She fancies herself cultured and knowing; if the conversation turns on Goya, she recites all she has heard about him. And yet the narrator chooses to see in her conversation a "greatness of spirit." Her replies to his declarations are invariably trivial: " 'I never thought I'd know you,' I said, taking both her hands together. 'You seemed like a romantic vision—the kind of thing one can't get over to from reality.' 'I never thought I'd know you either'. . . .'You still don't seem,' I pursued, 'to belong to the real world I live in—you don't belong with ordinary people.' 'You're not like other people either'" (130).

His attempts to take her to bed are repeatedly thwarted. She much prefers keeping him as the languishing adorer and hints that there is something wrong with her that he must not discover. They join in elaborate fantasies in which they imagine that they are married and live in exotic places. These please her and madden him. When he finally does bring her to bed, the experience is disappointing for both. Then she becomes hysterical and tries to make him feel guilty. Her secret, or taboo, seems to be a bad back (which looks perfect); she wears an elaborate, tight brace. When he goes to the public library to investigate her infirmity (Pott's disease), he discovers almost by chance a book called *The Hysterical Element in Orthopaedic Surgery* and learns melodramatically that "a large number of cases which had the aspect of spinal disease and even of congenital deformity had been found to be neurotic shams." All of Imogen's physical symptoms are counterfeit. At last, "empty and giddy," he is "delivered of Imogen" (275-6).

The eroticism of "Princess" established the notoriety of *Memoirs* in 1946. Acting on complaints by the Society for the Suppression of Vice, the New York police raided the local bookstores in July—as did the police in Philadelphia—and seized the book, which had been banned in Boston since April. The New York Public Library removed the book from its shelves in September. In November the Special Sessions Court in New York City voted two to one against the book as tending to deprave and corrupt the young and immature. The Court fined jointly the publisher, Doubleday and Company, and Doubleday Book Shops a thousand dollars (five hundred dollars on each of two counts); about a year later it fined Womrath's Bookshops and Libraries five hundred. (At a trial by jury in San Francisco, from September 29 to December 12, 1946, the book was absolved of immorality and the salesman was freed.) Doubleday appealed to the Appellate Division, which upheld the Special Sessions decision without opinion on May 16, 1947; on November 13, the United States Court of Appeals in Albany also unanimously upheld the conviction. On October 26, 1948, the United States Supreme Court upheld the conviction by a four to four tie vote, Justice Felix Frankfurter taking no part in the decision. Until 1959 the unexpurgated *Memoirs* was not published again in the United States and is still not for sale in New York State.[13]

The reviewers, too, were stirred by the book, although they assumed a sophisticated attitude toward the detailed sexual passages. They did not object to the sexuality, they said, but to the lack of passion; D. H. Lawrence at least wrote passionately. Mrs. Trilling was particularly taxed not to seem shocked: what disturbed her was not the daring of the sexual passages, but "the breach they make between sensation and emotion." Alfred Kazin wrote in the *Partisan Review*: "Mr. Wilson's descriptions of fornication ... are really pathetic.... Mr. Wilson's narrator is so locked up in his own mind that he seems to have his encounters only for what he shall think of them. Nothing could be further removed from passion; or even from neurotic conquest; or even from mechanical lechery."[14] This judgment is not entirely true; for, as Kazin himself admits later, the narrator does experience passion with Anna.

Surprisingly, the reviewers did not consider several explanations for the apparent lack of passion. First, in terms of the structure of "Princess," the narrator's bemused disappointment with Imogen after his voluptuous expectations makes a pleasing contrast, as well as an irony that is in keeping with the theme of self-deception. Furthermore, the narrator is in love with no one except Anna—he only *imagines* that he loves Imogen—and thus might be expected to be less passionate than analytical. What is also true is that it is just as much in his nature not to be passionate (except, again, in his imaginings) as it is to enjoy a maddening pursuit more than attainment. Therefore, his love-making, if detached, is characteristic of him.

At the time no one seemed to realize that the eroticism is essential for understanding "Princess" since it represents better than anything else could the differences between the two women. Anna, after some wooing, enters wholeheartedly into love-making —to enjoy her lover and be enjoyed by him. The setting need not be romantic: they make love at any time, in and out of bed, dressed and undressed, and—from the narrator's point of view— nearly always satisfactorily. Imogen, on the other hand, despite her superb body, which he describes in detail, is passive in and humiliated by the act of love. She is quite unable to abandon herself, and it is not until her perplexed lover has finshed that she brings herself to a feeble orgasm. The point is that Anna lives in the imperfect but real world of flesh and blood, and, determined to make the most of this world, expects nothing from any other. Imogen's world is entirely one of make-believe—the only one in which she feels comfortable, since her illness itself is a lie—and, when confronted with a situation where no pretense is possible, she responds with resentment and hatred.

Both women are important for the development of the narrator's imaginative *and* analytical thinking, although Imogen is far less important than Anna. Imogen arouses his imagination, but Anna presents him with the actuality of life that he has never known before. Neither woman alone can fill all of his psychological needs: Imogen, because she cannot respond to or even recognize reality; Anna, because she is too different from him culturally for a permanent relationship—she, of course, is aware of this difference and doesn't want to meet his friends for fear of not knowing what to say. His writings on nineteenth-century painting require both imagination and the ability to take the measure of environment, but he cannot depend on someone else for these; and perhaps, in the act of writing, he can unite imagination and reality and become fulfilled.

To be sure, *Memoirs* has faults: "Snapping Turtles" ends too abruptly; and it leaves the technical problem of how the first-person narrator could know about the murder, which no one witnessed but which is described as if he were an agent inside both Stryker's house and Latouche's mind. "Princess" is too long by perhaps twenty-five pages; the narrator is so confiding and so analytical that one sometimes wishes that he would be quiet and get on with the story. In "The Milhollands" the satire on the publishing industry may not be especially significant, but this point is debatable. And the four-page essay on refugees in America that opens "Blackburn" is tedious. But these minor faults are far outweighed by definite virtues.

For one thing, Wilson has converted rather unpromising material into good fiction. Three of the stories—"Snapping Turtles," "Ellen Terhune," and "Blackburn"—are basically improbable; but this fact is apparent only upon reflection. In the reading they are not improbable at all but credible and fascinating. It requires a great deal of skill, for example, to take the melodramatic, if not trite, elements of "Ellen Terhune"—the brilliant but doomed composer trying to work out a sense of guilt in a final opus based on a haunting four-note theme—and make them into a genuinely dramatic story of the narrator's own loss of touch with reality. Moreover, Wilson also succeeds with the first-person narrator in at least two stories out of the three in which the narrator has practically no part in the action—"Snapping Turtles," "Wilbur Flick," and "The Milhollands." In these he is almost only a reporter (in the last he is also a ruminator). Of course, he is seldom a disinterested reporter: the way that he sees things is interesting enough so that one hardly notices his "absence" from the action. Furthermore, as he himself tells us, the six parts of *Memoirs* are "tales," and therefore he may be excused from not always participating in them.

However, the most remarkable feat of all is that Wilson has transformed what could be case histories in a textbook of psychoanalysis into full, convincing people. One *knows* them as he does not know the people in *Daisy*. Most important of all, one knows the main character, the narrator, without ever feeling sympathetic for him: Wilson has not falsely engaged the reader's credulity by putting his hero in a position where one feels obligated to like or to feel sorry for a man whose reactions and thoughts are so honestly told that sometimes the reader recoils. For the narrator is a young snob who tries not to be one.

The convincing characterization depends a great deal on the dialogue, which seems more accurate than ever before—as when Anna is telling the narrator about her stepfather: " 'His name is

Alexis, but they call him Fatty. He's a big fat awful-lookin guy. We were measurin ourselves one day—we have a lotta fun when I'm not sore at-um—and he's as big aroun the thigh as I am aroun the waist—twenny-four.—And my mother supports-um, she gives-um money. When I think of my mother livin with-um! When I go past the door of her room and see her cuddlin up to-um in bed, I could just go in and smack her!' " (148-9).

Wilson's diction is concrete, explicit. The style is accretive, unlike that of Scott Fitzgerald, who often places a character quickly by a striking metaphor or by stringing together disparate qualities, as in his description of Irene Scheerer in "Winter Dreams": "Irene was light-haired and sweet and honorable, and a little stout...."[15] When Wilson, in "Princess," writes the same kind of hurrying sentence (and he doesn't do this often), he uses only elements from one class, such as physical attributes: "She was slim and rather pale and had reddish hair and was wearing a blue dress." In his deliberate manner, Wilson moves from one class of attributes to another, and the portrait of Anna evolves:

> I was struck by her complete unconcern. Instead of coming to meet me with alacrity the moment she saw me advancing, she stood without catching my eye; when I spoke to her, she said simply, "You want this one?"; and did not even smile. I noticed that she was not made up, did not seem to have put on even lipstick, where the other girls heavily depended on their artificial mouths and lashes in the peachy artificial light; and when I talked to her, she paid out no patter but answered my questions briefly, in a toneless but not unfriendly voice. Nor did she glue her knee against me: we danced with a conventional interval. I asked her what her name was and she said Anna. Her last name—when I asked for it—was Lenihan. It did not sound fancy enough to be one of their made-up names. (143)

Wilson's stylistic method is that of a stonemason, carefully chipping to fit the right word in the right place. In his precise use of "hard," concrete words, not only characters but situations and scenes become vivid, as for example, the seemingly simple description of Stryker's drained pond:

> The operation took the whole of one summer: it horribly disfigured his place, and it afflicted the neighborhood with the stench of the slime that was now laid bare. One family whose place adjoined Stryker's were obliged to go away for weeks during the

heaviest days of August, when the draining had become complete. Stryker, however, stayed and personally attended to the turtles, cutting off their heads himself; and he had men posted day and night at the places where they went to lay their eggs. At last someone complained to the Board of Health, and they made him fill up his pond. He was indignant with the town authorities and declared that he had not yet got all the turtles, some of which were still hiding in the mud; and he and his crew put in a mad last day combing the bottom with giant rakes. (5)

Surprisingly, Wilson's straightforward style with its frank diction can be used suggestively. The opening of "Princess," for example, implies a faint sordidness just by being so forthright: "I had found, in the course of the summer, that I was watching Imogen Loomis at parties. I had been seeing her and her husband for years, but I had always thought them rather boring—on the middle-class side of Hecate County. Then my regular girl of that period had had to go out to Pasadena, where she spent six months of the year with her children, and I had suddenly started gazing at Imogen. I wondered why I had never noticed how sensationally attractive she was" (111).

Another novelist's view of *Memoirs* may be useful here. John Wain, the British author who has written one of the few articles about *Memoirs*, says that the strength of Wilson's criticism is the personality behind it, which is also the weakness of his imaginative work.[16] Amusingly, Wain continues: "It is a conducted tour, skillfully and vividly done; Mr. Wilson has decided not to appear in the role of himself, and therefore comes before us in dark glasses and with a little crepe hair on his upper lip, but we know it's *him* all right." But if the personality of the author is recognizable in his work, how is that in itself a defect? The fiction of Proust, Gide, Kafka, Joyce, Hemingway, D. H. Lawrence, and perhaps most of the currently practicing novelists in England and America is full of "personality." Wain no doubt knows this, and it is likely that what he objects to is *Wilson's* personality (a "critical" one), but there is not much that Wilson can do about that.

Wain claims that the "sketches" in *Memoirs* aren't narratives but essays: "There is the same strong, idiosyncratic personality in control, the same logical step-by-step marshalling of the material, the same alternation of presentation and comment. . . . he gives us a slab of narrative and then talks about the significance of what he has told us." The same could be said about the novels of Henry Fielding or the tales of Hawthorne. Wain calls *Memoirs* ratiocinative and analytical but not imaginative, although he admits that, in part, so is all fiction.[17] His description of Wilson's narrative-commentary technique is generally correct, but it is truer of "Princess," "The Milhollands," and "Blackburn" than of "Snapping Turtles," "Ellen Terhune," and "Wilbur Flick."

But what would Wain say about *Memoirs* if he did not first know that Wilson was a critic? It may not really mean much when people speak of a "critical" intelligence as opposed to an "imaginative" one, or a "dramatic" intelligence as opposed to an "analytical" one. The best imaginative writer, such as James Joyce or W. B. Yeats, is a superior critic; and the best criticism is to some extent imaginative. A more meaningful distinction than the imaginative-critical dichotomy might be one of temperament, the temperament of the "pure" mathematician on the one hand and the "applied" mathematician on the other. The imaginative or "pure" writer is happiest with a hypothetical system; the critical or "applied" writer prefers to examine the hypothetical system empirically and perhaps to relate it to other kinds of knowledge.[18] The major Romantic poets, especially Coleridge and Shelley, enjoyed doing both. And many other "creative" writers—such as Matthew Arnold, Henry James, T. S. Eliot, and John Crowe Ransom—have been outstanding analysts of writing.

The quality of a novel depends upon the consistency of motive and action within its own "world," and in this respect *Memoirs* is stronger than *Daisy*. How far removed the hypothetical world of the novel is from "real life," or how much the author has "transformed" his materials, is beside the point. Wilson's fiction makes that kind of speculation easy since it contains parallels with his own life; furthermore, he continues in *Memoirs of Hecate County* to use the first-person narrator. But, as the book's title and form indicate, his narratives are "memoirs."

IV *Wilson's Major Fiction By His Own Standards*

Because Edmund Wilson is known primarily as a critic, the question sometimes asked in regard to his fiction is whether it succeeds by his own critical standards. This question begs still another, whether it should—whether, in fact, one's standards as a critic of fiction should also be his as a writer of fiction. But if the latter question is waived as requiring far too theoretical an answer, there remains the main difficulty, noted in Chapter 2: Wilson has no sharply defined standards. As was pointed out in Chapter 2, he is not a theoretical critic but a "public" or "practicing" one who depends on his own taste—the result of his long experience with literature—to evaluate it. He has no "rules" for what fiction should be and do other than the most obvious: it is human experience in an organized form; it portrays recognizable people; it has emotional impact; and, finally, it is useful in helping people to understand themselves.

This summation is related to William Faulkner's statement that a story should be "familiar to everyone in some very moving way ... so true that anyone would say, 'Why yes—that's so ...'" (*Faulkner at West Point* [1964], 50). But one difference between the two writers is that Faulkner in his fiction uncoils a meaning at once large and simple, or "universal"; Wilson, who of course knows that literature can have this dimension, directs his own fiction toward a sphere of human activity that is more topical and limited.

Faulkner's statement continues: "I think that no writer's got time to be drawing a picture of a region, or preaching anything— if he's trying to preach you a sermon, then he's really not a writer, he's a propagandist, which is another horse. But the writer is simply trying to tell a story of the human heart in conflict with itself, or with others, or with environment in a moving way" (50-1). Wilson would agree, despite his tendency to preach; but the scope of human activity and conflict in his fiction is fairly confined to the intellectual and to his attempts to find a place for himself in the life of a more or less urban and boorish America. The Wilson hero is usually bookish and aloof, yet he feels somewhat guilty about his intellectual pursuits. He wants to understand other people, but is invariably irritated by them. He belongs to no community and can manage only brief relationships. He has no identity (no name) and no tradition to sustain him spiritually. His isolation is clear in *I Thought of Daisy* and in *Memoirs of Hecate County*. In fact, the theme of the intelligent, idealistic, and rather snobbish protagonist who is forced to take some attitude toward his environment is already revealed in "The

Men from Rumpelmayer's" and even more clearly shown in "Galahad," both fairly early stories of 1927. In "Rumpelmayer's," he is cowed by his environment; in "Galahad," thoroughly beaten by it.

In *I Thought of Daisy* the protagonist struggles to overcome his snobbery and to attain harmony with his sometimes distasteful surroundings. He determines by the end that he will write about ordinary American people, such as Daisy, and not isolate himself from the common, actual world. He thereby hopes to accomplish two things: to solve the problem of his (and, in general, the artist's) alienation from his surroundings, and to contribute to the solution of economic and social inequality by portraying people on the underside of American life. The reader, however, is left in some doubt about the narrator and his goal: does he really have the heart for the true-to-life kind of writing (he has been a fairly sheltered intellectual), and will his efforts be quite as significant—especially to the unlettered Daisys—as he thinks? But his determination represents at least a positive attitude toward adjusting to the larger environment outside literary circles and trying to use it artistically.

The narrator's final realization, or *Daisy's* "meaning," depends upon his arriving at the truth about people and ideas after seeing them in a series of shifting attitudes; and these depend, in turn, upon the tightly knit, five-movement "musical" structure, which can be either a symphonic theme-and-variations or a dance in which the partners change rapidly. This structure certainly suggests experience organized—a second of Wilson's criteria. But *Daisy* does not live up to the others: characterization (recognizable people) is slight, and emotional power is therefore lacking.

Memoirs of Hecate County pursues the theme of the snobbish intellectual's having to take a moral position in regard to his social environment. The narrator is more educated in the ways of the world than either the schoolboy in "Galahad" or the literary young man in *Daisy;* thus he is not so vulnerable to defeat as the former or so prone to optimism as the latter. Although he manages to stay somewhat aloof from the diabolical world, he is nevertheless affected by it; and, after exhibiting a number of neurotic symptoms—not the least of which is his obsession to become the lover of a Hecate County "princess" who cannot bear to live in reality—he comes very close in the last of the six memoirs to a total nervous breakdown. The diabolism is a sickness more serious than social wrong and psychological maladjustment, although both of these are present. The main environmental defect is a spiritual and ethical disease: people have no inner space in which to grow and no principles by which to live. As the old Puritan Asa Stryker learned in "The Man Who Shot Snapping Turtles," right and wrong mean nothing in Hecate County; what matters is making the best deal for oneself. The novel suggests that the YMCA morality of "Galahad," ineffectual as it is in an environment of ridicule, has nevertheless been replaced by no other satisfactory way of life. The intellectual narrator is finally able to reject the "smart," dull, dishonest and neurotic upper-middle class. But he, too, is a victim of the disease and can never purge himself of it. He perfunctorily works on his book, but he never entirely finishes it; and, when he goes to the Southwest, he takes the boredom and despair of Hecate County with him.

Memoirs generally satisfies Wilson's criteria for fiction, most surprisingly in portrayal of character and in emotional power ("impact" is too strong a term) of a peculiar kind, involving the whole range of mental depression mentioned earlier. The book also attains a structural unity, looser than that of *Daisy* but nevertheless sustained by the Hecate County mood. It raises certain questions, too, such as whether the narrator is meant to be taken entirely seriously or whether he is included in the objects of satire, or both. But this question adds to the book's interest—it is appropriate to the perplexity of Hecate County—and is in no way a defect, as it is in *Daisy*. It suggests that Wilson has managed an ambiguity that annoyed him in Henry James. At any rate, *Memoirs* is the best of all his fiction and among the best of all his books.

CHAPTER *5*

Fact and Fiction: Conclusion

A S HAS BEEN NOTED, Wilson sees literature as an intellectual activity that gives "a meaning to our experience."
In this view, the main province of fiction is the presentation of
ideas in a manner so compelling or attractive that they will
readily possess the reader. This contrasts to a more widely held
attitude, also related to Faulkner's, that fiction should present "familiar" people and their experiences in a seemingly disinterested
way, permitting the reader to think that he draws his own conclusions. With the exception of "Galahad," *I Thought of Daisy,*
and *Memoirs of Hecate County,* Wilson deliberately mingles his
fiction with his articles, reviews, essays, and sketches because
fiction for him is another way of illustrating something that has
seemed to him true. Some of Wilson's reportorial pieces, mainly
from the 1930's, which show how he uses fictional techniques to
illuminate facts are examined in this chapter, as well as three
"later" stories, which show how Wilson *uses* fiction.

I *Follies and Jitters*

In *The Shores of Light* Wilson has placed a factual account,
"The Road to Greenwich Village" (1925), with a story, *"Fire-
Alarm"* (1927), under one title, "Greenwich Village in the Early
Twenties." The point is that the fictional and factual pieces are
both authentic views of the same environment—the Village just
before it passed into commercialism. "The Road to Greenwich
Village," a small portrait of one of the Village residents in the
1920's, concerns a woman who escapes what seems to her the
provincial, bigoted, great West by coming East to find her freedom as the manager of a Village dress shop. The companion
piece, *"Fire-Alarm,"* is the story of an expressionist play written

[163]

in eighteen scenes and dealing with the nervous breakdown of a worker in a paper-box factory. The story satirizes the expressionist movement in drama, to which Wilson himself had contributed *Cronkhite's Clocks* (see Chapter 3) at the height of intellectual antagonism toward big business. The play itself is of course nonsense: "The next scene is a long soliloquy: the stars have come out in the sky, and the Man can see them through the paper box. They are red, yellow and green and are continually going on and off.... The Man apostrophizes the stars: 'Oh, little jazz-babies,' he says, 'oh, little jazz-babies, twinkling so bright as you dance the shimmy of the spheres! Oh, little jazz-babies, winking, with the mascara of night on your eyelashes!— look down on the great smoky city and tell me where my sweetie is!' This goes on for some time."

The actors are inadequate, the director knows nothing about directing, and rehearsals and performances are chaotic:

> There was one man who ran a book shop who was jealous of one of the actresses, a girl with whom he had been living and whom he had begun to suspect of an interest in one of the members of the cast. He would come and sit there every day, and sometimes conceal himself behind the scenes, where the actors would fall over him as they were making their exits. Bob Mott had a police-dog named Hindenburg, which he always brought to the theater with him and which barked at the fire-alarm and the scenes in which people were knocked around. There was also a Polish girl, who drank and was in love with Bob Mott. We used to hear her sobbing in the pauses.... One night, during the final scene, when the Professor took the hero by the arm and led him toward the dawn of Truth, the electric rhomboid, at the back of the stage, instead of bursting into brightness, merely gave a momentary glow and then began to grow fainter and fainter. When the Professor delivered his exhortation, "Come with me into the Light!", the stage was entirely dark.

On the final night, one member of the audience, "a strange rigid woman—a spinster of about forty-five ... dressed in hideous clothes of some remote age and place"—comes backstage after the performance to speak with the author. She has been extremely moved by the play, seeing it as a portrayal of Gibson, Colorado, where she suffered as a schoolteacher. *Fire-Alarm* triggers her own creativity. "That was my first meeting with Isabelle Griffin.

I did not know that she was eventually to become the first woman dramatist of importance in the history of the theater.... Today, one speaks of Isabelle Griffin and Strindberg" (*Shores*, 82, 86-7, 89-90).

Again in *The Shores of Light* Wilson groups two other pieces—one factual, one fictitious—to reveal "Greenwich Village at the End of the Twenties," when it had been spoiled as a haven for the poor poets and radical prophets. In "15 Beech Street" (1927), fiction, the narrator visits Jane Gooch, an old-time Village resident who has been struggling for some time to keep her little magazine *Vortex* in business. From their conversation one learns of the change: people have moved away, died, committed suicide, broken up with their old lovers, or turned respectable. "And they used to be ashamed of getting married!" Jane says (360). The narrator discovers that Ralph Davis, a poet whose address he wants, is now a writer for the magazine of a Detroit automobile firm.

The second half of this pair, "Hans Stengel" (1928), is about a painter and caricaturist who committed suicide. Stengel's art was harsh and "too serious" for New York publications; the *Masses* had died long ago, as had even the *Liberator*. Stengel had to do hack cartoon work, some of it so silly that he would not sign it. "It is always difficult, in a given case, to estimate how far a good artist may have been discouraged from doing his best by a lack of demand for his work." Stengel was a proud man, and at one of his own parties "he shut himself into the coat-closet, tied a rope to his neck and the doorknob and, pulling against it, strangled himself" (364-6).

Like "*Fire-Alarm*" and "The Road to Greenwich Village," these two pictures of the Village are at once similar and different. Both are "true"; both are alike in style and tone. But the first never actually happened—there was no Jane Gooch, no *Vortex* magazine—while the second did. Yet there were people like Jane and magazines like *Vortex*. In Wilson's writings the difference between fiction and fact is not that one is imagined and the other documented; it is that one is a general and the other a specific truth; that one deals with a type, the other with a particular. How Wilson attempted to make fiction out of actual events that were often the subjects for articles provides for an interesting life-art study. But even when he did not use the

events he reported for fiction—and he did not write much fiction—
he came to report in a "creative" way by using fictional techniques and thereby gaining a wider range of implication than
straight reporting could have achieved.

Wilson's early reporting, however, was mainly simple observations, sometimes humorous and satirical in tone, as in "Thoughts
on Leaving New York for New Orleans" (1926): "Young poets,
who cannot afford night clubs, are writing poems on the hollow-
ness of modern life. The Brevoort and the Lafayette are being
unattractively renovated in the style of the lavatory of the Pennsylvania Station. . . . Detectives and tarts in collusion are framing
victims in the upper Forties." But among these rapid impressions
are bits of a profounder social criticism, as in the following juxta-
position: "Young lawyers in the District Attorney's office are
forswearing the use of alcohol in order that they may act as
agents provocateurs in fashionable bootlegging nightclubs. Young
lawyers in private firms are protecting the interests of the Consolidated Gas Company" (*The American Earthquake*, 121-3).

By the time Wilson dealt with his greatest subject, the Depression, his reporting was changing from observation, description,
and comment to a more vivid and moving kind of reporting that
employed techniques of fiction: sharp contrasts, irony, detail selected to heighten the inherent drama, illumination of character,
and various unifying devices—most of all, the *overtones* of fiction,
the suggestion of the "flavor" and significance of history in events
that might be lost in a newspaper. One of the best examples of
this fictionalized reporting is "Detroit Motors," a long essay about
the Ford empire that includes interviews with workers and a
review of the books on Ford, as well as Wilson's firsthand impressions of the Dearborn plant. A thorough piece of reporting,
it takes on the color of fiction in the discussion of Ford himself—
a capricious tyrant, a mechanical genius, an "unlettered idealist,"
an extremely ignorant man. But, ironically, Ford finally appears
as a small-town boy who is bewildered by the gigantic Ford
interests which he started and who is protected by a publicity
department "to prevent him from making a fool of himself in
public" (*Earthquake*, 244). He is out of his element as the head
of a complex organization.

Wilson's account is moving because of the fictional technique
of overlaying the heavily documented portrayal of an industrial

tycoon with the fainter image of the rustic boy. Surprisingly, this slight fictionalization helps to explain the curious personality of Ford, permitting a more balanced picture than the one-sided version, marked by anger and contempt, in Dos Passos' novel, *The Big Money*, or than the satirical suggestion in Aldous Huxley's *Brave New World* of Ford, the god of a completely mechanized society.

"May First: The Empire State Building; Life on the Passaic River," another example of Wilson's creative reporting, appears to be an account of two different things; but closer examination shows that it not only has fictional overtones but a unity so natural that one scarcely notices it. The Empire State Building is formally opened on May 1, 1931, by Al Smith, president of the owning company. Wilson inspects it and duly notes the statistics: "'The building contains 10,000,000 bricks and weighs 600,000,000 pounds—distributed, however, so evenly that 'the weight on any given square inch is no greater than that normally borne by a French heel'" (*Earthquake*, 293). To Wilson, this engineering marvel is an ostentatious and superfluous triumph in the midst of a bankrupt society. From the fifty-fifth floor one can see New Jersey; there, in Buchanan on the Passaic River live a Yugoslavian immigrant named John Dravic and his family. Dravic has been laid off from his job in a carshop, so he borrows three hundred dollars to go into business for himself as the owner of a cigar and candy store. He is very fond of his three sons and teaches the older two to play the violin and cello. But, when his store fails, he shoots his children, including the baby, and then himself. The main unifying device is the grand and hazy view of Buchanan from the fifty-fifth floor of the Empire State Building, although even the ironic contrast (splendor-squalor) of the two scenes is a kind of unity. What the irony implies is outrage against a society that tolerates such an expensive structure to exist beside starving and despairing people.

But the reports on America in *Travels in Two Democracies* (1936) are still more fictionalized than those (from *The American Jitters* [1932]) already mentioned; the narration seems more detached, there is more "camera work." *Travels* opens with a prologue, "The Man in the Mirror" (1935). This short story in dialogue is set "almost anywhere in the world." As a prologue, it is obviously intended to apply to the two "democracies" of the title

—New Deal America and Soviet Russia. Its theme is suspicion
and fear—of being spied upon, of being turned in to the police,
of being punished for unknown acts of disloyalty to "the cause."
Everywhere is a spy, "the man in the soft gray hat." In a restau-
rant the main character, a world traveler, orders "jellied gulls'
lungs." He detests them, but they are a dish of that country
and will not arouse suspicion. A man and a woman sharing his
table bicker in "Blankville," a dialect they think unknown to him,
over a missing letter, accusing each other of being a spy or at
least a *provocateur*. Then they quarrel as to whether the man
eating the jellied gulls' lungs is a spy—or is the waiter a spy?
But "the man in the soft gray hat" turns out to be only one's
reflection in the mirror, although the traveler does not realize
this. This little portrayal of self-suspicion is Wilson's comment
on the world of 1935, when he was disillusioned with the United
States of the Depression and with Russia under a dictatorship
worse than that of the Czars.

The thirteen sketches which follow "The Man in the Mirror"
show American life from a humane and rational position.
Delmore Schwartz called Wilson's outlook a "fundamental decency," a cliché which he deliberately used because he thought
it best described the "sensibility and honesty" which make *Jitters*
and *Travels* "far more than journalism" ("The Writing of Edmund
Wilson"). The political outlook is progressive—indeed, Marxist,
but anti-Stalin. In general, however, the events speak for themselves as Wilson selects and delineates them.

His glance in *Travels* is directed toward situations involving
both ordinary and famous people. "Election Night," the first
tableau, is simply the carping of a man in an unpretentious res-
taurant on election night in 1932: "Walker or O'Brien—O'Brien or
Walker! Turn the bums out—put more bums in!" (*Travels*, 11).
Never once during these rantings does Wilson intrude with his
own view. In part he must agree with him; but the man—ignorant
and unreasonable, as well as drunkenly perceptive—then rants
against women and Sacco and Vanzetti.

The last of the thirteen, "Japanese Cherry Blossoms," concerns
the Washington Cherry Blossom Festival in May, 1934. A representative of the Women's International League for Peace and
Freedom wants to make the parade "a gesture of friendliness
toward Japan." But the Parade Committee chairman and parade

leader is "a certain Major-General Fries," who says that a float with American and Japanese children and banners for peace "would amount to propaganda for peace." The parade "included, among the chiffon and pretty faces, thirty-four units of horse-drawn artillery, thirty-six units of motor-drawn artillery, a battalion of the regular army unit of the Third Cavalry and men from every other military unit in Washington. And among the floats was one of Commodore Perry arriving in Uraga Bay with his gunboats; and another which showed the development of the rifle" (112). Wilson's ironic "camera" makes commentary unnecessary.

Indeed, in "Shaw at the Metropolitan" (1933), the narrative technique is in part consciously that of the motion picture camera, which focuses on the austerely elegant Bernard Shaw, white whiskers against pink skin, widens its lens to include the dignitaries on the platform behind him, and then pans over the audience: "thousands and thousands of people who have bought seats to a show at the Metropolitan." First there are the members of the Academy of Political Science ("old ladies and old gentlemen in evening clothes"), which is sponsoring Shaw's lecture. Most of the rest are "the eerie half-human attendants at anything that is new on Broadway—the dead-pans of the Theatre Guild openings. They never laugh and they never applaud—they never seem to know what the play is about—if they ever respond at all, it is only to grumble a little when it is over. They have turned out tonight to see Shaw with the same simple phototropic instinct which draws them to the other entertainments by which they never seem to be entertained. . . . Before this awful tribunal of trolls, then, more dismaying because they never pass sentence—poor Bernard Shaw appeared" (51-2). Finally, way up in the gallery, beyond the camera's eye in the dollar seats, are the radicals—the only ones who really understand and want to hear what Shaw has to say.

Wilson's subject is not Shaw's speech but the strained relationship between the speaker and his audience. At first surprised and even "driven to comment on the silence which followed his most emphatic points," Shaw gradually becomes aware that only those in the dollar seats care about what he is saying and that the deadness in the five-dollar seats is that of well-fed people who have never bothered about Karl Marx and are blank at the name of Henry George. Apparently Shaw supposed the Academy of Political Science to be "a serious and alert organization," and he navigates with difficulty between the larger uncomprehending and the smaller enthusiastic segments of his audience. Wilson concludes that the ambiguity of the occasion is Shaw's own: he has allowed himself to become a "favorite public character."[1]

In "Sunshine Charley" (1933), Wilson contrasts Charley Mitchell as an emperor of the Boom to the man on trial for income tax evasion. He "looks cheap in court," but just a few years earlier he was the super-broker who hounded his salesmen to sell fifteen billion dollars of securities in ten years; he headed the National City Company, which was legally distinct from, but actually a subsidiary of, the National City Bank, and whose purpose was to sell securities which the bank was prohibited from selling. In the courtroom of 1933, "ledgers, suitcases, crammed briefcases, are all that is left of those days.... The great salesman of salesmen is washed up, and the two Jewish lawyers fight over him":

> The perfect type of the big executive of the cigarette and success-course advertisements undergoes a degradation. Confronting the lawyers with his blue suit, his robust torso and grizzled crest, with his scowling brows of power and his forceful nose joined by coarse lines to his wide and common mouth, he throws out his hands in stock gestures of frankness and exposition, making things clear weakly; tries to put over points with a finger that no longer carries conviction; breaks down in the middle of sentences, frowning helplessly, his mouth hanging open. In reply to questions featured by his attorney, "I did!" "I certainly did!" he declares with the ham dramatic emphasis of a movie actor playing the role of a big executive. (58-60)

Wilson's account of this trial is reminiscent of H. L. Mencken's account of the Scopes "Monkey Trial" ("In Memoriam: W. J. B.") —as, indeed, is much of Wilson's reporting. But Wilson is kinder in portraying Mitchell, whom he loathes, than Mencken was with prosecuting attorney William Jennings Bryan. In general, Wilson's reporting is less partial, less sarcastic, and less trenchant than Mencken's; the reporting of both is full of sharp observations. What most annoys Wilson about Charley Mitchell is not the man himself but the labors of the "prosperity writers these many years ... to build up Charley Mitchell as a respectable public figure. And they are still at it. . . ." These reporters "provide him with a firmness of front which he certainly did not display when I saw him"; they describe his testimony as "melting" and himself as a "tragically mistaken leader" (61-2).

This little essay with its restraint and its rather formal presentation of contrasts is much like fiction in its suggestion of a vast social illness behind poor wriggling Charley—"the mania of the public to believe in him." Wilson uses the image of the sea monster, which he got from William Beebe's account of South Sea diving, to suggest that the American business-tycoon-monster was, after all, the result of his environment: ". . . the climate and soil of the boom . . . nurtured this being and his fellows. So the eyes of the fishes of the dark ocean depths become eventually atrophied and blind, so they learn to excrete their luminous mucus; so dwelling below the level where a diet of plants is possible, they develop their valise-like carnivorous jaws" (61).

Perhaps the most lingering impressions from the American half of *Travels* are of the quick, graphic portrayals of poverty and strife. For example, "Hull House in 1932" concerns Chicago, particularly the area just south and west of the Loop. The settlement house, an old Victorian mansion owned by Jane Addams, philanthropist and labor agitator, is one of the cheerier aspects of the Depression in Chicago. But the reader moves from Hull House to sights of increasing horror: to people with nothing to eat living in little apartments on South Halsted; to overcrowded, stinking flophouses occupied by men without work, where the disease underlying all others is starvation—even hoboes do much better by stealing and begging.

From the shelters one is taken to the Angelus Building on South Wabash; during the World's Fair of 1892, it was the popular Ozark Hotel, but now it houses sixty-seven Negro families in its seven stories, the top two of which have been condemned. Toilets won't flush, bathtubs won't drain; there is no heat; no one can afford electricity; and, of course, the inhabitants are starving. But even this place is better than the "Hoovervilles," where people live in tarpaper shacks, if they are lucky, or in packing boxes and old car bodies. Wilson finishes the picture with a nauseating, two-page description of people ferreting out things to eat in garbage dumps and dining on chicken-claw soup and maggoty meat.

"Hull House" is included in this discussion not as a fictional-ized piece, but as an example of Wilson's straight reporting. It is much like an objective documentary film. If it exploits an artistic technique at all, it is the downward progression from one scene of misery to a worse one, something like a Naturalistic drama. Nor is there anything suggestive about it—it simply registers a terrible situation in one city and the author's not entirely re-strained shock at beholding it. There are moments in writing when nothing is so effective as the relentless accretion of data, and "Hull House" is quite successful.

But all of the thirteen pieces are told differently, and "Illinois Household" (1933), like dramatic fiction, is told in the dialogue of the people it portrays. This sketch is the story of the organiz-ing in 1933 of the Progressive Miners of America. Coal miners in Illinois who demand better working conditions and better pay are set upon by small-town thugs, police, business men, and coal-company "goons." But they manage to organize anyway, only to be harassed by John L. Lewis' United Mine Workers, sheriffs, and National Guardsmen. The Progressives detest Lewis, who, they feel, has his own rather than the miners' interests at heart. The events are narrated by an actual mining family, including the miner, his wife, and, from time to time, their eleven-year-old son:

They had baseball bats and billiard cues and clubs! They smashed the headlights and the windshields, and they'd reach in and club people's arms. The people left the cars and ran to the farmhouses—and they turned the machine-guns on the fields to keep them back. They could see the machine-gun fire mowing down the corn and there was a panic.—The people in the houses just about went insane—they were afraid to go out. They just sat inside and heard it over the radio! Some of the men got shotguns and wanted to go out to fight, but they couldn't get enough cour-age to go up against the machine-guns.—People couldn't eat for a week, they were so sick. There was blood all over the concrete —and food all alongside of the road!—loaves of bread hanging on the fenceposts!—those crazy hoodlums had come down there and stamped on the tomatoes and things! (33)

The point of this account is simply to show the lawlessness, in-justice, lack of legal protection, and downright danger for Pro-gressive Miners in Illinois. But what makes the point so telling—aside from the details—is the quiet, colloquial, unhurried narrative. Only the boy seems to raise his voice, and Wilson's own silence conveys the sensation of shock.

These examples clearly indicate Wilson's attention to form. It is impossible to read such articles without a sense of indignation and a desire to do something about the wrongs, and this involvement could not occur thirty-five years afterward were it not for the skillful arrangement of material—the way a situation is "staged" for the reader or is discussed by those who are part of it.

One more reportorial piece which deserves mention is "Inaugural Parade" (1933), Wilson's account of the parade for Franklin D. Roosevelt, which ominously takes place while banks are closing across the nation. "Everything is gray today," the account begins. This time a narrator, Wilson himself, describes and interprets everything for the reader. "The people seem dreary," he says as he waits in front of the Capitol, "and they are curiously apathetic." Even Roosevelt's speech seems gray, "the echoes of Woodrow Wilson's eloquence without Wilson's exaltation behind them . . . . professions of plain-speaking followed by the old abstractions. . . . There is a warning, itself rather vague, of a possible dictatorship" (43-5).

The parade itself is stupid and tawdry. "Roosevelt smiles his smug public smile. . . ." "Chief of Staff, General Douglas Mac Arthur, who drove the veterans out of Washington last summer. . . Negroes in khaki, always with a white officer at their head. . . ." The parade continues in the gray cold for three hours more, degenerating with every passing group to a circus: "The fairy drum major . . . is followed immediately by Governor Ritchie, who looks like a silk-hatted Mr. Woodchuck out of one of Thornton Burgess's Bedtime Stories . . . and you expect to see the automobile go off with a blaze and a bang, and the silk hats tumbling in the arena." "The National Indian War Veterans are old men in a big green bus." The American Legion Posts wear "bright blue coats and canary-yellow trench helmets." "Are these the implacable guardians of Americanism?" (46-7).

Then "the spectacle becomes phantasmagoric" as the lodges pass—"in curled-up shoes and fezzes . . . in hideous greens, purples and reds. . . . A very large loose old Negro in a purple fez and yellow-edged cloak, carrying the prong of an antler as if it were the Golden Bough. . . . The Spirit of '76 have all the appearance of being cockeyed: one of the trio is always getting behind and then running to catch up with the others." The parade goes on and on: the New York Police Band and Tammany politicians (these two more dignified than any other group); Al Smith, Tom Mix, and the Hollywood contingent on a "Better Times Float"; and still more absurd marching clubs. Finally, "a small group from the Virgin Islands, soberly uniformed and quietly behaved, and a float of chilly-looking trained nurses, incongruously end the procession" (47-9).

By now, of course, the reader is in a mood to believe the narrator as he concludes: "If the parade went on any longer, it would be too dark to see, too cold to stay out. And you are glad when it is over, anyway. The America it represented has burst, and as you watched the marchers, you realized that it had been getting sillier and sillier all the time." Then, the final sentence: "The America of the boom definitely died today, and this is the ghost it just gave up" (49).[2]

Regarding the sickness of the early 1930's, Wilson has written in his foreword to *The American Earthquake*: "how difficult it is for persons who were born too late to have memories of the depression to believe that it really occurred, that between 1929 and 1933 the whole structure of American society seemed actually to be going to pieces." This theme of breakdown or illness also characterizes the one piece of fiction among the thirteen. "What To Do Till the Doctor Comes" (1934) is a breathlessly told first-person narrative concerning a pointless, frantic round of drinking bouts, full of sudden misunderstandings and rages, mad fondlings in taxicabs, irrational blubberings, and so on. It is reminiscent of Carl Van Vechten's *Parties* (1930), but the life it represents is even more futile than that portrayed in *Parties*, for these people are not pursuing even pleasure.

What the thirteen New Deal pieces mainly comprise are fictionalized facts—facts presented in part by fictional techniques. Carried far enough, as in "What To Do Till the Doctor Comes," they become factualized fiction: what has previously been referred to as the truth generalized, so that the people and events are drawn from life but also enlarged and made to seem typical of the time. To Wilson, a factual and a fictional account are opposite aspects of the same reality, or idea, or meaning—opposite approaches to the same thing.

Perhaps it would be clearer to classify this kind of fiction under the term "anatomy," Northrop Frye's name for literature that deals more with mental attitudes and types than with individual people—the kind of literature that comprises satire, fantasy, utopian visions, the novel of ideas, and the proletarian novel of the 1930's—that views the world in terms of an intellectual pattern in contrast to both the "confession" and the "romance" (*Anatomy of Criticism*, 309). Wilson's "social" or "public" fiction, like his criticism, is concerned with recognizing and trying to do something about problems that affect many people in real life. It allows Wilson not only to comment on his environment but to moralize about it.

There are several disadvantages to the kind of fiction that deals mainly with public issues. It risks being inadequately imagined and becoming propaganda. It usually does not allow the reader to withdraw from patterned attitudes (often conventional moral categories) and to behold the subject in a new and personal way. Philip Roth in "Writing About Jews" speaks eloquently on this point. After the publication of *Goodbye, Columbus*, Roth came under attack in the synagogues and in letters to the Anti-Defamation League for allegedly showing the Jew in a bad light. He replied, in part:

> And generally speaking, what draws most readers and writers to literature is this "something more"—all that is beyond simple moral categorizing. It is not my purpose in writing a story of an adulterous man to make it clear how right we all are if we disapprove of the act and are disappointed in the man. *Fiction is not written to affirm the principles and beliefs that everybody seems to hold, nor does it seek to guarantee us of the appropriateness of our feelings. The world of fiction, in fact, frees us from the circumscriptions that the society places upon feeling; one of the greatnesses of the art is that it allows both the writer and the reader to respond to experience in ways not always available in day-to-day conduct.* . . . Ceasing for a while to be upright citizens, we drop into another layer of consciousness. (*Commentary* [December, 1963], 446-7, italics added.)

What Roth says seems similar to what Edmund Wilson, in "Marxism and Literature," calls "a complex vision of things [in] works of the highest order." But one should point out that the writer of social fiction willingly gives up the advantage of which Roth speaks because he wants to share common attitudes with his readers in order to sway them to his point of view; he *aims* at persuasion. It should also be noted that Wilson is nevertheless concerned with portraying characters as having problems of their own. Furthermore, there is no good reason to believe of Wilson's fiction that the author himself is the observer, at least not more than partly; in his mature fiction he allows his narrators the freedom to be characters.

Wilson's social fiction is like his fictionalized reporting in that it presents social situations with a definite attitude, but it differs from his reporting in that the facts are generalized and thereby to some extent disguised. The reader should not think that the events literally happened, but that they represent events that did. The story is a generalization of an experience that, if it is not itself a common one, stands for a common one.

II *Three Later Stories*

"Lieutenant Franklin" is called a "flashback," and it appears as a sort of punctuation mark between the American and Russian sections of *Travels*.[3] The action, which takes place in Germany just after the 1919 Armistice, concerns a lieutenant who has been assigned as a censor in a German town with three other American officers. He knows no German, only French; but this lack is not supposed to matter. But after he urges leniency for the editor of a German newspaper who ran an anti-British editorial and was consequently suspended from publishing for ten days, his commanding officer has him transferred to another town on the grounds that he doesn't know German. At Trèves on the Moselle River he is assigned the role of assistant district defense commander, but there is nothing for him to do. He lives in the household of the burgomaster and becomes friendly with the Germans, which he has been warned against doing. Eventually, he is sent back to France for fraternizing.

This story presents a moral dilemma: to whom should Lieutenant Franklin be loyal? As a victor, he is officially expected to hate the Germans and to side always with the French in the continual bickering. But he is uncomfortable: he has nothing against the Germans; and, after all, the war is over. His superior, Captain Scudder, who has little use for either Germans or French, points out to him that an armistice is not officially the end of a war; it is Scudder, apparently, who files an intelligence report against Franklin and who is promoted to major. The social or public side of the story is the problem of how to treat a fallen enemy. The "personal" side, with its emphasis on revealing character, is Franklin's obeying his conscience and defying his military role to remain decent and fair. But this private struggle remains fairly undeveloped because he acts almost automatically.

A story which develops the social and personal themes more thoroughly and combines them more dramatically appears in *Europe Without Baedeker* (1947). Bearing the unpromising title of "Through the Abruzzi with Mattie and Harriet," it apparently is so closely based on fact that Wilson felt obliged to apologize in the preface "for the roles that my characters are made to play" and to indicate that he had tried "to create a *typical situation*" [italics added]. Mattie Nugent, an American, and her superior, Harriet Locker, English, are field workers for the United Nations Relief and Rehabilitation Administration (UNRRA) shortly after World War II. Their job is to see that food and clothing are properly distributed among the destitute people in the bombed-out villages of the Abruzzi region of Italy. Working against them is the black market, which bribes local officials to obtain supplies intended for the poor. Mattie, new to her work, takes a great interest in the people and culture of Italy: she practices her Italian, enjoys looking at churches, and to some extent comes to know the Italians among whom she works. Harriet, on the contrary, takes no interest in Italy beyond what is required by her duty. Hardened to suffering, she is an efficient, practical overseer of the dole. Yet her lack of zeal also becomes a lack of thoroughness: she cannot be bothered to stay and see that the mayor of a little town distributes all of the goods; if a pair of scales won't balance, she doesn't concern herself with correcting it.

Gradually the two women become more and more opposed to each other. Mattie thinks that the dole cannot really solve the problems of the Italians; she thinks they need assistance in rebuilding, and, above all, their own democratic government to allow them self-respect. To her, the Allied Command is just another dictatorship. Harriet, on the contrary, says that the Italians are precious lucky to get anything and that a conquered people do not deserve self-government.

These differing views lead to an open rift at Pescara on the Adriatic. Mattie meets two Italians who work for ten cents a day finding and neutralizing land mines. Their old-fashioned American mine detector finds only those mines made of metal and not those of wood or bakelite. They describe the most dangerous kind of mine, which detonates twice: the first charge lifts the device into the air; the second, more powerful, kills in a wide radius. The women are leaving Pescara in their jeep to return to Aquila, their home base, when they hear a dull thud followed by an unmistakable blast: " 'I hope that isn't those boys!' said Mattie. 'There'd be nothing we could do,' said Harriet. But Mattie was deeply disturbed: 'I think we ought to stop and make sure, though!' 'The nuns would be able to look after them. They must be prepared for accidents. They have a hospital in the convent.' 'If you don't mind, I'd like to go back and see. There might be *something* we could do, and we wouldn't want to—' Harriet cut her off: 'I don't think we've got time, you know—we have to make another stop' " (153).

Shortly after this incident, Harriet tells Mattie to stay in Aquila while she goes out to do the field-work herself. Mattie complains to the American major at the hotel, but he avoids taking her side because things are a little "sticky" between the Americans and the British, and he is there "to promote cordial relations." Moreover, it really won't do for her to give the impression that she is what the British call a "Bolshie." Besides, he is outranked by a British colonel who recently moved into the hotel; and he has, indeed, adopted many British mannerisms. When Mattie carries the battle to the colonel, she cannot shake his imperturbable condescension: " 'As for the Eye-tyes,' the Colonel pronounced, 'I think they deuced well get more than they deserve when we send them such charming young ladies to minister to their needs!' " (157). The story ends with the major's leaving Mattie alone at the bar and joining the colonel and two other British officers, who need a fourth at bridge.

"Abruzzi" is a good short story, one of Wilson's best. The characterization both of individuals and types is distinct in dialogue and action. The accumulation of differences between the two women is well timed. Also, the haranguing which marred Wilson's earlier fiction is completely absent—an improvement partly due to his use of the third-person narrator, as in "Lieutenant Franklin," although the point of view is of course Mattie's and her attitude becomes increasingly anti-British. Finally, the environment is graphically described, and the sense of destruction is inescapable.

Wilson's greatest achievement in this story is the combination of social and personal themes. On the one hand, there is the actual problem immediately following World War II of aiding people who, officially at least, were enemies. What is the "decent thing" to do with the vanquished? How should aid be administered? How can the black market be stopped? How can the allies stay on good terms with each other and share authority?

Closely joined to these things are Mattie's private problems. She has a clear duty, and she must cooperate with others in doing it. Yet she is increasingly tormented by the feeling that it is all wrong, that it really works toward no good end. The starving and abject people who need food *and* self-respect are not merely Italians but fellow human beings not wholly responsible for their plight. The Fascist government they had helped to power had in some ways benefited them. Had not Mussolini built schools, roads, hospitals? What point is there in humiliating the enemy after he has been defeated? Worst of all for Mattie is the gnashing futility that she encounters when, in her subordinate role, she runs against the established administration. When everyone upholds official policy, or is at least too discreet and cowardly to oppose it, there is nothing that one person can do, especially when she is just another pretty girl—a bitter lesson for an intelligent, impulsive, good-natured idealist. Her relationship with Harriet, who is as true to her principles as Mattie is to hers, is a subtler theme. Mattie rather likes Harriet; she admires her ability, her dauntlessness; she would like to know her better. Yet the disagreement between them can only widen.

"Through the Abruzzi" is also superior fiction because Wilson was not only familiar with, but unusually sensitive to, the postwar problems of Italy in general and those of the UNRRA in particular. By contrast, his most recently published short story, "The Messiah at the Seder" (in *A Piece of My Mind*), is interesting but not compelling—perhaps because Wilson does not really see the problem it presents from the "inside."

Eight Jews celebrating the Seder with a traditional dinner on the first evening of the Passover are visited by the Messiah and his prophet Elijah. The Messiah is a contemporary Jew, a nuclear physicist in a business suit; Elijah has been lent him from the Old Testament. Visiting all Seder celebrants in New York City simultaneously, the Messiah announces that he has come at last; that they should all prepare to leave for Israel, where he will establish his kingdom; and that the Arabs will be painlessly killed by "a simple vibration" to make more room for the Jews. Although their first impulse is to regard him as a fake, the Jews give him a hearing and are, indeed, enthusiastic. But gradually they quarrel with him and one another as to who will be redeemed and who not—can a Marxist Jew be redeemed?—what about a Freudian? Freud and Marx, after all, were Jewish prophets. Then they have not imagined that the Messiah would look like an ordinary Jew. And who is this Elijah?—somebody from the Yiddish stage?

When the Messiah awakens from his trance the next morning, he painfully realizes that every Jew found something objectionable about him or Elijah and rejected him—and after he had given up his profession for the Cause! He takes up the problem with the Lord, who does not know what to make of it: "I am no longer quite omniscient, as I used to be." The Messiah complains that the Jews never could agree: "They're getting to be just like the Protestants—they believe in themselves, not you. Yet they got it out of our Bible. . . ." The Messiah becomes indignant when the Lord tells him that He's going to spare the Arabs because killing them would simply convince the Jews "that the Middle East is a dangerous place to live"; besides, He feels a little sorry for the Arabs and is somewhat annoyed by the Messiah's presumption. "Go back to your old work," He finally tells him. "Go on raising money for Israel. Maybe some good will come of it" (*A Piece of My Mind*, 133-5).

Certainly this story reveals knowledge of the contemporary Jew and of what is often his perhaps ambivalent attitude toward Judaism: not really taking it seriously as a religion, he nevertheless maintains the old customs; comfortably placed in American life, he nourishes pride in the idea of a homeland. Although Wilson has been much interested in Jewish culture and has "acquired a little Hebrew" (88), it is impossible for him to see Jewish life from the inside, as, for example, Philip Roth can. "Messiah" therefore lacks the closeness of good fiction and is only a sort of narrative essay. This characteristic is most noticeable at the beginning, where for six pages Wilson ploddingly describes the dinner, noting the tradition behind each dish. Then the dialectic of the Jews and the Messiah and, later, of the Messiah and the Lord becomes informative and even entertaining without ever evoking how it feels to be a Jew. Incidentally, the lesson underlying the story is that the Jews should stop regarding themselves as a "chosen people" and should concern themselves with a brotherhood of peoples.

As this chapter has attempted to show, Wilson employs techniques of fiction in a number of his social documentaries. In "May First" he uses irony as a *structural* device as well as a non-fictional means of commenting on the incongruity of splendor-and-despair. In "Detroit Motors" he uses it dramatically to help reveal the remarkably inconsistent character of Henry Ford. Some of his other fictional devices are a camera-like objectivity ("Shaw at the Metropolitan"), dialogue ("Illinois Household"), illumination of character ("Sunshine Charley"), selected detail to heighten the foolishness of an inaugural parade against a national background of moral and economic sickness ("Washington: Inaugural Parade"), and the metaphor of a sea monster to suggest a social and political environment conducive to the breeding of financial monsters ("Sunshine Charley").

What he achieves in his reporting by the use of fictional techniques is vividness and immediacy while yet preserving a valid social documentation. For Wilson, an event is never just an event, but a statement of the moral and economic welfare of his society. Fictional devices make the statement more compelling, and the reader attends more carefully. However, when Wilson moves from fictional reporting to plain social fiction, he can perhaps more completely involve the reader in the subject: this is the main justification for writing fiction where an essay would serve. Furthermore, fiction allows him to generalize from facts and thus to interpret freely his subject, which in two of the three stories just discussed is the responsibility of the victor among the vanquished.

An appropriate way to approach Wilson's later fiction, then, is by means of social and personal themes—by noting the large public issues which cause or contribute to the protagonist's own dilemma. Of the three later stories, "Through the Abruzzi" most successfully unites these two themes. It combines the international problem of the proper attitude toward a fallen enemy and the private problem of an individual's attempt to act humanely and rationally in the face of an international bureaucracy. Although Wilson's social fiction sometimes fails because, as in "The Messiah," it is insufficiently realized, it offers an interesting study of how fact can be generalized into fiction.

III *Conclusion*

To estimate how a writer will be remembered is always difficult because the preferences of a literary public are no more predictable than those of any other public. It is easier to observe that Wilson has produced four excellent books—more than one man's share—three of which have been considered in this monograph: *Memoirs of Hecate County,* one of the few worthwhile works of fiction from the 1940's; *Patriotic Gore,* an outstanding example of biography and cultural history; and *The American Earthquake,* a fine collection of little documents on American life during the upheaval of the 1920's and 1930's which linger like good fiction in the mind's eye. With these must be included another brilliant biography and intellectual history, *To the Finland Station,* now considered a classic study of the development of Marxism. In the second rank—not so thoroughly satisfying—are *Axel's Castle,* the pioneer analysis of the Symbolistic revolution; the three literary chronicles from the 1920's to the 1960's, *The Shores of Light, Classics and Commercials,* and *The Bit Between My Teeth;* the very good and, I think, neglected survey of contemporary Canadian culture, *O Canada;* and the essays on Dickens, Kipling, Hemingway, *Finnegans Wake,* Pushkin, Chapman, Shaw, and "Mr. Rolfe" in *The Wound and the Bow* and *The Triple Thinkers,* as well as several autobiographical essays.

These and his other works are all a kind of reporting, for Wilson is pre-eminently the intelligent, humane observer. As Richard Gilman wrote in the essay cited in Chapter 2, Wilson came to the literary situation after World War I "eager, erudite, with piety for the cultural past but also with an appetite for the new"—surely prerequisites for a self-taught course in literary reporting. Add to his gift for thoughtful observation his talents for summarizing, analyzing, and clear prose writing (which his early "infatuation" with Flaubert did not intimidate), and one recognizes what a very good critical reporter Wilson is.

But, to a large extent, Wilson observes the facts with a mind made up, with an intelligence that shares, more than the younger Wilson would ever have admitted but which his writings again and again admit for him, the Humanist values of Irving Babbitt and Paul Elmer More, as well as those of his teacher Christian Gauss—the "fundamental decency" noted by Delmore Schwartz. Ironically, his moral sense betrayed him as a literary critic. For one thing, as Gilman indicated, "the primness of his imagination" kept him from taking the measure of "the really disturbing and aberrant writers of our time." For another, Wilson, in whom, like Kipling, there has always been a bit of the preacher, has apparently never been content simply to criticize. The ultimate justification for criticism is the pleasure—in continual oscillation with the primary response to a work of art—of analyzing the work's effect, of determining how it makes its impression. But for Wilson this task is not enough: he always needs to make a social or moral application. Concerned more with what literature should do for life ("a critic," according to Gilman, "who for a very long time has not really criticized"), Wilson has avoided as "academic" esthetic questions, skirting the work of art itself to confront on its periphery thinkers and moralists.

When, despite his belief in mastering "new combinations of elements," he could not view contemporary literature as "an attempt to give a meaning to our experience"—as, indeed, he could not wholly do even as early as *Axel's Castle*, which deplores the artist's tendency toward isolation and social irresponsibility— Wilson was left with connoisseurship, research, and journalism. In 1929 he wrote to Gauss "the diet of symbolism, early and recent, which I have lately been consuming, has had the effect in the long run of wearying and disgusting me with this kind of subjective literature" (*The Papers of Christian Gauss*, 259). It is no wonder that the writer whose hope for literature has been its lessons and whose fictional protagonists try so hard to do something about their world should be disappointed and bored with so much new fiction, solipsistic or not; just as it is not surprising that his belief in "the victory of the human intellect" should strengthen with age as he ponders such topics as the Dead Sea Scrolls, the

Russian language, the Iroquois Indians, or the despotism of big government. And yet how can his late pedantry concerning correct English usage be explained? Do such pieces as "Current Clichés and Solecisms" and "More Notes on Current Clichés" in *The Bit Between My Teeth* represent merely an old man's crankiness? Is his fussy preoccupation with correct expression something that he can be absolutely right about and can therefore hold on to?—the last refuge of the man of letters? Or does it, like a similar irritation in the late James Thurber, express the bitterness of other things?

It is difficult, then, to precisely determine Wilson's contribution to criticism, just as it would be difficult to say exactly what he has contributed to the long tradition of travel literature, in which he is also superior. He is not as fine a scholar-critic as Wellek, Frye, Ransom, and Warren, mentioned in the Preface; nor perhaps as several others of his generation, notably Erich Auerbach. But as a public critic in Frye's sense of the term (Chapter 2), he has no peer: W. H. Auden writes as well, but does not match the tremendous concentration of Wilson as he turns a subject that really interests him over and over again; nor did T. S. Eliot, who was one of the best public critics. Except when his work is damaged by a psychobiographical theory or becomes ponderous, Wilson provides a common-sense approach to literature which has earned him the silent gratitude of many a graduate student and teacher. The serious reader returns to Wilson for fresh air when the atmosphere of theoretical and academic critics either thins out or becomes stale. But the common-sense approach is ultimately unsatisfactory to the serious student, who learns that to view literature as an attempt at making experience meaningful is not to see it wholly.

In biography and intellectual history his contribution is more readily summarized. For anyone interested in Western culture from the late eighteenth to the early twentieth century, *To the Finland Station, Patriotic Gore*, and *Axel's Castle* have "caught" many of the leading thinkers and literary artists. Likewise, Wilson's "chronicles" and "notes" have provided a valuable record of literary activity in twentieth-century America and Canada, especially from 1920 to 1950. But he deserves to be as well remembered for a different kind of cultural history in his succinct, powerful pieces on American common life during the Boom, the

Slump, and the New Deal. In 1927 he wrote to Gauss, "What should be done about America?"—and, in 1931, "I think that the world is in a pretty bad way, don't you?" In 1932 Gauss, having read *The American Jitters* with complete satisfaction, in effect answered these questions when he wrote to Wilson an evaluation that I believe will stand (*The Papers of Christian Gauss*, 247, 275, 283): "You certainly are doing the future a service in spreading the sense of the problem. . . . . I don't know any book that has done this more tellingly than you have by your realistic presentments. You have made them all so simply reasonably human. . . . . You have etched any number of actors in the drama to the life."

Notes and References

Chapter One

1. Wilson, " 'Mr. Rolfe,' " *The Triple Thinkers* (New York, 1948), pp. 248-49. For information on Wilson's early and uncollected writings, I am indebted to Arthur Mizener's bibliography, "Edmund Wilson: A Checklist," *Princeton University Library Chronicle*, V (February, 1944), 62-78; and also to Wilson's own reminiscence, *A Prelude: Landscapes, Characters, and Conversations from the Earlier Years of My Life*, I, *New Yorker*, XLIII (April 29, 1967), 50-131. *A Prelude* also suggests the originals for some of Wilson's fictional figures, such as the Streetfields in *The Crime in the Whistler Room* and the protagonists in "Lieutenant Franklin" and "Glimpses of Wilbur Flick."

2. Gauss, "Edmund Wilson, the Campus and the Nassau 'Lit,' " *Princeton University Library Chronicle*, V (February, 1944), 46. See also William Goldhurst, *F. Scott Fitzgerald and His Contemporaries* (Cleveland and New York, 1963), pp. 43-73. On Wilson's contributions to the *Lit*, see Sherman Paul, *Edmund Wilson* (Urbana, 1965), pp. 16-19.

3. Wilson then and later was not enthusiastic over sociology as a formal course of study. See *A Prelude*, III, *New Yorker*, XLIII (May 13, 1967), 150.

4. *Devil Take the Hindmost* (London, 1932) is the English edition of *The American Jitters* (New York, 1932); most of this book was later included in *The American Earthquake* (New York, 1958). For Wilson's feelings on his own generation before World War I, see the first part of *A Prelude, New Yorker*, April 29, 1967, which is haunted by the motif of brilliant young friends who later did not succeed. For further information on Wilson's experiences in the army, see the third part of *A Prelude*, May 13, 1967.

5. "The Old Stone House" was first published in *Scribner's Magazine*, December, 1933, pp. 368-72. *Travels in Two Democracies* was published in New York in 1936.

6. "At Laurelwood" first appeared as "A New Jersey Childhood: 'These Men Must Do Their Duty!' " *New Yorker*, XV (November 18, 1939), 65-72. *Wilson's Night Thoughts* was published in New York in 1961.

7. On the change in American life from 1870-1910, see Norman Podhoretz, "Edmund Wilson: Then and Now," *Doings and Undoings*

(New York, 1964), pp. 30-32. See also one of Wilson's finest biographical essays, "John J. Chapman: The Mute and the Open Strings," *The Triple Thinkers*, pp. 133-64, which was based on M. A. DeWolfe Howe's *John Jay Chapman and His Letters* (Boston and New York, 1937).

8. See "Newton Arvin's *Longfellow*," *The Bit Between My Teeth* (New York, 1965), pp. 552-55.

9. Edel, " 'Am I, Then, in a Pocket of the Past?' " *New Republic*, CXXXV (December 17, 1956), 25-26.

10. Geismar, "Apostles of the Rational Mind," *Nation*, CLXXXIII (December 8, 1956), 502-3.

11. Frederick C. Crews, "Lessons of the Master," *New York Review of Books*, V (November 25, 1965), 5.

12. "We Don't Know Where We Are" (interview by Henry Brandon), *New Republic*, CXL (March 30, 1959), 14.

13. See V. J. Jerome, "Edmund Wilson: To the Munich Station," *New Masses*, XXXI (April 4, 1939), 23 ff. During this period, Dorothy Parker, among others, supplied *New Masses* with anti-fascist sentiment tinged with hysteria: "I don't feel funny any more. I don't think these are funny times, and I don't think Franco is funny" ("Not Enough," March 14, 1939, p. 4).

14. Hicks, "The Intransigence of Edmund Wilson," *Antioch Review* (Winter, 1946-47), p. 554.

15. Aaron, *Writers on the Left* (New York, 1961), p. 182. Mr. Aaron's book is the most informative account of leftist American writers. Two other useful works are Murray Kempton's *Part of Our Time* (New York, 1955) and Walter B. Rideout's *The Radical Novel in the United States, 1900-1954* (Cambridge, 1956).

16. Gilman, "The Critic as Taxpayer," *New Republic*, CXLIX (November 30, 1963), 25.

17. "Wilson v. the U.S.," *Time*, LXXXII (December 6, 1963), 124-27.

18. Epstein, "Wilson's Amerika," *New York Review of Books*, I (November 28, 1963), 9-11.

19. Sheed, "Mr. Wilson and the Cold War," *Commonweal*, LXXIX (January 10, 1964), 434-35.

20. Bazelon, "Some Deductions," *Commentary*, XXXVIII (August, 1964), 67-68.

21. See "The Old Stone House," *Travels in Two Democracies*, pp. 65-66, 71.

22. Wilson presents the United States and Soviet Russia as two voracious sea slugs, each with a record of having devoured smaller organisms (*Patriotic Gore* [New York, 1962], pp. xi ff.).

23. Irving Howe, in "Edmund Wilson and the Sea Slugs," *A*

World More Attractive (New York, 1963), writes: "... the comparison with the sea slug is too grandiose, too monolithic, too apocalyptic. ... One need not cling to theories of inevitable progress in history to find purpose and direction, morals and sentiments, ideas and ideals, all contributing to the outcome of events and all a good deal more than mere disguises for the urge to power" (303-4). See also Marius Bewley, "Northern Saints and Southern Knights," *Hudson Review*, XV (Autumn, 1962), pp. 431-39. Bewley writes: "The one disappointing aspect of the book lies in Mr. Wilson's failure to correlate convincingly this 'Monster' of modern 'Centralism' with what he considers to be its seeds germinated in the Civil War" (439).

24. Howe, "Edmund Wilson: A Reexamination," *Nation*, CLXVII (October 16, 1948), 433.

25. Culver, *Scrutiny*, I (September, 1932), 199.

26. Buckley, "Here We Go Again," *National Review*, XVII (July 13, 1965), 578-79.

Chapter Two

1. Christian Gauss was the most important single influence in Wilson's career. The correspondence between the two men from 1916 to Gauss's death in 1950 (in *The Papers of Christian Gauss* [New York, 1957]), although incomplete, clearly shows that Gauss was not only a great friend but a tactful, judicious critic of Wilson's work, particularly in the first half of the younger man's career. Gauss encouraged, curbed, steered, and praised him; and *Axel's Castle* and *To the Finland Station* were no doubt improved because of Gauss's interest. Incidentally, he was tremendously pleased over Wilson's dedication of *Axel's Castle* to him.

2. Fiess, "Edmund Wilson: Art and Ideas," *Antioch Review*, I (February 1, 1941), 356-67.

3. Notice, for instance, Virginia Woolf's impressions of *Ulysses* in 1922, after T. S. Eliot had praised it to her: "I finished *Ulysses* and think it a mis-fire. Genius it has, I think; but of the inferior water. The book is diffuse. It is brackish. It is pretentious. It is underbred, not only in the obvious sense, but in the literary sense. A first rate writer, I mean, respects writing too much to be tricky; startling; doing stunts. ..." (*A Writer's Diary* [New York, 1954], p. 48). By 1927, however, many intellectuals expressed their admiration for the book by signing an "International Protest" against Samuel Roth's pirated American edition.

Among the better, more recent studies of the Symbolists are C. M. Bowra's *The Heritage of Symbolism* (London, 1954) and Anna Balakian's *The Symbolist Movement: A Critical Appraisal* (New York, 1967). The latter contains a good bibliography.

4. The English critic Frank Kermode has accurately described the method of *Axel's Castle* as "passionate identification with the work under discussion; followed by detached appraisal; followed by historical inference, which does not neglect the primary response" ("Edmund Wilson and Mario Praz," *Puzzles and Epiphanies* [London, 1962], pp. 55-63).

5. F. O. Matthiessen, who praised Wilson's essays on Joyce and Proust in a 1931 review of *Axel's Castle*, noted that Wilson's treatment of the poets was less satisfactory; he said that Wilson spent too much time showing the evolution of Yeats's ideas and Eliot's debt to the French Symbolists and not enough time analyzing the poetry (*The Responsibilities of the Critic* [New York, 1952], pp. 159-61).

A case *for* the presence of the poet in the poem is made by George T. Wright, *The Poet in the Poem: The Personae of Eliot, Yeats, and Pound* (Berkeley and Los Angeles, 1960). Wright argues that apparently impersonal art is really and distinguishably personal. But this argument, successful or not, cannot invalidate the position that a poem has what John Crowe Ransom has called its own "ontology."

6. Freeman, "Edmund Wilson's Globe of Glass," *New Masses*, XXVII (April 12, 1938), 73-79.

7. Wilson, incidentally, has met his match more than once. Two of his notable exchanges were with John Crowe Ransom in 1927 and with Vladimir Nabokov in 1965. In the former incident Wilson had written that the poetry of Ransom and others was distinguished in style but not sufficiently interesting, "perhaps because the poets themselves do not lead very interesting lives." Ransom's reply was scathing: "I admire your natural taste all the more, since your reasoning, by which you go through the motions of fortifying your judgment, seems to me brutal and absurd. . . . It is my thesis that you judge well of poetry without knowing why you judge, and that you invite the world to judge of poetry on grounds which are thoroughly insufficient" ("The Muses Out of Work," *The Shores of Light*, pp. 197-211).

In 1965 Wilson wrote a surprisingly pedantic review of Nabokov's translation into English of Pushkin's *Eugene Onegin;* Wilson picked out what he called errors in Nabokov's Russian (the latter's native language) and listed them in an article of tedious length. Nabokov, replied with haughty sarcasm, stating that Wilson understood neither Russian prosody nor linguistics. Wilson's counterstatement was singularly mild, as it had been to Ransom's letter, when he had said that Ransom had misunderstood him; he acknowledged some of his own mistakes that Nabokov had noted and even sounded apologetic when he wrote, ". . . in rereading my article, I felt that it sounded more damaging than I had meant it to be, and this has given him a chance to score" ("The Strange Case of Pushkin and Nabokov," *New*

York Review of Books, V [July 15, 1965], 3-6; and, Nabokov's reply, as well as those of other readers, "The Strange Case of Nabokov and Wilson" [August 26, 1965], p. 25 ff.).

8. "Marxism and Literature" and "The Historical Interpretation of Literature," *The Triple Thinkers,* pp. 205, 269. Sherman Paul identifies Wilson with the Humanism of Christian Gauss, who was "flexible, humane, and worldly" as opposed to the "rigid and provincial More." Gauss's Humanism, writes Paul, "is neither Romantic nor Classic, but a compound of both. It respects the individual, his depth of participation in life . . . and it respects self-discipline" (*Edmund Wilson,* pp. 23-27).

9. Schwartz, "The Writing of Edmund Wilson," *Accent,* II (Spring, 1942), 185n.

10. Because I refer to the "revised and enlarged" *Triple Thinkers* of 1948, rather than to the first edition of 1938, I am discussing it after *The Wound and the Bow.*

11. For a thorough discussion of Wilson's view of James's governess, see the exchange between Marius Bewley and F. R. Leavis in *Scrutiny,* XVII (Summer, Autumn, 1950), 90-127, 255-63.

12. See Austin Warren, "Henry James," *The New England Conscience* (Ann Arbor, 1966), pp. 143-56.

13. Wilson's carelessness also appears in other writings during the 1930's and 1940's. See his 1944 article, "A Long Talk About Jane Austen," *Classics and Commercials* (New York, 1950), pp. 196-203, in which he attempts to discuss *Mansfield Park* after confessing that he has not read it for thirty years.

14. To gain a convincing impression of James's agonizing introspection, see his reactions to the deaths of Minny Temple and Constance Fenimore Woolson, especially the former, who was a powerful influence on his work after 1870; in Edel's *Henry James,* Vol. I, *The Untried Years* (Philadelphia and New York, 1953), pp. 323-33; and Vol. III, *The Middle Years* (1962), pp. 356-89.

15. The *American Historical Review* did not review *Patriotic Gore.* Paul Fatout reviewed it favorably in the *Mississippi Valley Historical Review,* XLIX (September, 1962), 341-42; Bruce Catton, less favorably, in *American Heritage,* XIII (August, 1962), 109-10. Perhaps the fullest evaluation by a professional historian is Henry Steele Commager's "Myths, Morals and a House Divided," *New York Times Book Review,* April 29, 1962, pp. 1 and 24. This review qualifies its praise by noting that Wilson excludes certain deserving writers, exaggerates the importance of Alexander Stephens, and, in the Introduction, oversimplifies American military policy from the Civil War to the present.

16. Howe, *A World More Attractive,* p. 300; Kazin, "Our Amer-

ican Plutarch," *Reporter*, XXVI (May 24, 1962), 43-46.

17. *The Bit Between My Teeth*, pp. 1-5. Wilson expressed much the same view when he was interviewed by Harvey Breit for the *New York Times Book Review*, November 2, 1952; see Breit's *The Writer Observed* (Cleveland and New York, 1956), pp. 267-69.

18. Wilson's favorite contemporary poets are Robert Lowell and W. H. Auden; after those two he prefers Elizabeth Bishop and John Berryman.

One disturbing, indeed aberrant, writer that Wilson has taken an interest in and written about in two fine essays for *The New Yorker* is the Marquis de Sade. In the first essay, "The Vogue of the Marquis de Sade" (XXVIII [October 18, 1952], 163-64 ff.), Wilson is concerned with the revival of interest in "the prophet of human self-immolation" and his "worth to the world" as the first systematic cataloguer of sexual abnormalities; as an anticipator of Sigmund Freud regarding infant sexuality; and, in his annihilism, as "a reminder that the lust for cruelty, the appetite for destruction, are powerful motivations that must be recognized for what they are." The second essay, "The Documents on the Marquis de Sade" (XLI [September 18, 1965], 175-86 ff.), based on Gilbert Lely's biography and on Sade's correspondence edited by Lely and George Dumas, is one of Wilson's best biographical pieces and successfully presents Sade as a pathetic man (*The Bit Between My Teeth*, pp. 158-73, 174-227). But Sade has been dead for over a hundred and fifty years, and Wilson's interest is not primarily literary.

19. Michael Gold's *Jews Without Money*, an autobiographical account of growing up among impoverished Jews on New York's Lower East Side, is characterized by an explosive, swift, and sometimes incantatory style. Graphic and sensational, it went through seventeen printings between 1930 and 1938.

Chapter Three

1. Neither this dialogue nor three other appendices are included in the Anchor paperbound edition of *To the Finland Station*.

2. Graves, "Edmund Wilson, A Protestant Abroad" (review of *Red, Black, Blond and Olive*), *New Republic*, CXXXIV (April 30, 1956), 13-16.

3. I discuss only those early poems that appeared later in *Poets, Farewell!* (New York, 1929) and not those that had been published in the *Hill School Record*, the *Nassau Literary Magazine*, and *A Book of Princeton Verse* (1916), which Wilson wrote with John Peale Bishop.

4. Zabel, "Marginalia of a Critic," *Poetry*, XXXV (January, 1930), 222-26. Zabel's title may indicate a more candid opinion of *Poets, Farewell!* than his review does.

5. Wilson later changed the third line to read: "Was laid with dog-tagged soldiers in a trench" (*Night Thoughts* [1961], p. 5).

6. See *Night Thoughts,* pp. 233-45, 265-74.

7. Wilson republished, with minor changes, the first two of the four dialogues in *The Shores of Light* and the last one, "In the Galapagos," in *A Piece of My Mind.* "Mrs. Alving and Oedipus," like *Cronkhite's Clocks,* has never been republished; and *Discordant Encounters* has long been out of print.

8. Gibbs, "The Odd Case of Mr. Wilson," *New Yorker,* XXVII (May 12, 1951), 49-50.

9. Marshall, "Drama," *Nation,* CLXXII (May 12, 1951), 450.

10. Kerr, "The Stage," *Commonweal,* LIV (May 18, 1951), 141-42.

11. Atkinson, *New York Times,* XVII (April 30, 1951), 2.

12. Clurman, "Theatre: Wilson and Pirandello," *New Republic,* CXXIII (September 18, 1950), 21-22.

13. Clurman, "Theatre: From Booth to Shakespeare," *New Republic,* CXXIV (May 14, 1951), 20-21.

14. Cosman, "Edmund Wilson, Playwright," *Theatre Arts,* XXXIX (August, 1955), 13.

15. This play has recently been published as *The Duke of Palermo* with two new plays—*Dr. McGrath,* a drama about a religious and political bigot; and *Osbert's Career,* a satirical farce on American life and culture in the last forty years.

Chapter Four

1. When Wilson republished "The Hero" in *A Prelude,* he left off the moralistic harangue at the end (*New Yorker,* [May 13, 1967], pp. 91-92).

2. Fitzgerald, incidentally, thought highly of "The Death of a Soldier" and praised it in a letter to Wilson in 1922. See *The Letters of F. Scott Fitzgerald,* ed. Andrew Turnbull (New York, 1963), p. 339.

3. The attitude expressed in *Garland* of America as prudish and tasteless had already been held by Wilson during the war and perhaps earlier. In France he made the following "historical" observation in his notebook: "Human bodies in the twentieth century were so unsightly that it was considered indecent to expose them, and sexual relations had become so sordid that as topics of conversation they were regarded as low. In America, the word *beautiful,* which, among the Greeks and the French had covered all good taste, loveliness, and nobility, became so outlawed and seldom heard that it made people self-conscious to use it. This was the greatest age of America's industrial prosperity" (*A Prelude,* p. 102).

4. In 1925 Wilson wrote another, briefer monologue, "A Dandy Day," not since republished in any of his collections. The speaker is a little girl named Betty who spends a day at the beach and over-hears her parents discuss what should be done with her the following winter. Her father will be traveling for his company, and her mother does not like the prospect of staying at home with the girl. Nor does Aunt May want to take little Betty this winter because she might make Grandma nervous. The mother wants to be free either to return to the stage or to accompany the father. Despite her parents' re-strained arguing and the unpleasant tone of the outing, Betty has a good time. Eventually her father reluctantly decides not to travel but to work at home; the implication is that he may thereby miss a promotion. The monologue is a sharp observation on American "fam-ily" life. But Wilson's main interest is the character of Betty, who has an appealing sense of humor: "Vreeland Fox is just a shout in a bath-ing suit" (*New Republic*, LXXIII [August 19, 1925], 348-49).

5. It is difficult to tell exactly which appeal this refers to. Between 1921 and 1927 Webster Thayer, the Massachusetts Superior Court judge who tried the case, denied eight motions for a retrial. At least four of these motions were appealed to the Supreme Judicial Court of Massachusetts, which dismissed them, finding no evidence that the trial had not been conducted legally. But the appeal probably referred to in "Rumpelmayer's" is the seventh and most sensational, "the Medeiros motion." Celestino F. Medeiros was a young Portu-guese under sentence of death in the Dedham jail, where Sacco was confined, for the holdup-murder of a bank cashier. In a dramatic note scrawled in a magazine and sent to Sacco on November 18, 1925, Medeiros said: "I hearby confess to being in the south Braintree shoe company crime and Sacco and Vanzetti was not in said crime." Then, in an affidavit tendered to Judge Thayer on May 26, 1926, Medeiros further stated that he and four Italians, members of the "Morelli gang," had committed the crime. Thayer denied the motion on the grounds of Medeiros' doubtful probity. On April 5, 1927, the Su-preme Judicial Court of Massachusetts affirmed the denial. Sacco, Vanzetti, and Medeiros were electrocuted at the Charlestown State Prison shortly after midnight on August 23. Notable writers besides Wilson who protested were Edna St. Vincent Millay, Upton Sinclair, and John Dos Passos. The case has since been examined in great detail, but for a quick, well-documented review, see *Commonwealth vs. Sacco and Vanzetti*, ed. Robert P. Weeks (Englewood Cliffs: Prentice-Hall, 1958).

6. In *The Armed Vision* Stanley Hyman says that *Daisy* ends "in a real frenzy of phallic imagery, a sequence on the last page running from lipstick to mouth-organ to pistol to snake." His assertion is mis-

leading since there is nothing frenzied about the ending and since he does not mention the other gimcracks obtained at Coney Island—a baby doll, a minature roulette wheel, and a pair of moccasins. If there is "phallic imagery," Hyman does not suggest how it is employed. Probably both the phallic and non-phallic gimcracks are simply a little commentary on American amusement parks and on the people who are amused there.

7. Christopher Ricks, *New Statesman*, LXV (February 8, 1963), 208. *Daisy* had recently been published in paperback by Penguin.

8. Mary Ross, "The Atlantic Bookshelf," *Atlantic Monthly*, CXLIV (December, 1929), 32, front advertising section. *Daisy* was reviewed in most of the popular American literary magazines, and the reviews were generally favorable. But it apparently was not a popular success. In a letter to Maxwell Perkins, the famous Scribner editor, Scott Fitzgerald wrote: "Sorry Bunny's book didn't go—I thought it was fine, and more interesting than better, or at least more achieved, novels" (November 15, 1929). But earlier, in a letter to Hemingway in Paris, Fitzgerald (in Cannes) was more critical: "Bunny Wilson's book has a fascinating portrait of [John] Dos [Passos] in it, and is full of good things, and to me is interesting throughout. Oddly enough what it lacks is his old bogey, form. It is shapeless as Wells at his wildest, or almost" (August 23, 1929; *The Letters of F. Scott Fitzgerald*, pp. 216, 305).

9. Some of these characters were obviously drawn from living people. Rita is modeled on Edna Millay, and the narrator, to an uncertain extent (see note 10), on Wilson himself. Hugo Bamman, as note 8 indicates, is John Dos Passos. Sue Borglum may be drawn from Mabel Dodge, hostess of "evenings" for the New York intelligentsia, but the omission of any reference to Wilson in her four-volume *Intimate Memories* (New York: Harcourt, Brace), 1933 to 1937, especially in Vol. III, *Movers and Shakers* (1936), concerning her life, mostly in New York, during the nineteen-teens, suggests that he was not part of her circle; and it could be that in *Daisy* Mabel Dodge is referred to merely as Myra Busch, another party-giver. Bobby McIlvaine may be drawn from Robert Edmond Jones, the set designer. Professor Grosbeake is undoubtedly based on Christian Gauss, as the latter noted in "Edmund Wilson, the Campus and the Nassau 'Lit'" (cited in Chapter 1).

But far more interesting than this sleuthing is Edna Millay's opinion of *Daisy*. Apparently Wilson sent her the manuscript sometime in 1928. When she did not respond promptly, he seems to have thought that she was offended by the portrait of her. In two letters that she wrote to him on February 6 and 10, 1929, she assured him that she was "not offended," apologized for having kept the manuscript so long, and begged him not to publish it yet: "It is really not ready to be published, & I swear that you will do yourself a great injury if you publish it just as it is—it is very uneven—I like much of it tremendously—but it is not a whole—it needs a whole lot of working on still. *Please* don't have it published this spring—no matter what your publisher says—your reputation is the principal thing,—& it really isn't good enough, yet, Bunny, I swear it isn't.—You can make a grand book of it, but it's not finished" (*Letters of Edna St. Vincent Millay*, ed. Allan Ross Macdougall [New York, 1952], pp. 230-32). Since the first reviews of *Daisy* appeared in August of 1929, it is doubtful that Wilson reworked the manuscript as much as Edna Millay wanted him to, if at all.

10. How much Wilson portrayed himself in *Daisy* is conjectural. In the only totally unfavorable review of 1929, Norah Meade called Wilson "the Puritan in search of a clean soul": "Somewhere in Mr. Wilson lurks a Puritan who seems to be suffering from the hang-over of a Greenwich Village adolescence. The book may, then, be regarded as the purgative open confession that is supposedly so good for the soul. . . ." ("Greenwich Villagers," *Nation*, CXXX [January 1, 1930], 20).

Miss Meade's review is not very good, and her vehemence is curious, but other reviewers have since felt that a Calvinist background is an influence in his work. See Robert Graves's review of *Red, Black, Blond and Olive*, "Edmund Wilson: A Protestant Abroad," *New Republic*, CXXXIV (April 30, 1956), 13-16. See also Frederick C. Crews's "Lessons of the Master" (cited in the Preface) and R. W. B. Lewis' "The Professional," *New York Times Book Review*, December 12, 1965, pp. 1, 43-45; both of these articles are in part reviews of *The Bit Between My Teeth* and in part reviews of the first book to be published on Wilson, Sherman Paul's *Edmund Wilson* (cited in Chapter 1), which makes a good deal of Wilson's "religious disposition."

11. The three reviews mentioned are Mrs. Trilling's "Fiction in Review, *Nation*, CLXII (March 30, 1946), 379-81; Smith's "The Devil in the Suburbs," *Saturday Review*, XXIX (March 22, 1946), 22; and Cowley's "Limbo-by-the-Sea," *New Republic*, CXIV (March 25, 1946), 418-19.

12. *The Papers of Christian Gauss*, p. 252. Sherman Paul identifies the book which was so difficult to finish as *To the Finland Station* (1940)—see his *Edmund Wilson*, p. 164.

13. This information on the suppression of *Memoirs* has been taken from the *New York Times*, which also published a cartoon on April 28, 1946, showing a wife reading *Memoirs* and saying to her husband: "Poor Mr. Wilson—hasn't he any nice friends?"

14. Kazin, "Le Misanthrope," *Partisan Review*, XIII (Summer, 1946), 375-80.

15. Fitzgerald, *Babylon Revisited and Other Stories* (New York, 1960), p. 127.

16. Wain, "Edmund Wilson: The Critic as Novelist," *New Republic*, CXLII (January 18, 1960), 15-17.

17. See Wayne Booth, *The Rhetoric of Fiction* (Chicago and London, 1961), pp. 3-20.

18. See Northrop Frye, *Anatomy of Criticism* (Princeton, 1957), pp. 74, 79, 92-93.

Chapter Five

1. Actually Shaw had been a "public character" for a long time. Leonard Woolf, in *Beginning Again: An Autobiography of the Years 1911 to 1918* (New York, 1963), recalls an amusing incident in 1913, when Shaw stopped on a Hyde Park sidewalk to tell Leonard and Virginia Woolf about his recent travels and quickly drew a crowd (p. 122).

2. The inaugural parade for Franklin D. Roosevelt contrasts to the "more impressive" *Physcultúr* Parade that Wilson saw in Moscow in 1935 and described in *Travels* (219-22) and again in *Red, Black, Blond and Olive* (238-41).

3. So far as I know, "Lieutenant Franklin" was not published before its inclusion in *Travels*, and its restrained tone indicates that it is not an early story. It has been republished in the first part of *A Prelude*, where Wilson says that it combines an experience of his own with one of his friend George Perkins, Jr., and that he wrote it later than 1918—but he does not suggest how much later (*New Yorker*, May 13, 1967, p. 120).

Selected Bibliography

PRIMARY SOURCES

(In Order of Publication) *

"The Oppressor," *Liberator*, IV (May, 1921), 25-26, 28. Story.
"The Hero," *Liberator*, V (February, 1922), 12. Exemplum.
"Night Thoughts in Paris: A Rhapsody," *New Republic*, LXVI
    (March 15, 1922), 75-77.
The Undertaker's Garland [with JOHN PEALE BISHOP]. New York:
    Alfred A. Knopf, 1922. Fiction and poetry.
"A Dandy Day," *New Republic*, LXXIII (August 19, 1925), 348-49.
    Monologue.
Discordant Encounters: Plays and Dialogues. New York: Albert and
    Charles Boni, 1926. Four dialogues, a skit (*Cronkhite's Clocks*),
    and Wilson's first play (*The Crime in the Whistler Room*).
"Galahad." *The American Caravan*. Ed. VAN WYCK BROOKS *et al*.
    New York: Literary Guild of America, 1927, pp. 222-61. Story.
I Thought of Daisy. New York: Charles Scribner's Sons, 1929; Lon-
    don: W. H. Allen, 1952; New York: Farrar, Straus and Young,
    1953; Harmondsworth, Middlesex: Penguin Books Ltd., 1963;
    New York: Farrar, Straus and Giroux, 1967 [with "Galahad"].
    Novel.
Poets, Farewell! New York: Charles Scribner's Sons, 1929. Poems and
    prose sketches.
Axel's Castle: A Study in the Imaginative Literature of 1870-1930.
    New York and London: Charles Scribner's Sons, 1931. Criticism.
The American Jitters: A Year of the Slump. New York and London:
    Charles Scribner's Sons, 1932. English title, *Devil Take the
    Hindmost*. Journalism.
Travels in Two Democracies. New York: Harcourt, Brace and Co.,
    1936. Journalism.
This Room and This Gin and These Sandwiches: Three Plays. New
    York: The New Republic, 1937. Includes *The Crime in the
    Whistler Room, A Winter in Beech Street* (later titled, *This
    Room . . . etc.*), and *Beppo and Beth*.
The Triple Thinkers: Ten Essays on Literature. New York: Harcourt,

*Not every edition of each work is included.

Brace and Co.; Oxford: Oxford University Press, 1938. *The Triple Thinkers: Twelve Essays on Literary Subjects.* New York: Oxford University Press, 1948. Criticism.

To the Finland Station: A Study in the Writing and Acting of History. New York: Harcourt, Brace and Co.; London: Secker and Warburg, 1940; Garden City, N. Y.: Doubleday and Co., 1953. Biography and history.

The Boys in the Back Room: Notes on California Novelists. San Francisco: The Colt Press, 1941. Later included in *Classics and Commercials.* Criticism.

The Wound and the Bow: Seven Studies in Literature. Cambridge, Mass.: Houghton Mifflin Co., 1941; London: Secker and Warburg, 1942; New York: Oxford University Press, 1947, 1959. Criticism.

Note-Books of Night. San Francisco: The Colt Press, 1942. Poems and prose sketches.

The Shock of Recognition: The Development of Literature in the United States Recorded by the Men Who Made It. Garden City, N. Y.: Doubleday, Doran and Co., 1943. An anthology of "literary documents," mostly essays, by contemporaries of American writers who flourished between 1845 and 1938.

Memoirs of Hecate County. Garden City, N. Y.: Doubleday, Doran and Co., 1946; New York and Boston: L. C. Page and Co., 1959 (rev. ed.). Novel.

Europe Without Baedeker: Sketches Among the Ruins of Italy, Greece and England. Garden City, N. Y.: Doubleday, Doran and Co., 1947. Journalism.

The Little Blue Light: A Play in Three Acts. New York: Farrar, Straus and Co., 1950.

Classics and Commercials: A Literary Chronicle of the Forties. New York: Farrar, Straus and Co., 1950; Random House, 1962. Criticism.

The Shores of Light: A Literary Chronicle of the Twenties and Thirties. New York: Farrar, Straus and Young, 1952; Random House, 1961. Criticism.

Night Thoughts. New York: Farrar, Straus and Co., 1961. Poems and prose; most of this material was published earlier in *Poets* and in *Note-Books.* A small part of it, *Three Reliques of Ancient Western Poetry Collected by Edmund Wilson from the Ruins of the Twentieth Century,* has been published in pamphlet form with no publisher, place, or date given.

Eight Essays. Garden City, N. Y.: Doubleday and Co., 1954. Criticism and biography; the essays on Dickens and Hemingway were previously published in *Wound,* and those on Housman and Shaw in *Thinkers.*

Selected Bibliography

Five Plays. New York: Farrar, Straus and Young, 1954; London: W. H. Allen, 1954. One new play, *Cyprian's Prayer,* in addition to the four published previously.

The Scrolls from the Dead Sea. New York: Oxford University Press, 1955; London: W. H. Allen, 1956. Journalism.

A Piece of My Mind: Reflections at Sixty. New York: Farrar, Straus and Cudahy, 1956; London: W. H. Allen, 1957. Personal essays.

Red, Black, Blond and Olive: Studies in Four Civilizations: Zuñi, Haiti, Soviet Russia, Israel. New York: Oxford University Press, 1956. Journalism; the section on Russia is an expanded version of the same material in *Travels.*

A Literary Chronicle: 1920-1950. Garden City, N. Y.: Doubleday and Co., 1956. An Anchor Book containing selections from *Classics* and *Shores.*

The American Earthquake: A Documentary of the Twenties and Thirties. Garden City, N. Y.: Doubleday and Co., 1958. Journalism; most of this material was previously published in *Jitters* and *Travels.*

Apologies to the Iroquois (with "The Mohawks in High Steel" by JOSEPH MITCHELL, 1949). New York: Farrar, Straus and Cudahy. 1959. Journalism.

Patriotic Gore: Studies in the Literature of the American Civil War. New York: Oxford University Press, 1962. Criticism and biography.

The Cold War and the Income Tax: A Protest. New York: Farrar, Straus and Co., 1963. Polemic.

O Canada: An American's Notes on Canadian Culture. New York: Farrar, Straus and Giroux, 1965. Journalism.

The Bit Between My Teeth: A Literary Chronicle of 1950-1965. New York: Farrar, Straus and Giroux, 1965. Criticism.

Europe Without Baedeker: Sketches Among the Ruins of Italy, Greece and England together with Notes from a European Diary: 1963-1964. New York: Farrar, Straus and Giroux, 1966. Journalism.

The Lamentable Tragedy of the Duke of Palermo by Henry Chettle and William Shakespeare Now First Discovered and Transcribed by Homer R. Winslow, M. A. Hillsdale, Ph.D. Harvard, Presented by Edmund Wilson. New York Review of Books, VII (January 12, 1967), 13-23. Play.

Galahad and *I Thought of Daisy.* New York: Farrar, Straus and Giroux, 1967. Fiction.

A Prelude: Landscapes, Characters and Conversations From the Earlier Years of My Life. New York: Farrar, Straus and Giroux, 1967. Autobiography.

The Fruits of the MLA. New York: New York Review, 1969. Polemic.
The Duke of Palermo and Other Plays, With an Open Letter to Mike Nichols. New York: Farrar, Straus and Giroux, 1969.
The Dead Sea Scrolls: 1969, New Yorker, XLV (March 22, 1969), 45-84; (March 29, 1969), 45-96; (April 5, 1969), 45-94.

SECONDARY SOURCES

(Most of the articles on Wilson and his work are book reviews, and many of these, even in respectable periodicals, are mediocre or worse. The following list by no means includes all of the articles and books consulted in the preparation of this study, nor even all of the pieces cited in the text, but only those of some merit or interest.)

AARON, DANIEL. *Writers on the Left: Episodes in American Literary Communism*. New York: Harcourt, Brace, 1961. The best study I have seen of modern American left-wing writers.

BEWLEY, MARIUS. "Northern Saints and Southern Knights," *Hudson Review*, XV (Autumn, 1962), 431-39. Good review of *Patriotic Gore*.

COMMAGER, HENRY STEELE. "Myths, Morals and a House Divided," *New York Times Book Review*, April 29, 1962, pp. 1, 24. Review of *Patriotic Gore* which takes issue with Wilson's Introduction.

CORBETT, E. P. J. "America's Sainte-Beuve," *Commonweal*, LXXII (May 13, 1960), 173-75. Appreciative article. Christian Gauss, too, once referred to Wilson's writing (on Sinclair Lewis and H. L. Mencken) as having a "Sainte Beuvian sense of enjoyment"; but Wilson would rather be compared with Taine.

COSMAN, MAX. "Edmund Wilson, Playwright," *Theatre Arts*, XXXIX (August, 1955), 13.

COWLEY, MALCOLM. "Edmund Wilson's Specimen Days," *New Republic*, CXXVII (November 10, 1952), 17-18. Favorable review of *The Shores of Light*.

————. *Exile's Return: A Literary Odyssey of the 1920's*. New York: Viking Press, 1951. Interesting account of the disillusionment of American expatriates.

————. "Limbo-by-the-Sea," *New Republic*, CXIV (March 25, 1946), 418-19. Review of *Memoirs of Hecate County*.

CREWS, FREDERICK C. "Lessons of the Master," *New York Review of Books*, V (November 25, 1965), 4-5. Review of *The Bit Between My Teeth;* one of the better recent articles on Wilson.

DUPEE, F. W. "Wilson Without Reputation," *New York Review of Books*, VII (November 17, 1966), 3-5. Review of the 1966 edition of *Europe Without Baedeker* by a professor and former acquaintance of Wilson who seems to lament the passing of their friendly relationship. In a letter to the editor in the December 15, 1966, issue of the *Review,* Wilson corrects a mistake that Dupee made in quoting from *Europe.*

EDEL, LEON. "'Am I, Then, in a Pocket of the Past?'" *New Republic,* CXXXV (December 17, 1956), 25-26. Review of *A Piece of My Mind.*

EPSTEIN, JASON. "Wilson's Amerika," *New York Review of Books,* I (November 28, 1963), 9-11. One of the few favorable reviews of *The Cold War and the Income Tax.*

FIEDLER, LESLIE. "Edmund Wilson's Criticism: A Re-examination," *New Leader,* December 13, 1947, p. 15. Judicious article with an air of disillusionment over a former idol.

FIESS, EDWARD. "Edmund Wilson: Art and Ideas," *Antioch Review,* I (February 1, 1941), 356-67. Early, still good essay dealing mainly with *Axel's Castle* and "Marxism and Literature."

FRAIBERG, LOUIS. *Psychoanalysis and American Literary Criticism.* Detroit: Wayne State University Press, 1960. The best case from a psychological standpoint against Wilson's wound-and-bow theory.

FREEMAN, JOSEPH. "Edmund Wilson's Globe of Glass," *New Masses,* XXVII (April 12, 1938), 73-79. Marxist complaint.

GAUSS, CHRISTIAN. "Edmund Wilson, the Campus and the Nassau 'Lit,'" *Princeton University Library Chronicle,* V (February, 1944), 41-50. Biographical value.

————. *The Papers of Christian Gauss.* Ed. KATHERINE GAUSS JACKSON and HIRAM HAYDN. New York: Random House, 1957. Especially valuable for the letters between Gauss and Wilson; these form the best biographical document available on Wilson between 1916 and 1950.

GILMAN, RICHARD. "The Critic as Taxpayer," *New Republic,* CXLIX, (November 30, 1963), 25-27. Review of *Cold War.*

————. "Edmund Wilson, Then and Now," *New Republic,* CLV (July 2, 1966), 23-28. Review of *The Bit Between My Teeth* and the finest essay on Wilson yet to appear.

GRAVES, ROBERT. "Edmund Wilson, A Protestant Abroad," *New Republic,* CXXXIV (April 30, 1956), 13-16. Interesting review of *Red, Black, Blond and Olive* with shrewd insights into Wilson as writer and observer.

HICKS, GRANVILLE. "The Intransigence of Edmund Wilson," *Antioch Review* (Winter, 1946-47), 550-62. Mr. Hicks admires Wilson, but is disturbed by his apparent truculence.

HOWE, IRVING. *A World More Attractive: A View of Modern Literature and Politics.* New York: Horizon Press, 1963. Praises *Patriotic Gore* but objects to the sea-slug metaphor in the Introduction.

————. "Edmund Wilson: A Reexamination," *Nation*, CLXVII (October 16, 1948), 430-33. Notes certain failings in Wilson as critic and suggests that his main contribution to letters is his recording of American life.

HYMAN, STANLEY E. *The Armed Vision: A Study in the Methods of Modern Literary Criticism.* New York: Alfred A. Knopf, 1948. Validly classifies Wilson as a "translator" of literature; but personal abuse ruins the discussion. Hyman omitted the chapter on Wilson in the Vintage edition (1955).

JEROME, V. J. "Edmund Wilson: To the Munich Station," *New Masses*, XXXI (April 4, 1939), 23-26. Marxist attack.

KAUFMANN, R. J. "The Critic as Custodian of Sanity: Edmund Wilson," *Critical Quarterly*, I (Summer, 1959), 85-98. Sane article.

KAZIN, ALFRED. *The Inmost Leaf: A Selection of Essays.* New York: Harcourt, Brace, 1955. Contains a favorable review of *The Shores of Light.* Except for the review of *Memoirs* listed below, nearly everything Kazin writes about Wilson is favorable.

————. "Le Misanthrope," *Partisan Review*, XIII (Summer, 1946), 375-80. Review of *Memoirs*.

————. *On Native Grounds: An Interpretation of Modern Prose Literature.* New York: Reynal and Hitchcock, 1942. Contains a good discussion of Marxist criticism and a eulogy of Wilson.

————. "Our American Plutarch," *Reporter*, XXVI (May 24, 1962), 43-46. Review of *Patriotic Gore*.

KEMPTON, MURRAY. *Part of Our Time: Some Ruins and Monuments of the Thirties.* New York: Simon and Schuster, 1955. Contains a good chapter, "The Social Muse," on Wilson and other social critics of the 1930's.

KERMODE, FRANK. *Puzzles and Epiphanies: Essays and Reviews, 1958-1961.* London: Routledge and Kegan Paul, 1962. Contains a useful discussion of *Axel's Castle*.

KRIEGEL, LEONARD. "The Politics of Edmund Wilson." Unpublished dissertation, New York University, 1960. Microfilm 60-5284: University Microfilms, Inc., Ann Arbor, Michigan. Study of Wilson's "political evolution"; a competent and well-researched review of Wilson's career up to 1940, but weak on the later Wilson and generally inadequate in critical analysis; the attack on Kenneth Burke as a "new critic," in the Conclusion, is superfluous and flaccid.

KRUTCH, JOSEPH WOOD. "Reflections of a Mature Man," *Saturday Review*, XXXIX (November 17, 1956), 22. Review of *A Piece of My Mind*.

LEAVIS, F. R. "An American Critic," *Scrutiny*, XI (Summer, 1942), 72 ff. Qualified praise of *The Wound and the Bow*.

Selected Bibliography

LEWIS, R. W. B. "The Duke of Palermo," New York Times Book Review, March 2, 1969, pp. 4, 46-48. Favorable review of Wilson's recent plays and of his idea for an American National Theater.

————. "The Professional," New York Times Book Review, December 12, 1965, pp. 1, 43-45. Laudatory review of The Bit Between My Teeth.

MACDOUGALL, ALLAN ROSS (ed.). The Letters of Edna St. Vincent Millay. New York: Harper and Bros., 1952. Biographical value.

MATTHIESSEN, F. O. The Responsibilities of the Critic: Essays and Reviews. New York: Oxford University Press, 1952. Contains a review of Axel's Castle.

MIZENER, ARTHUR. "Edmund Wilson: A Checklist," Princeton University Library Chronicle, V (February, 1944), 62-78. Definitive bibliography of Wilson's writings through 1943.

PARRY, ALBERT. Garrets and Pretenders: A History of Bohemianism in America. New York: Dover Publications, 1960. Informative and entertaining; especially valuable for information on Greenwich Village. Includes a new chapter by Harry T. Moore, "Enter Beatniks."

PAUL, SHERMAN. Edmund Wilson: A Study of Literary Vocation in Our Time. Urbana: University of Illinois Press, 1965. Useful biographical study; first book devoted to Wilson.

PERENYI, ELEANOR. "Wilson," Esquire, July, 1963, pp. 80-85, 118. Biographical article, not completely reliable.

PODHORETZ, NORMAN. Doings and Undoings: The Fifties and After in American Writing. New York: Farrar, Straus and Giroux, 1964. Contains a chapter on Wilson.

PRITCHETT, V. S. "A Commitment to Letters and Life," New York Times Book Review, October 2, 1966, pp. 1, 36. Judicious review of the recent Europe Without Baedeker by an Englishman who enjoys discussing Wilson's attitude toward the English.

RICHLER, MORDECAI. "Wilson in Canada," New York Review of Books, V (September 30, 1965), 6, 8-9. Review of O Canada by a Canadian who finds the book not entirely satisfactory.

RIDEOUT, WALTER B. The Radical Novel in the United States: 1900-1954. Cambridge: Harvard University Press, 1956. Has little to do with Wilson, but a useful study of left-wing fiction in his time.

RUBIN, LOUIS D., JR. "Edmund Wilson and the Despot's Heel," Sewanee Review, LXXI (January-March, 1963), 109-15. Good review of Patriotic Gore.

SCHWARTZ, DELMORE. "The Writing of Edmund Wilson," Accent, II (Spring, 1942), 177-86. Early study which concentrates on The Wound and the Bow; still one of the better essays on Wilson.

TURNBULL, ANDREW. "Cool, Crisp, a Little Tart," *Harper's Magazine*, CCXXXV (September, 1967), 120-23. Favorable review of *A Prelude* which notes Wilson's puritanism and compares him to the French Encyclopedist, Diderot.

————. (ed.). *The Letters of F. Scott Fitzgerald.* New York: Charles Scribner's Sons, 1963. Biographical value.

WAIN, JOHN. "Edmund Wilson: The Critic as Novelist," *New Republic*, CXLII (January 18, 1960), 15-17. Interesting article on *Memoirs* by a critical British novelist.

WARREN, ROBERT PENN. "Edmund Wilson's Civil War," *Commentary*, XXXIV (August, 1962), 151-58. Thorough, balanced review of *Patriotic Gore*, with which Warren sometimes takes issue.

Index

Index

Gide, André, 43, 72, 158
Gilman, Richard, 26, 72, 182, 183, 187, 201
Gissing, George, 46
Goethe, Johann Wolfgang von, 84
Gold, Michael, 38, 74; *Jews Without Money*, 74, 191
Goldhurst, William, *F. Scott Fitzgerald and His Contemporaries*, 186
Gorman, Herbert, 132
Gottfried von Strassburg, 152
Goya, Francisco José de, 153
Grant, Ulysses S., 60, 63, 65
Grass, Günter, 72
Graves, Robert, 77, 191, 195, 201
Grayson, William, 63
Greeley, Horace, 66

Hardy, Thomas, 53
Harris, George Washington, 62
Hawthorne, Nathaniel, 32, 60, 137, 159; *The Blithedale Romance*, 115
Haydn, Franz Joseph, 125
Healy, William, A. F. Bronner and A. M. Bowers, *The Structure and Meaning of Psychoanalysis*, 57
Helper, Hinton
Hemingway, Ernest, 13, 42, 102, 103, 158, 182, 194, 198
Hercules, 43
Herndon, William, 60
Hesse, Hermann, 72
Hicks, Granville, 25, 38, 39, 130-1, 187, 201
Hitler, Adolf, 139
Holmes, Oliver Wendell, 62, 64-5
Homer, Homeric, 34-5, 68
Housman, A. E., 198
Howe, Irving, 29, 201-2; *A World More Attractive*, 65, 187-8, 190, 201
Howe, M. A. De Wolfe, 49, 187
Howells, William Dean, 51
Humanism, Humanists, 14, 37-42, 70, 84, 149, 183, 190
Huxley, Aldous, *Brave New World*, 167
Hyman, Stanley, *The Armed Vision*, Preface, 77, 82, 193-4, 202

Ibsen, Henrik, 33
Impressionism, Impressionists, 122, 149
Iphigenia, 115

Jackson, Katherine Gauss, and Hiram Haydn, 201; eds., *The Papers of Christian Gauss* (*see* Gauss)
James, Henry, 49-55, 60, 61, 93, 115, 137, 140, 159, 162, 190
Jerome, V. J., 187, 202
Johnson, Samuel, 65
Jones, Robert Edmond, 194
Jonson, Ben, 55-8
Joyce, James, 34-5, 42, 46, 68, 70, 73, 117, 118, 122-3, 125, 138, 158, 159, 182, 188, 189

Kafka, Franz, 68, 72, 158
Kaufmann, R. J., 202
Kazin, Alfred, 39, 65, 154, 190-1, 196, 202; *The Inmost Leaf*, 202; *On Native Grounds*, 39, 202
Kempton, Murray, *Part of Our Time*, 187, 202
Kennedy, John F. (President), 15
Kennedy, John Pendleton, 62
Kent, Rockwell, 30
Kermode, Frank, *Puzzles and Epiphanies*, 189, 202
Kerr, Walter, 92, 93, 192
Kipling, Rudyard, 44, 46-8, 55, 71, 182, 183
Kriegel, Leonard, 202
Krook, Dorothea, *The Ordeal of Consciousness in Henry James*, 50, 51, 55
Krutch, Joseph Wood, 202

Laforgue, Jules, 37
Lanier, Sidney, 61, 62
Lardner, Ring, Jr., 30
Lawrence, D. H., 154, 158
Leavis, F. R., 190, 202; *The Great Tradition*, 55
Lee, Robert E., 64
Le Gallienne, Eva, 100
Lely, Gilbert, and George Dumas, 191

FICTION

PLAYS AND DIALOGUES: